Cosmic

B1+

Students'
Book

Fiona Beddall

Unit	Reading	Vocabulary	Grammar	Listening	Speaking	Writing
1 **Who Do You Think You Are?** **Page 5**	Choosing a title / Gist reading Mixed questions	People Prepositions, phrasal verbs Personality: adjectives Word formation: nouns from adjectives with -ty/-ity, -ence, -tion Appearance: descriptive nouns and adjectives	Present simple, Present continuous, Stative verbs Articles	Multiple choice True or False	Talking about yourself	Descriptive article
Revision 1 page 16						
2 **Days to Remember** **Page 17**	Becoming an adult is never easy Matching photos with parts of text Multiple choice	Life experiences Word formation: nouns and verbs Collocations Time: times of day, expressions with time Dates Days out	Past simple, Past continuous, used to / would	Sentence completion Multiple choice	Comparing pictures	Letter to a newspaper
Revision 2 page 28						
3 **Fact or Fiction?** **Page 29**	Freeze-time Missing sentences Multiple choice	Stories Verb-noun collocations Compound words Adverbs Verbs: ways of looking, speaking, walking Verbs + prepositions	Present perfect simple, Present perfect continuous Past perfect simple, Past perfect continuous	Dictation Multiple choice	Making a choice	Story
Revision 3 page 40						
4 **The World's Your Oyster** **Page 41**	The Big Apple Multiple choice	Transport Word formation: verbs and nouns Adjectives Places Phrasal verbs British and American English Holidays: accommodation, activities	The future Future time clauses	Multiple matching Table completion	Making a decision	Informal email
Revision 4 page 52						
5 **Best Mates** **Page 53**	Ask Alice ... Matching texts with photos Multiple matching	Relationships Useful phrases Phrasal verbs Word formation: suffixes -ship, -hood Adjectives + prepositions Verb antonyms Verbs + prepositions	Modal verbs Past modals	Notes completion Picture multiple choice	Roleplay	Essay
Revision 5 page 64						

Hi, guys! Everyone's different, but what makes us who we are? Who has had the biggest influence on your life?

1 Who Do You Think You Are?

Vocabulary Starter
People

1 Explain the difference between the following:

1 a **half-brother** and a **stepbrother**
2 a **niece** and a **nephew**
3 a **grandparent** and a **great-grandparent**
4 a **sibling** and a **twin**
5 a **relative** and an **ancestor**
6 a **mother-in-law** and a **stepmother**
7 a **first cousin** and a **second cousin**
8 a **great-aunt** and a **great-uncle**
9 an **only child** and a **lonely child**

2 Match the underlined words with the definitions below.

1 Your rich great-aunt dies and you <u>inherit</u> everything.
2 Your best friend moves to another town and you <u>lose touch</u>.
3 There's a new person in your class and the two of you <u>have</u> a lot <u>in common</u>.
4 At your birthday party, your mum shows your friends a video of your <u>birth</u>.
5 You travel back in time and repeat your early <u>childhood</u>.
6 Friends keep saying that you look <u>similar</u> to your favourite film star.
7 You and a friend arrive at a party wearing <u>identical</u> clothes.
8 Your parents decided to <u>adopt</u> a baby.

a almost the same _____
b exactly the same _____
c time as a child _____
d share the same interests _____
e make another person's child your own child by law _____
f time when a baby comes out of its mother's body _____
g stop speaking or writing to someone _____
h get money from someone who dies _____

CHATROOM

How would you feel if the things in Exercise 2 happened to you? Why?

Reading

1 You are going to read a magazine article. Read the article quickly and choose the most suitable title.

a Life as an only child

b Growing up with an identical twin

c Twins reunited

> **Reading Tip:** reading quickly
>
> When you first read a text, read it quickly to find out what it is about. Don't read every word. Read the first and last paragraphs, and the first sentence of the other paragraphs.

2 Read the article again and answer the questions.

1 When Kathryn was a young child, what aspect of her life did she want to be different? _____

2 What started happening when she moved house? _____

3 Why was Kathryn angry when someone kissed her? _____

For questions 4–8, tick (✓) the box.

4 Maddy and Kathryn are identical twins.
  True ☐ False ☐

5 Maddy and Kathryn grew up in similar families.
  True ☐ False ☐

6 Compared to Maddy, Kathryn is
  A more generous. ☐
  B more sociable. ☐
  C more self-confident. ☐

7 What has increased since Maddy and Kathryn met?
  A Kathryn's weight ☐
  B Maddy's weight ☐
  C Kathryn's self-confidence ☐

8 Maddy is worried that
  A boys don't like identical twins. ☐
  B her boyfriend might prefer Kathryn. ☐
  C Kathryn hasn't got a boyfriend. ☐

For questions 9–10, write the words.

9 Find the word or phrase in the passage which means the same as:
  wanted very much (paragraph 2) _____
  people you don't know (paragraph 3) _____
  meetings that haven't been arranged (paragraph 4) _____

10 Find the word or phrase in the passage that follows in these word sequences:
  none, a few, … (paragraph 2) _____
  possibly, probably, … (paragraph 6) _____

1 In many ways, only children are lucky. Compared to children with siblings, they get more attention from their parents, more presents, more help with homework, more space to themselves. But for some, life as an only child can be very lonely.

2 Kathryn Greet grew up as an only child in the north of England. 'I had a happy childhood,' she says, 'but I always longed for a brother or sister. I had several pets, but it wasn't the same. I was adopted at birth, and I sometimes wondered if my genetic parents had had any other children. I dreamed that I would meet them one day.'

3 When she was sixteen, she and her parents moved to Bristol, in southwest England, and within a week the strangest things started to happen. 'Strangers kept coming up to me in the street,' she remembers with a laugh. 'They started talking about their party last night, or their homework – all sorts of things that I knew nothing about. One guy came and gave me a kiss, and I'd never met him in my life. I was really angry!'

4 Kathryn started to realise that there was a girl in Bristol who looked very like her. In one of Kathryn's strange encounters on the street, she found out that the girl's name was Maddy. She asked for Maddy's email address and soon got in touch. It turned out that Maddy had been having similar experiences over the past few months, and that she too had been brought up by adoptive parents. They arranged to exchange photos by email. Neither of them could believe what they saw when they opened the photos on their computers. The two girls looked absolutely identical: the same green eyes, the same long dark hair, the same smile. They were even holding their heads in exactly the same position in the photos!

5 Later that week, the twin sisters met up for the first time, and since then they have become good friends. 'We are doing the same course at university,' says Kathryn, 'so we see each other almost every day.'

6 'We get on incredibly well,' continues Maddy, 'and we have a lot in common. But we've got completely different personalities. I grew up with two older brothers, and I'm probably more outgoing and sociable than Kathryn, and more energetic too! Kathryn's definitely lazier. She's always chilling out instead of studying. But she's also more generous, and much more sensible than I am.'

7 What's the best thing about having an identical twin? 'It sounds silly,' says Kathryn, 'but it really helped my self-confidence. I used to think that I was too fat, but Maddy is the same size as me and she looks great. So now I know that my worries about my weight are just in my head.'

8 And the worst thing? 'Introducing your boyfriend to your twin sister,' laughs Maddy. 'You want to believe that you are the only person in the world for him. But if he likes the way you look, he likes the way your sister looks too. You definitely don't want to give him the chance to work out which one of you he prefers!'

CHATROOM

- If you have brothers and sisters, would you like to be an only child? Would you like more siblings? Why/Why not?
- If you are an only child, would you like brothers and sisters? Why/Why not?

WebSearch

http://en.wikipedia.org/wiki/Twins
www.twin.com

Vocabulary
Words from the text
Prepositions

1 Choose the correct word to complete the sentences.

1 He's the same size _____ me.
   A of   B to   C with   D as

2 What's the worst thing _____ living in your town?
   A about   B with   C of   D in

3 I haven't introduced him _____ my parents yet.
   A for   B to   C with   D at

4 Can you send me that photo _____ email, please?
   A on   B in   C with   D by

5 You aren't the best in the class, but you're good compared _____ me.
   A at   B to   C as   D by

6 Tonight I'm going to see my new baby brother _____ the first time.
   A on   B for   C at   D with

7 A journalist got _____ touch with me last week.
   A on   B to   C at   D in

Phrasal verbs

2 Complete the phrasal verbs in the text with *out* or *up*.

Charlie Murphy **grew** ¹_____ on the same street as me. We were best friends until Charlie's mum married someone from Ireland and they decided to **bring** ²_____ Charlie there. We weren't very good at emailing, so we lost touch.
   Later I tried to **find** ³_____ what had happened to Charlie, but I couldn't. There were a lot of people called Charlie Murphy in Ireland and I couldn't **work** ⁴_____ which one he was. Then, last year, I went on holiday to Ireland with my family, and I saw a big poster for a new TV show. Charlie was in the poster! It **turned** ⁵_____ that he was a big star in Ireland. I sent him an email, and soon after that we **met** ⁶_____ . After all those years, we still got on really well. Now Charlie has moved back to England and we see each other every week. He's a great person to **chill** ⁷_____ with.

3 Match the phrasal verbs from Exercise 2 with these definitions.

1 spend your childhood _____
2 meet by arrangement _____
3 decide after thinking carefully _____
4 look after a child _____
5 happen in a particular way _____
6 relax _____
7 get information about something _____

Personality
Adjectives

4 Complete the crossword with adjectives from the box.

> outgoing   energetic   loyal   polite   romantic
> modest   brave   moody   sensible   cautious
> mean   naughty   generous   ambitious   honest

Someone who:

1 behaves badly is …
2 isn't easily scared is …
3 always supports his/her friends is …
4 dreams of perfect love is …
5 doesn't often talk about his/her abilities and achievements is …
6 enjoys meeting and talking to people is …
7 wants to get an important job is …
8 is careful to avoid danger and risk is …
9 gives a lot of presents is …
10 is very active and full of energy is …
11 behaves and speaks in the correct way and is never rude is …
12 isn't kind is …
13 gets upset easily is …
14 always tells the truth is …
15 shows good judgement is …

5 Make a list of other personality adjectives that you know.

Word formation: nouns from adjectives

6 Complete the table.

	adjective	noun
		-ty/-ity
1		loyalty
2	honest	
3	modest	
4		generosity
5	creative	
6		responsibility
7	mature	
		-ence
8		self-confidence
9	impatient	
		-tion
10	ambitious	
11		caution

7 Decide which of the nouns in Exercise 6 are qualities, which are faults and which are neutral.

Appearance

8 Match the words with the parts of the face.

> cheek   eyebrow   chin   forehead
> nose   lip   fringe   ponytail

2 _____

3 _____

1 _____

4 _____

5 _____

6 _____

8 _____

7 _____

9 Where on the body do you find these things? Do you think any of them are attractive? Which ones?

> wrinkles   a tattoo   a beard
> a moustache   freckles   a scar   make-up

10 Complete the table with these words. You can write some words twice.

> slim   wavy   elderly   pale   straight   curly
> middle-aged   teenage   well-built   blond
> pretty   shoulder-length   tanned   dark
> overweight   skinny   good-looking   ugly
> handsome   fair   spiky   cute

Hair	Body	Skin	Age	Opinion

11 Answer the questions about the words in Exercise 10.

Which word:

1 means *thin in a good way*?
2 means *thin in a bad way*?
3 is a more polite way to say *fat*?
4 is usually only used to describe men and boys?
5 is usually only used to describe women and girls?
6 means *a little bit curly*?
7 means *not long and not short*?

12 Describe these people.

CHATROOM

- Describe the appearance of your favourite film star or singer.
- Talk about friends and family. What do they look like? What are they like?

Grammar
Present simple and Present continuous

1 Match the examples (a–g) with the forms and uses in the grammar notes.

a We're doing the same course at university.

b A class is held every morning.

c We see each other almost every day.

d She's always chilling out instead of studying.

e Only children get more attention from their parents.

f They are being photographed for the magazine.

g They're holding their heads in the same position.

Present simple
- a regular action or habit [1]_____
- a permanent situation or general truth [2]_____

Passive form: [3]_____

Present continuous
- an action that is happening at the moment [4]_____
- a temporary situation [5]_____
- a habit with *always* (often annoying) [6]_____

Passive form: [7]_____

See **Grammar File**, page 158.

2 Complete the text with the present simple or present continuous, active or passive.

Logged in ⊗

I've got relatives all over the world. My half-brother Mark [1]_____ (live) in New York this year, but he's coming home after Christmas. Mum will be happy when he's back. She [2]_____ (complain always) that Mark [3]_____ (phone never) us. Dad grew up in Australia and my grandparents [4]_____ (live still) over there. Flights from Australia to Britain [5]_____ (take) at least twenty-two hours, and they [6]_____ (cost) hundreds of pounds, so we [7]_____ (not see) each other very often. I've also got relatives in Canada. I [8]_____ (study) really hard at the moment because every year the top student in Year Nine [9]_____ (chose) for an exchange programme to Canada!

> The grandkids say the Internet has made the world a smaller place, but I'm not so sure.

Stative verbs

3 Read the grammar notes and circle the correct options.

Stative verbs include:

agree, be, believe, like, love, hate, have, hear, imagine, know, mean, need, own, prefer, promise, realise, remember, see, understand, want

We usually use stative verbs in the [1]**present simple / present continuous**, even when they are describing a temporary situation.

I **don't understand** the question.

I **love** your hair today.

Some words can be stative verbs with one meaning and ordinary verbs with another meaning.

I **have** a new watch. (have = possess) [2]**stative verb / ordinary verb**

I'm **having** lunch. (have = eat) [3]**stative verb / ordinary verb**

I **think** she's cool. (think = believe) [4]**stative verb / ordinary verb**

I'm **thinking** of learning French. (think = consider) [5]**stative verb / ordinary verb**

See **Grammar File**, pages 158–159.

4 Complete the phone conversation with the present simple or present continuous.

Mark: Mum! Hi! It's Mark.

Mum: Hello, Mark. It's great to hear your voice. [1]_____ (you / have) a good time in New York?

Mark: It's OK, but I [2]_____ (not know) enough people here. I [3]_____ (think) of joining a basketball club so that I can make some new friends.

Mum: That's a good idea! But don't worry. You [4]_____ (have) lots of friends in England, and you'll be back here soon.

Mark: But New York is great in lots of ways. I definitely [5]_____ (prefer) the weather here. It [6]_____ (snow) at the moment. A lot of New Yorkers [7]_____ (not like) the winter, but I [8]_____ (think) this cold weather is wonderful.

Mum: Oh, I [9]_____ (not agree) with you. Warm weather is so much nicer. In fact, at the moment we [10]_____ (try) to organise a winter holiday to Tunisia.

Articles

5 **Match the rules in the grammar notes with the groups of examples, a, b and c.**

a Children without siblings are lucky.
  I love music.
  We both like eating chocolate.
b I always longed for a brother or sister.
  There was a girl in Bristol who looked very like Kathryn.
c Later that week, the twin sisters met up.
  What's the best thing about it?
  The girl's name was Maddy.
  The music at the concert was lovely.

> *a/an* + singular countable noun
> • to talk about something or someone that is not specific, or one of many, or mentioned for the first time
> *(See examples ____)*
>
> *the* + countable, uncountable or plural noun
> • to talk about something or someone that is specific, unique, mentioned before, or with superlatives
> *(See examples ____)*
>
> no article + uncountable or plural noun
> • to talk about things or people in general
> *(See examples ____)*

See **Grammar File**, page 159.

6 **Complete the email with *a, an* or *the*. Leave the gap empty if no article is needed.**

○○○

✉ New   ✉ Reply

Hi Ed,

Thanks for ¹_____ your email. It was nice to hear from you!

I had ²_____ interesting day yesterday. My dog ³_____ Biggles loves digging in ⁴_____ garden, and yesterday he dug up ⁵_____ big pile of earth. I was looking at ⁶_____ pile when I saw ⁷_____ ring! It turns out that ⁸_____ ring had been my great-great-grandmother's. She gave it to my grandmother and she lost it ⁹_____ ten years ago. My great-great-grandfather was ¹⁰_____ King's ¹¹_____ doctor and my great-grandmother was ¹²_____ politician!

Come and visit in ¹³_____ summer. We can meet in ¹⁴_____ centre of ¹⁵_____ London and see ¹⁶_____ sights. Would you like to go for ¹⁷_____ walk next to ¹⁸_____ River Thames?

Write soon!

Love Jess

Back up your grammar

7 **Choose the correct word or phrase, A, B, C or D to complete the sentences.**

1 Look! That girl _____ at you!
  A smiles   C smiling
  B is smiling   D smile
2 My birthday is on _____ July.
  A the last day in the   C last day in
  B a day in the   D the last day in
3 She _____ Italian boy in her class.
  A doesn't like a   C isn't liking
  B is liking an   D likes the
4 Because it's so sunny at the moment, I _____ lots of freckles.
  A am having   C has
  B having   D have
5 They spend _____ school every day.
  A a long time at   C long time at the
  B the long time at D a long time at the
6 I _____ generosity is a very important quality in people.
  A think the   C am thinking the
  B think   D am thinking
7 Egypt is _____ Africa.
  A a country in the   B a country in
  C the country in the D country in
8 I _____ teacher when I'm older.
  A want to be   C am wanting to be
  B want to be a   D am wanting to be a

CHATROOM

Talk about the following:

• what your friends and family are doing right now.
• what you enjoy doing with them.
• what annoying habits they have.

11

Listening

Cancer June 22 – July 23

Aries March 21 – April 20

Taurus April 21 – May 21

Gemini May 22 – June 21

Scorpio Oct 24 – Nov 22

Leo July 24 – Aug 23

Virgo Aug 24 – Sept 23

Libra Sept 24 – Oct 23

Capricorn Dec 23 – Jan 20

Sagittarius Nov 23 – Dec 22

Aquarius Jan 21 – Feb 19

Pisces Feb 20 – Mar 20

ShyBoy27 Logged in

My cousin's really into star signs and reads her horoscope every day. I wonder if any of it's true.

What star sign are you? Do you read your horoscope? Do you think your star sign has any influence on your personality?

More soon ... Watch this space.

Listening 1

1 Listen to this conversation and circle the correct answer.

Listening Tip: multiple choice

Read the questions carefully before you listen, and underline the key words.

1 Where was Ethan last night?
 A at Sam and Max's house
 B at his girlfriend's house
 C at a party
 D with Katie

2 What does Rebecca look like?
 A She's tall.
 B She's got dark hair.
 C She's pretty.
 D She wears glasses.

3 Ethan and Rebecca don't like the same
 A sports.
 B music.
 C teachers.
 D books.

4 Ethan's star sign is
 A Scorpio.
 B Libra.
 C Capricorn.
 D Sagittarius.

5 Katie knows about star signs from
 A a book that she got for her birthday.
 B her friend Jasmine's book.
 C Kyle and Liam.
 D a book from the library.

6 What does Ethan think of Katie's ideas about star signs?
 A He wants to learn more about them.
 B He doesn't believe them.
 C He thinks they will make her unhappy.
 D He thinks they're true.

7 Ethan wants to
 A get in touch with Rebecca.
 B find out when Rebecca's birthday is.
 C keep talking to Katie.
 D apologise to Katie.

Listening 2

2 You are going to hear a radio interview with Tom Bevan, who is talking about his research. Decide if the statements are true (T) or false (F).

1 Tom is explaining how we inherit our character from our parents. ☐
2 There are a lot of politicians who are eldest children. ☐
3 Eldest children hate making mistakes. ☐
4 The second child is usually the naughtiest member of the family. ☐
5 Second children are often competitive. ☐
6 Middle children often think they're very lucky. ☐
7 A lot of scientists are middle children. ☐
8 Youngest children usually choose very serious, responsible jobs. ☐
9 Only children usually help their parents a lot at home. ☐
10 A lot of only children are very creative. ☐

CHATROOM

Think of some people you know and the position they have among their siblings. How well does Tom's description fit their personality?

WebSearch

www.birthorderandpersonality.com

12

Speaking
Talking about yourself

1 How well do you know your classmates? Tell a partner two true sentences and one false sentence about yourself. Your partner has to ask questions and work out which sentence is false.

2 Listen to the conversation. Underline the words in blue in the Language Upload box that you hear.

3 Work with a partner. Take turns being the interviewer and giving information about yourself. Talk about these things:
- your family
- your home
- your local area
- free time

Speaking Tip:
talking about yourself

Try not to give one-word answers.

If you don't understand a question, say calmly: *Sorry. Please could you repeat the question?*

Mum, it'll only take me five minutes to install this new software. My friend Jason and I are really into a new game. I'll do my homework later ...

Language Upload

Questions
Could you tell me something about ...?
Could you describe ... to me?
What do you like about ...?
Is there anything you'd like to change about ...?
How often do you go to ...?
What (else) do you like doing in your free time?

Your family
(See pages 5, 8 and 9.)

Your home
I live in [1] a flat / a house.
My home has got [2] three bedrooms / a balcony / a garden.
It's on [3] the ground floor / the first floor / the top floor.
It's in [4] the city centre / a quiet residential area / a town / a village / the countryside.

Your local area
It (only) takes me five minutes to walk to [5] the shops / the station / the bus stop / school.
A lot of my [6] friends / relatives live nearby.
There's (not) a lot to do in the area.
It would be good if there were more [7] shops / sports facilities / restaurants.
It would be good if there was [8] a cinema / a bowling alley / a school nearby.

Free time
I go to the city centre [9] every week / about once a month / three times a year.
We sometimes go [10] clothes shopping / to a café for a chat / to the cinema.
I'm really into [11] football / video games / dancing.
I love going to [12] the mountains / the beach / my friend's house.

Writing: Descriptive article
Before you write

1 Read the writing task and answer the questions.

> You have seen this notice in your school magazine. Write an article for the magazine. Use 120–180 words.

Writers Wanted!

Write about someone who has had a big influence on your life. Describe the person's appearance and personality, and explain the influence that he or she has had on you.

The best articles will be published next month!

1 What should the article be about?
2 Who is going to read the article?
3 What important information should you include?
4 On which pages of this unit will you find useful vocabulary for the article?

2 Read Jason's article. Who is it about? Would you like a person like this in your family? Why/Why not?

My grandfather

I love sport, and one of the main reasons for that is my grandfather. He comes to every tennis and basketball match that I play in and he always shouts words of encouragement. He's ¹_____ wonderful person, and he has had a huge influence on my life.

When you first see ²_____ grandfather, you only notice one thing: his moustache. It's big and grey, and covers half his face. He's got a nice smile, red cheeks and kind brown eyes. He hasn't ³_____ much hair, but his eyebrows are big and grey and move a lot when he talks. ⁴_____ tall and well-built. He's ⁵_____ old man, but when he's playing sport with me he seems like a teenager because he's very energetic.

He's very patient, and he's never moody. He's ⁶_____ honest too.

When he says that I've done well, I know that he means it.

My grandfather has taught me that you can only succeed in something if you work hard at it. It's my ambition to become ⁷_____ professional basketball player. Because of my grandfather, I have the confidence to achieve that ambition.

3 Now complete the gaps with a suitable word or phrase.

4 Complete Jason's plan for his article.

Writing Plan

Paragraph 1	Introduce the person and his/her importance to me	• my grandfather and sport • huge influence on my life
Paragraph 2	Describe his/her appearance	• face: big grey _____, nice smile, red _____, kind brown _____, big grey _____ • hair: not much • body: tall, _____ • age: an old man (but very energetic)
Paragraph 3	Describe his/her personality	• patient • never _____ • honest
Paragraph 4	Say what influence he/she has had on me	• hard work • confidence to achieve my ambition

5 Find some examples of these connecting words in Jason's article.

Connecting words

Giving reasons

because + clause

I'm interested in sport **because** my grandfather has always encouraged me.

because of / thanks to + noun

Because of my grandfather's encouragement, I'm quite a confident person.

Thanks to my grandfather's encouragement, I've won lots of matches.

noun + is the reason for + noun

My grandfather's encouragement **is the reason for** my successful sporting career.

6 Rewrite the sentences using the connecting words from Exercise 5.

1 People don't think I'm good at things because I'm very modest.

   Because of my modesty, people don't think I'm good at things.

2 Thanks to my stepmother's generosity, I can buy a new MP3 player.

   Because my stepmother _____

3 We know what happened to the money because you were honest.

   Thanks to _____

4 I'm impatient because I stay up too late at night.

   My late nights are the reason _____

7 Write sentences about the following, and the reasons for them. Use the connecting words from Exercise 5.

1 a fantastic day

   Last Saturday was fantastic because I was with my best friends all day.

2 your results in a test

   _____

3 an achievement in a hobby or sport

   _____

4 a time when you were very angry

   _____

5 a time when you were very late for something

   _____

Time to write

8 You are going to do the writing task in Exercise 1. Choose a person to write about then make a plan for your article using the plan opposite to help you.

9 Now write your article. Use the Memory Flash and Connecting words box to help you.

Writing Tip

Remember to read the task very carefully. Include everything that it mentions.

Memory Flash

Introducing the person	Describing appearance	Describing personality	Explaining the person's influence
He's a wonderful person.	When you first see my grandfather, you only notice one thing: his …	He's very …	Because of my grandfather, …
He has had a huge influence on my life.	He's got a nice smile.	He's never …	My grandfather has taught me that …
	When he …, he seems/ doesn't seem …	He can …	

Vocabulary

1 Complete the sentences with the correct form of the word in capitals.

1 She paints beautiful pictures, and she's a writer too. She's so _____ . CREATE

2 He's thirteen, but he looks and behaves much older. His _____ is very unusual. MATURE

3 _____ is needed when you cross busy roads. CAUTIOUS

4 Why are you so _____? Just wait – I'll be ready soon. PATIENT

5 Thanks to her _____ , I always have a friend when I need one. LOYAL

6 Is it possible to learn _____ , or do we inherit it from our parents? SELF-CONFIDENT

2 Choose the correct word, A, B, C or D to complete the sentences.

1 I hope we don't lose _____ when we leave school.
  A touch   C common
  B relative   D friend

2 He isn't skinny. He's _____ and very handsome.
  A well-built   C ugly
  B shoulder-length   D pretty

3 My parents _____ me at birth.
  A adopted   C brought up
  B inherited   D meant

4 She's got long blond hair that she wears in a _____ .
  A cheek   C moustache
  B tattoo   D ponytail

5 Don't be so _____ . You're not OK at music, you're fantastic!
  A romantic   C naughty
  B modest   D moody

6 I can't _____ how I know you.
  A chill out   C work out
  B turn out   D grow up

7 He's got a lot of wrinkles on his _____ .
  A fringe   C forehead
  B scar   D beard

8 I've got five _____ – two brothers and three sisters.
  A twins   C ancestors
  B siblings   D nieces

9 She only looks good if she wears a lot of _____ .
  A lips   C eyebrows
  B make-up   D chin

10 He'd never do anything so silly. He's always very _____ .
  A energetic   C sensible
  B mean   D brave

Grammar

3 Complete the mini-dialogues with the present simple or present continuous.

1 **A:** _____ (you / have) a good time at the party?
  B: Yes, but I _____ (not know) many people here.

2 **A:** Where _____ (your stepdad / be)?
  B: He _____ (visit) his nephew in Manchester.

3 **A:** I _____ (not understand) my homework. Can you help me?
  B: Oh, you _____ (always ask) for help!

4 **A:** _____ (you / remember) how to get to Jack's?
  B: Yes, it's easy. My grandparents _____ (live) on the same street.

5 **A:** You _____ (not drink) anything. I've got some juice, if you like.
  B: Yes please. I _____ (prefer) juice to tea or coffee.

4 Complete the gaps with *a, an* or *the*. Leave the gap empty if no article is needed.

¹_____ Sassy is ²_____ friend of ³_____ mine. In fact, she's ⁴_____ best friend I've ever had. ⁵_____ last year, our families went to ⁶_____ Wales on ⁷_____ holiday together. She's got ⁸_____ little brother. He's ⁹_____ very energetic boy. He can cycle ¹⁰_____ hundred kilometres in one day! We had ¹¹_____ pool, and spent ¹²_____ hours in it every day.

5 Complete each gap with a suitable word.

What does your pet say about you?

If you are ¹_____ of buying a pet, be warned! People can find out a lot about your personality from your choice of pet. ²_____ you have a cute little dog that goes with you everywhere? ³_____ he sitting in your bag at this moment? Then you are a kind and generous person, and are probably interested in fashion. If, however, you ⁴_____ a larger dog, this shows that you are energetic and outgoing.

Perhaps you have a cat ⁵_____ home. Is it ⁶_____ on your bed now, waiting for you? Then you are ⁷_____ hard-working and loyal person.

Owners of reptiles like snakes and lizards don't like to be ⁸_____ same as others. They see themselves as brave and independent. If goldfish are your thing, that may be because you ⁹_____ a cautious person who likes routine. Tropical fish, however, tell a different story. They show that you are romantic and ¹⁰_____ adventure.

We all remember some days more than others. What have been the biggest moments in your life so far?

2 Days to Remember

Vocabulary Starter
Life experiences

1 Complete the sentences with words from the box.

> culture   adolescents   tribes
> ceremony   tradition   wedding

1 In some places, people are expected to get married as _____ , around the age of fifteen.

2 People usually get married in their twenties or thirties in European _____ .

3 In England two thousand years ago, there were many different _____ , each with a different language.

4 It's a _____ in Britain that the woman getting married wears something old, something new, something borrowed and something blue.

5 My stepbrother Charlie's getting married! I'm going to his _____ tomorrow.

6 The _____ starts at three o'clock, and after that they will be officially married.

2 Which clue? Number the clues to the adjectives crossword below.

☐ boring
☐ making your face go red when you think about it
☐ very unusual or surprising
☐ very impressive and exciting to look at
☐ strange
☐ liked by a lot of people
☐ very interesting
☐ making part of your body hurt
☐ difficult in an interesting way
☐ very good
☐ too painful or difficult
☐ making you rest and stop worrying
☐ providing useful or interesting information
☐ making you want to achieve something, even if you have to work hard

Crossword:

4 UNBEARABLE (across)
10 EXTRAORDINARY (across)
13 DULL (across)
14 MOTIVATING (across)

Down clues:
1 WEIRD
2 PAINFUL
3 RELAXING
5 FASCINATING
6 CHALLENGING
7 SPECTACULAR
8 EMBARASSING
9 INFORMATIVE
11 POPULAR
12 BRILLIANT

- How do you think the people in the photos would describe their experience?
- Have you experienced any of the events in the photos? What were they like?

Reading

1 You are going to read an article about teenage ceremonies. Read the article quickly and find out where the photos were taken and what they show.

2 Read the article again and choose the best answer, A, B, C or D.

> **Reading Tip: multiple choice**
>
> First read the text. Then read the questions, but not the multiple-choice answers.
>
> Find the relevant part of the text.
>
> Read the multiple-choice answers and choose the best one.

1 Which sentence about land diving is correct?
   A It is a newer sport than bungee jumping.
   B It is done to make sure there is enough food on the island.
   C It isn't very dangerous.
   D It is important that the shoulders don't touch the ground.

2 Why was David's mother holding a toy car?
   A Because she planned to give it to David after his jump.
   B Because she used to like playing with it.
   C Because a car is the symbol of becoming an adult.
   D Because she planned to throw it away after his jump.

3 Why did David decide to jump?
   A Because this allowed him to become a man.
   B Because his mother could see him.
   C Because he wanted to be injured.
   D Because he knew that he wouldn't be seriously injured.

4 Since jumping, how has life changed for David?
   A Everyone now sees him as an adult.
   B He is more interested in girls.
   C He is more attractive to the opposite sex.
   D He is no longer interested in toys.

5 What is special about the ceremonial gloves of the Satere Mawé people?
   A Young men are shot by a bullet when they wear them.
   B They are full of wasps.
   C They cause a great deal of pain.
   D Only over-18s are allowed to wear them.

6 What happened to Mari while he was wearing the gloves?
   A The gloves permanently damaged his hands.
   B His uncle took away his pain.
   C He screamed and screamed.
   D His brother tried to help him.

7 What are Mari's intentions for the future?
   A To wear the gloves many more times.
   B To go on a journey.
   C To wear the gloves for three hours.
   D To find other ways to prove that he's grown up.

Becoming an adult is never easy

'Can't you see that I'm not a child any more? What do I have to do to prove that I've grown up?' It's a question that is asked time after time by teenagers around the world, and in every culture there's a different answer.

1 For David, growing up on Pentecost Island in the South Pacific, the answer had always been clear. He had to become a land diver. Land diving is a tradition on Pentecost Island which inspired the better known sport of bungee jumping. Land diving, however, is much more dangerous.

2 Every year at a ceremony called Naghol, the men of the island jump off towers thirty metres tall, with long vines, not elastic, tied to their feet. A perfect jump is one in which the shoulders land gently on the ground. People believe that this will help the crops on the island to grow. If the vine is too short and the jumper's fall is stopped before the shoulders touch the ground, the jumper is considered a coward. If the vine is too long, the result can be serious injury or death.

3 As David climbed the tower, his mother watched from below. She was holding a toy car that he used to play with when he was younger. After a boy's first land dive, his favourite toy is thrown away to show that he is no longer a child.

4 'Before my jump, I felt very nervous,' remembers fourteen-year-old David. 'As a child, I always used to watch the land divers at Naghol.

Every year someone would get an injury. For a second, I panicked. I thought about changing my mind … but you can't become a proper man without being a land diver.'

5 David jumped. While the people down below were playing drums and singing, he fell head-first to the ground. Luckily, he landed safely and walked away with just a few bruises. And does he feel like a man now? 'Well, I certainly feel more mature,' he smiles. 'And the girls in my village are much more interested in me than they were before.'

6 The people of Pentecost Island are not alone in giving their adolescents a dangerous, painful or challenging task to prove their maturity. In the Amazon, the teenage boys of the Satere Mawé tribe have to go through the terrible pain of the glove ceremony. A pair of big ceremonial gloves are filled with 400 highly poisonous bullet ants. Bullet ants have their name for a reason: a sting from one of these two-centimetre-long ants feels like a gun shot. It causes thirty times the pain of a wasp sting.

7 Fourteen-year-old Mari recently went through this extraordinary ceremony. 'All my family was there with me, helping me and giving me advice,' he remembers. 'I had to keep the gloves on for ten minutes. The pain was unbearable and I wanted to scream, but that wasn't allowed. It was important not to make a noise in front of the rest of the tribe. I was being held up by my uncle and my older brother because I couldn't stand on my own. My brother was saying encouraging things in my ear, but I wasn't listening. The pain was too great. When the gloves were taken off, the pain didn't stop. The next three hours were the worst of my life. My hands were twice their normal size. Twenty-four hours later, though, I was fine.'

8 So, is Mari now seen as an adult by the rest of his tribe? 'Not yet,' says Mari with an uncomfortable smile. 'I have to put on the bullet ant gloves twenty times in total. I don't think I'll ever get used to that pain, but it's still worth it. After the twentieth time I'll be a man.'

9 Becoming an adult is rarely an easy journey, but it's easier in some places than in others. What would you do to prove you've grown up?

---

3 **Find words or phrases in the article that match these meanings.**

1 gave people an idea (paragraph 1) _____
2 plants grown for food (paragraph 2) _____
3 someone who isn't brave (paragraph 2) _____
4 felt so scared that it was impossible to think clearly (paragraph 4) _____
5 purple or brown marks on the skin, caused by falling or being hit (paragraph 5) _____
6 a small piece of metal that comes out of a gun (paragraph 6) _____
7 a yellow and black insect that stings (paragraph 6) _____

WebSearch

www.spotlightradio.net/listen/
becoming-an-adult

Vocabulary

Words from the text
Word formation: nouns and verbs

1 **Complete the table. You can find the words in the article on page 19.**

	Noun	Verb
1	proof	
2	growth	
3		result
4	cause	
5		injure
6	dive	
7		shoot
8		advise

2 **Complete the sentences with a word from Exercise 1.**

1 If you jump from too high, you might _____ your legs.
2 I told you not to do it, but you never listen to my _____ !
3 The _____ of the town has been very fast. It was only a small village ten years ago.
4 We've found some of his hair in the room. We've now got _____ that he was there.
5 Please don't _____ ! Put the gun down before you do something that you'll regret!
6 Your fantastic score in the test is a _____ of all your hard work this term.
7 Sports injuries can sometimes _____ health problems in later life.
8 Let's _____ off the boat and into the sea.

Collocations

3 **Choose the best word to complete the sentences. Then look back at the text on page 19 to check.**

1 She dived head- _____ into the swimming pool.
   A down   B first   C ways   D forward
2 I suggest you bring a _____ of gloves with you.
   A couple   B pair   C double   D two
3 Have you got any cream to put on a wasp _____ ?
   A bite   B sting   C injury   D hurt
4 I don't like travelling on _____ .
   A myself   B own   C my own   D alone
5 Sorry, I'm not coming after all. I've changed my _____ .
   A choice   B decision   C thought   D mind
6 They don't enjoy playing with toys _____ more.
   A for   B now   C any   D at
7 We've been to the rainforest seven times _____ total.
   A in   B at   C on   D for

Time
Times of day

4 **Match the times of day with the definitions. Then say what you are usually doing at each time.**

1 sunrise
2 dawn
3 dusk
4 sunset
5 noon
6 midnight

a twelve o'clock – also called 'midday'
b the time when the sun disappears in the evening
c the time of evening when it starts to get dark
d the time when the sun first appears in the morning
e the time of day when light first appears
f twelve o'clock, the middle of the night

Expressions with *time*

5 **Read the sentences and match expressions 1–8 with definitions a–h.**

1 They always get up **on time**.
2 We arrived just **in time** to see the start of the film.
3 You've been studying for hours. Take some **time off**.
4 I'm studying **full time** at the moment.
5 Next year she wants to work **part time** in a restaurant.
6 Oh no! It's six o'clock already. How **time flies**!
7 I enjoy going to the cinema **from time to time**.
8 **Time's up**! That's the end of the exam.

a sometimes _____
b time passes quickly _____
c at the right time _____
d less than thirty-five hours per week _____
e more than thirty-five hours per week _____
f early enough to do something _____
g time when you are not working _____
h there's no more time _____

6 Complete the sentences with expressions from Exercise 5.

1 _____ , I'm afraid. Did you manage to finish?

2 The train didn't leave the station _____ . It was ten minutes late.

3 They took some _____ last week and had a relaxing day on the beach.

4 He works _____ so he goes to work three days a week.

5 I can't believe it's so late! _____ when you're having fun!

6 She sees him _____ , but not very often.

7 Their mum works _____ , so she's out for most of the day.

8 We want to get home _____ to watch our favourite programme on TV.

Dates

7 Put these times in the past into the correct order.

a in the late 1950s ☐

b in the early twentieth century ☐

c the day before yesterday ☐

d in prehistoric times ☐

e in the first millennium BC ☐

f a decade ago ☐

g in 79 AD ☐

h the year before last ☐

i in the Middle Ages ☐

8 Match these events to times from Exercise 7. Then write your own sentences for the remaining three times in your notebook.

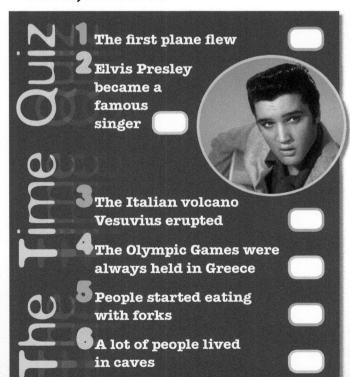

The Time Quiz

1 The first plane flew ☐

2 Elvis Presley became a famous singer ☐

3 The Italian volcano Vesuvius erupted ☐

4 The Olympic Games were always held in Greece ☐

5 People started eating with forks ☐

6 A lot of people lived in caves ☐

Days out

9 Match the words with the places 1–12.

> bowling alley   safari park   ice rink   temple
> seaside resort   aquarium   beauty spot   zoo
> art gallery   stadium   concert hall   museum

1 _____   2 _____

3 _____   4 _____

5 _____   6 _____

7 _____   8 _____

9 _____   10 _____

11 _____   12 _____

10 Explain the difference between the following:

1 a **zoo** and a **safari park**.

2 a **fire** and **fireworks**.

3 a **picnic** and a **meal out**.

CHATROOM

What places do you like going to on a day out with your friends or family? What places do you hate going to? Give reasons.

21

More practice on pages 128–129.

Grammar
Past simple and Past continuous

1 Read the grammar notes and complete the gaps.

> **Past simple**
> - a completed action at a specific time in the past
> *I¹_____ (go) to Pentecost Island last year.*
> - a sequence of completed actions in the past
> *He landed safely and ²_____ (walk) away.*
> - a past habit or regular past event
> *In past years, David always ³_____ (have) fun at Naghol.*
> - a situation in the past
> *I⁴_____ (feel) very nervous.*
> **Past simple passive:** *The gloves were taken off.*
>
> **Past continuous**
> - an action in progress at a particular time in the past
> *At the time of David's jump, his mother ⁵_____ (hold) a toy car.*
> - two actions in progress at the same time in the past
> *My brother ⁶_____ (say) encouraging things in my ear, but I ⁷_____ (not listen).*
> - an unfinished action interrupted by a short action
> *While I⁸_____ (stand) there, I panicked for a second.*
> - the background information in a story
> *The people down below ⁹_____ (play) drums and singing. David jumped.*
> **Past continuous passive:** *I **was being held** up by my uncle.*
>
> **Remember!** Stative verbs cannot be used in the past continuous.

See **Grammar File**, page 160.

2 Complete different people's memories below with the past simple or past continuous, active or passive.

☹ Moments

Embarrassing

1 Three weeks ago I [____1____] (write) in my diary about a cute boy in my class. The next day, my sister [____2____] (read) it to everyone in the lunch queue!

2 I was acting in a very sad play at school and hundreds of people [____3____] (watch) me. Suddenly my mobile phone [____4____] (start) playing the *Star Wars* theme tune!

3 When I was ten, my parents [____5____] (be given) a pink car by my dad's boss. I [____6____] (be driven) to school in it every day.

4 As I [____7____] (talk) to my teacher, I [____8____] (call) her 'mum' by mistake.

5 While we [____9____] (visit) a forest on a school trip, I [____10____] (climb) up a tree. Unfortunately, I [____11____] (not manage) to climb down again!

3 Complete the text with the past simple or past continuous, active or passive.

Kate would never forget her Prom night.

Prom night is a big deal here in the USA. It's a party at the end of your last year at high school.
Before my Prom, I ¹_____ (drive) to my girlfriend Kate's house. She ²_____ (still get) ready. An hour later, when she finally ³_____ (come) downstairs, she ⁴_____ (wear) a long red dress. She looked wonderful.
But then – disaster! As we ⁵_____ (walk) to the car, I ⁶_____ (not see) a step in the path. I ⁷_____ (fall), and landed on the bottom of Kate's dress. The dress ripped. It ⁸_____ (be ruined)!
The next few minutes were terrible. Kate ⁹_____ (cry) and her dad ¹⁰_____ (shout) at me. I felt really bad. Eventually, though, a dress ¹¹_____ (be borrowed) from Kate's cousin, and we could drive to the Prom. By the time we finally ¹²_____ (arrive), all our friends ¹³_____ (have) dinner. They were very pleased to see us – even if we were three hours late!

> **CHATROOM**
> - Describe an embarrassing moment in your life.

4 Read the grammar notes.

---

used to + infinitive
- a past habit or regular past event

*As a child, I always **used to watch** the land divers at Naghol.*
- a past state

*He **used to be** a good friend of mine.*

would + infinitive
- a past habit or regular past event (but NOT a past state)

*During my childhood, someone **would get** an injury every year.*

be used to + *–ing* form
- to say that something is no longer strange because we have experienced it so often

*I'**m used to seeing** enormous insects. I've lived in the rainforest for years.*
get used to means *become used to*.
*I'**ll** never **get used to** that pain.*

See **Grammar File**, pages 160–161.

5 Choose the best word or phrase, A, B, C or D to complete the sentences.

1 Rich Americans living in the north of the USA _____ to like their cold winters.
  A didn't use   C wasn't used
  B wouldn't   D didn't used

2 Some of them _____ come and spend the winter in a small Californian village called Hollywood.
  A used   C would
  B got used to   D didn't use

3 New York _____ be the centre of the American film industry back then.
  A was used to   C would
  B used to   D use to

4 The first film makers arrived in Hollywood in 1910, and they soon _____ to the friendly people and the long sunny days.
  A get used   C used
  B got used   D be used

5 The first films with sound were made in the late 1920s. They amazed their audiences, who _____ to silent films.
  A used   C get used
  B would   D were used

6 The first Disney film, *Snow White*, was released in 1938. Did you _____ enjoy watching Disney films when you were a little kid?
  A used to   C use to
  B would   D get used to

Back up your grammar

6 Read the text. Complete each gap with <u>one</u> suitable word. Don't forget to read the whole text before you complete the gaps.

Shia LeBeouf

is now a famous Hollywood actor, star of the latest *Indiana Jones* and *Transformers* films, but he ¹_____ his show business career at the age of ten, telling jokes in comedy clubs.

Every weekend he ²_____ go surfing. One of his surfing friends always used ³_____ have cool stuff – new games consoles, new shoes, new watches. Shia ⁴_____ not have any of these things, and he was jealous. He found out that his friend acted in a TV show and Shia decided to try something similar.

A few days later he walked into an agent's office, and before long he ⁵_____ chosen to be the star of the Disney TV show *Even Stevens*. It was challenging at first because he wasn't ⁶_____ to the long working days. When he ⁷_____ filming, he hardly saw his parents. But he soon ⁸_____ used to it.

CHATROOM

- What were your favourite films and TV shows when you were little? What did you use to enjoy most about them?
- Talk about a big and exciting change in your life. What was life like for you before and after that moment? How did you adapt to your new life?

More practice on pages 130–131.

Listening

Logged in

LizzieLu

I'm really looking forward to New Year's Eve. I'm going to a friend's house to celebrate. At midnight, they're going to have a fireworks display in the garden. I can't wait! What do you usually do at New Year?

More soon ... Watch this space.

Listening 1

🔊 **1** You are going to hear a radio programme describing the first moments of the twenty-first century. Listen and complete the sentences.

> **Listening Tip:** sentence completion
>
> Read the sentences before you listen and try to guess what kind of information is missing: a person's name, a place name, a date ...?

Kiribati was the [___1___] place to celebrate the new millennium.

There was a big [___2___] display in Sydney, Australia.

There was a [___3___] for two thousand couples in Bangkok, Thailand.

In Germany, [___4___] were born in different millennia.

The world's first millennium baby was born in a city in [___5___] .

The baby's parents didn't want to talk to people who worked for [___6___] .

Many people were worried about the problems that [___7___] might cause.

There weren't a lot of people travelling by [___8___] that night.

A German man was paid lots of money by his [___9___] .

At a video store in the USA, there was some confusion about which [___10___] it was.

Listening 2

🔊 **2** You are going to hear Emma talking about what she did on New Year's Eve, 1999. Listen to the conversation and the questions, then choose the best answers, A, B or C.

> **Listening Tip:** multiple choice
>
> Look at the possible answers before you listen, and try to guess what sort of question it might be: *What ...? How ...? Who ...? Why ...?* or a *yes/no* question.

1　A　ride on a big wheel
　　B　visit relatives in London
　　C　buy tickets to a concert

2　A　angry　　B　embarrassed　　C　excited

3　A　Her grandparents bought them.
　　B　Her mother won them.
　　C　Her friends changed their minds about going.

4　A　Yes.
　　B　No, because the wheel wasn't safe.
　　C　No, because Emma and her mother weren't well.

5　A　have a meal out in London
　　B　buy some fireworks
　　C　have fun at home

6　A　by boat　　B　by car　　C　by train

7　A　a meal in a restaurant
　　B　some food from a shop
　　C　some fruit

8　A　They were all friendly.
　　B　They were all from London.
　　C　They were all from other countries.

9　A　rainy　　B　snowy　　C　cold

10　A　very colourful　　B　quite short
　　C　not very good

CHATROOM

What traditions are associated with New Year's Eve in your country?

WebSearch

www.everything2000.com

Speaking
Comparing pictures

1 What makes a birthday fun? Work with a partner and try to agree on the three most important things.

- a   being with your best friends
- b   getting some cool presents
- c   being with your family
- d   having a special meal
- e   having a big party
- f   doing an activity that you don't often do
- g   staying up late

2 Look at these photos of different birthday celebrations. Listen to a person doing the task below and decide which two photos she is talking about.

> Compare these two photos of birthday celebrations. Whose birthday do you think it is? Which celebration would you prefer to go to, and why?

A

B

C

D

3 Listen again and complete the table.

Similarities	
Differences	
Whose birthday she thinks it is First picture: Second picture:	
Which celebration she would prefer to go to, and why	

4 Now read the task in Exercise 2 again and take it in turns to compare photos A and D and B and C. Use the Language Upload box to help you.

Speaking Tip: comparing pictures

Read the task carefully before you start speaking. Make sure you cover all parts of the task.

You have to speak for about one minute.

Think about the similarities and differences in: the people, the place, what they are doing, how they feel.

Language Upload

Describing a picture

The picture shows …
The people in the picture look happy.
They seem to be having a great time.
In the background / foreground …
In the top left hand corner there's …
At the bottom of the picture you can see …

Talking about similarities and differences

Both the pictures are of …
In one picture, … . In the other (picture), …
In the first picture, … . In the second (picture), …

Taking a guess

I'm guessing it's … 's birthday.
I don't think it's … 's birthday.
It's probably … 's birthday.

Expressing a preference and a reason

I think I'd prefer to be at …
I'd definitely rather go to …
… because I'm not too keen on …
… because I've never been to a party like that before.
… because … is better than …

Writing: Letter to a newspaper
Before you write

1 Read the newspaper extract and the task below. Then answer the questions.

> vulput ina reuisvaus aciii
>
> ### The *Daily Times* Best London Museum Competition
>
> The *Daily Times* is sponsoring a competition to find the best museum in London. We want readers to tell us about their favourite museum and explain its appeal. Please send your nomination to the editor.
>
> te fengiatio comm ⁓dana

Write a letter to the editor of the *Daily Times*. Name the museum that you think should win the competition. Describe your experience(s) at the museum. Start your letter 'Dear Editor' and write 140–180 words.

1 Who or what can win the competition?
2 Who are you going to write to?
3 What information should your letter contain?
4 Should you use formal or informal language in your letter?

2 Read Rick's letter. Complete each gap with the correct sentence.

a This was really fascinating.
b I am writing to nominate Madame Tussauds for the Best London Museum Competition.
c I would thoroughly recommend it to anyone.
d We had to walk through a dark room where scary-looking actors were hiding.

> Dear Editor,
>
> ¹_____.
>
> Madame Tussauds has life-size wax statues of the world's most famous people: Hollywood stars, sports stars, politicians and musicians. I went last year with a group of friends and it was a fantastic experience.
>
> The great thing about it was that we could touch the statues and ask our friends to take photos of us with our favourite celebrities. We were also impressed with the Chamber of Horrors. ²_____. The actors would jump out at us suddenly and give us the shock of our lives. It was terrifying, but fun too. Another aspect of the visit that we particularly enjoyed was the 'Spirit of London' section, where we learnt about the history of the city from the sixteenth century to the late 1980s. ³_____.
>
> All in all, Madame Tussauds is a brilliant place for a day out. ⁴_____.
>
> Yours faithfully,
>
> Rick

3 Complete Rick's plan for his letter.

Writing Plan

Paragraph 1	Explain your reason for writing	• Dear …, • nominate _____ for competition
Paragraph 2	Brief introduction to the place	• life-size wax _____ • Hollywood stars, sports stars, _____ , musicians • fantastic experience
Paragraph 3	Say what was good about the place	• touch the statues • take _____ with the statues • Chamber of Horrors, with scary-looking _____ • 'Spirit of London' section
Paragraph 4	Summarise your impression of the place and close	• a _____ place for a day out • Yours faithfully, …

4 Which of the phrases in bold can you find in Rick's letter?

Connecting words

Summarising

All in all, I would thoroughly recommend it.

To sum up, it's a place that everyone can enjoy.

In conclusion, I believe that there's no better museum in London.

All things considered, it's a fantastic day out for the whole family.

In short, the play is not appropriate for young children.

To conclude, I wasn't impressed by the book.

5 Complete the gaps with one suitable word.

1 _____ sum up, it's a fantastic film in every way.

2 _____ conclusion, my visit to the museum was one of the worst experiences of my life.

3 All _____ considered, I won't be going back to the bowling alley soon.

4 _____ in all, the new safari park is superb for all the family.

5 _____ conclude, Mrs Johnston was by far the best teacher I'd ever had.

6 _____ short, the performance could have been better.

Memory Flash

Time to write

6 Read the writing task below. Then make a plan for your letter, using the plan opposite to help you.

vuipul ma teuis ans acii

The *Daily Times* Best Days Out Website

The *Daily Times* is creating a new website covering the best places for days out in your region. We want readers to tell us about their favourite place for a day out and explain its appeal. Please send your nomination to the editor.

te fengiatio comm digna

Write a letter to the editor of the *Daily Times*. Name your favourite place for a day out in your local area. Describe your experience(s) there. Start your letter 'Dear Editor'.

7 Now write your letter (140–180 words). Use the Memory Flash and the Connecting words box to help you.

Writing Tip: formal letters and emails

Remember to use formal language, especially when you close your letter. Use *Yours faithfully* if you don't know the name of the person you are writing to, and *Yours sincerely* if you use their name.

Opening a formal letter	Saying what was good about a place	Making recommendations	Closing a formal letter
Dear …,	The great thing about it was that we could …	I would thoroughly recommend it to anyone.	Yours faithfully,
I am writing to nominate … for …	We were also impressed with …	It is a brilliant place for a day out.	Yours sincerely,
	Another aspect of the visit that we particularly enjoyed was …		

Vocabulary

1 Circle a word or phrase in the second sentence so that it has a similar meaning to the first sentence.

1 I don't have to study during the school holidays.
I can have some **part time / time off / time up** during the school holidays.

2 I really hate this.
This is **unbearable / brilliant / spectacular**.

3 In European culture, few people get married as teenagers.
There aren't many weddings between **adolescents / tribes / pairs** in European culture.

4 He was born in 1998.
He was born **in the early 1990s / in the 19th century / more than a decade ago**.

5 I was bored by the TV show.
The TV show was **fascinating / dull / painful**.

6 I was late, so I didn't see the first part of the concert.
I didn't arrive **in / on / from** time to see the first part of the concert.

7 Everyone liked the ceremony.
The ceremony was **relaxing / challenging / popular**.

2 Complete each mini-dialogue with a suitable word.

1 A You said you'd come to that new art _____ with me today.
B Oh, sorry. I've changed my _____ . I'm going to the ice _____ with Ellie instead.

2 A The train arrives at twelve o'clock.
B Twelve midnight or twelve _____?

3 A You can get a lot of people into a concert _____ .
B Maybe, but you can get more into a football _____ .

4 A He's a farmer, isn't he? Does he work hard?
B He works from _____ to _____ . Whenever there's daylight, he's working.

3 Complete the text with the correct form of the word in capitals.

1 In races, you should start running when you hear a _____ from a gun. SHOOT

2 Milly has always found running races very _____. MOTIVATE

3 She was the fastest runner in her class until she got a foot _____. INJURE

4 When she hurt her foot, her doctor _____ her to stop running for three months. ADVICE

5 While she was resting, she read a very _____ book about sport psychology. INFORMATION

6 When she started running again, the _____ in her self-confidence was amazing. GROW

7 Milly's extraordinary success is _____ that a book can change lives. PROVE

Grammar

4 Complete the text with the past simple or past continuous.

When I was younger, we ¹_____ (go) to the park every year on 5th November to celebrate Bonfire Night. We ²_____ (always enjoy) ourselves there … until two years ago. That year we ³_____ (have) a new dog, Pogo, and we ⁴_____ (decide) to take him with us. While we ⁵_____ (watch) the fireworks, Pogo ⁶_____ (run) away because the loud noises ⁷_____ (scare) him. We ⁸_____ (look) for him for ages before we finally ⁹_____ (find) him. He ¹⁰_____ (hide) under our car. Poor Pogo! He really ¹¹_____ (not like) those fireworks.

5 Complete the second sentence so that it has a similar meaning to the first sentence, using the word given. Use between two and five words.

1 Were you at the cinema last night?
go
_____ to the cinema last night?

2 This hot weather is becoming normal for us.
getting
We are _____ this hot weather.

3 She met some nice people during her visit to Norway.
while
She met some nice people _____ visiting Norway.

4 It still feels weird living in my new house.
used
I'm still _____ living in my new house.

5 Every Saturday, I watched the football with my dad.
would
Every Saturday, _____ the football with my dad.

6 At the time of the accident, he was having a shower.
when
_____ , he was having a shower.

Everyone loves a good story – but what do you prefer?
Fiction, or true stories?

3 Fact or Fiction?

Vocabulary Starter
Stories (1)

1 Which types of story do you think the photos illustrate? Which do you like to read?

> adventure story   horror story   fairy tale
> science fiction (sci-fi)   thriller
> historical novel   romance   detective story
> biography   autobiography   comic book   fantasy

2 Circle the correct word. Then make sentences about the other words. Use your dictionary to help you.

1 The main female character in a story is called the **hero** / **heroine**.
2 A bad character in a story is called **a villain** / **a vampire**.
3 The time and place of a story is called the **plot** / **setting**.
4 A person with extraordinary powers is **an alien** / **a superhero**.
5 If you do something bad to someone because they've done something bad to you, you take **revenge** / **victims**.
6 A story about people that don't really exist is **fact** / **fiction**.

3 Do the quiz. Choose *fact* or *fiction*, then check your answers on page 125.

Fact or Fiction?

1 A 15-year-old future king narrowly escaped death when a bullet hit the medal that he was wearing on his chest. — **Fact** / Fiction

2 Alligators have for many years been living in the dark, wet tunnels under the city of New York. — **Fact** / Fiction

3 The Greeks won their ten-year war against the Trojans by hiding in a wooden horse. — **Fact** / Fiction

4 The first two types of creature that travelled from our planet into space were flies and monkeys. — **Fact** / Fiction

5 Italian teenagers Romeo and Juliet got married in secret because their families hated each other. — **Fact** / Fiction

CHATROOM

- Talk about one of your favourite stories: mention the type of story, setting, characters and plot.
- If you were writing stories based on the sentences in Exercise 3, what type of story would you choose for each one?

freeze

Nina was fourteen when it first happened. She'd been at her cousin's wedding all weekend and hadn't studied for Mr Emsworth's Geography test. [1]

'Conrad's much better looking than Robbie.'

'Yeah, but he can't sing.'

Waiting for Mr Emsworth's lesson, Nina hardly listened to her friends' conversation about the latest talent show on TV. She was too worried about the test. ¹_____ 'I need more time. I haven't done enough revision … more time,' she thought. The words went round and round inside her head [10] like a dog chasing its tail.

And then it happened. One minute her friends were arguing about the competition, and the next minute they had stopped mid-sentence, open-mouthed. Frozen. She stared at them, not understanding. She glanced into the classroom. Mr Emsworth was there, walking towards the classroom door. Except, he wasn't moving. ²_____ A statue. One foot was in the air ready to take another step. Nina got out her books hurriedly and spent a few hours reading her geography notes. Then finally she started to relax. She [20] scratched her ear.

'… His singing's really bad! It's not surprising no one voted for him.'

Her friends were back. The conversation went on as if it had never stopped. Mr Emsworth called them into the classroom to start the test. It was not too difficult now that Nina had studied for it. It was lunchtime before Nina could talk to anyone about what had happened.

'While we were waiting outside Mr Emsworth's classroom, did you notice anything strange?' she asked her best [30] friend Jaz.

'What, apart from people liking Robbie more than Conrad?'

'Yeah. I … well … time seemed to …'

'Come on, Nina. Tell me later. Let's get some lunch.'

There never was a right time to talk to anyone about it. 'Time stopped, and I studied for the test for three hours that didn't exist.' She could imagine Jaz's response. 'Nina, stop being weird. You've been reading too many sci-fi stories.'

Reading

1 **You are going to read a short story. Six sentences have been removed from the text. Choose from sentences A–G the one which fits each gap (1–6). There is one extra sentence that you do not need.**

Reading Tip: missing sentences

Use the nouns and pronouns in the sentences to help you. The pronouns often refer to people and things that have been mentioned in the previous sentence. The nouns may be referred to again in the following sentence.

A He paid her well.

B With her extraordinary powers, she felt no pain.

C She pushed a pot of paint off her desk, then focused her mind.

D In horror, Nina realised that the woman was talking to her.

E Anyone who failed it had to do extra work every night for a month.

F He was like a man in a photograph.

G Nina saw the car centimetres from the boy's nose, and focused her mind.

time

But in her bedroom, in secret, she practised. ³_____ The
40 pot stopped in mid-air, and Nina caught it safely before paint
went all over the floor.

• • • • • • • • • • • • • • •

'Hey, Jaz, do you want to come and see that new fantasy film
later? I'll pay.'

Since that Geography test last year, Nina had been
delivering newspapers around town. Her boss couldn't
understand how a schoolgirl could deliver 20,000 newspapers
each week, but he didn't ask too many questions. ⁴_____
She could invite her friends to all the films, pop concerts and
meals out that they'd ever dreamed of. She had never been
50 more popular.

She always did her homework on time these days. After all,
it never interfered with having fun. She spent freeze-time days
relaxing on the beach. She stayed up all night, but froze time
whenever she needed to sleep. Once, when her mum asked
her to tidy her room, she froze time for a month so that she
could lie in bed eating crisps and popcorn. Life couldn't get
any better.

• • • • • • • • • • • • • • •

Nina spent a lot of time shopping.

'For older skin like yours, you might prefer this,' said the
60 woman in the make-up shop. ⁵_____

She studied her face in the mirror. With her finger, she
followed the lines of her wrinkles. The woman was right. Nina
had the face of a thirty-year-old.

She rushed out of the shop. This was terrible. She was
becoming middle-aged, and the only explanation was her
freeze-time lifestyle. Each time everyone froze and she
continued living, she got older than her friends. There had been
too much freeze-time. It had to stop.

A car came down the street, too fast. The driver hadn't
70 noticed the little boy crossing. ⁶_____ The car froze. Gently,
she moved the boy out of the way of the car, then touched
her ear. The driver sped on, and the boy ran into the park after
his mother.

'Sometimes you have to make an exception,' she thought.
'But that's it. Freeze-time has finished.'

She walked past a TV shop. A news report caught her eye.
A bus had had an accident on a mountain road. Rescuers
were getting the passengers off but they didn't think they would
have time to save them all.

80 Nina didn't want to be a heroine, and she didn't want to be
middle-aged. Not yet. But she knew that she could help these
people. Reluctantly, she focused her mind again.

WebSearch

www.superherodb.com
www.thesuperheroquiz.com

---

2 Read the story again. For questions 1–6, choose
the answer, A, B, C or D which you think fits best
according to the text.

1 What was happening the first time Nina froze time?
   A Nina's friends were dancing.
   B Someone was taking a photograph.
   C Nina was thinking about a dog.
   D Mr Emsworth was walking across the classroom.

2 When did Nina tell Jaz about the strange incident?
   A Before lunch.
   B After lunch.
   C After reading some sci-fi stories.
   D Never.

3 What did Nina practise in her bedroom?
   A Freezing time.   C Throwing and catching.
   B Painting.   D Keeping secrets.

4 Which sentence is **incorrect** about Nina a year after
   the Geography test?
   A She was a good student.
   B She enjoyed her life.
   C She didn't get enough sleep.
   D She always ate healthy food.

5 What did Nina realise during her shopping trip?
   A That she wasn't wearing make-up.
   B That she looked thirty years older than she was.
   C That she was ageing faster than her friends.
   D That the woman in the shop could freeze time.

6 At the end, what did Nina decide to do?
   A Never freeze time again.
   B Freeze time in order to help people.
   C Help people without freezing time.
   D Never become middle-aged.

3 Match the words and phrases from the story with
their definitions.

1 chase (line 11)   a reply or reaction
2 response (line 37)   b person who saves someone
3 deliver (line 45)   from danger
4 interfere (line 52)   c someone who is travelling
5 rescuer (line 77)   in a car, train, bus, etc.
6 passenger (line 78)   d take something to the
                             place where it's being sent
                           e follow someone or
                             something quickly in order
                             to catch them
                           f stop something from
                             happening

Do you think Nina is lucky or unlucky? Why?

Vocabulary

Words from the text
Verb-noun collocations

1 **Complete the sentences with the words in the box.**

| catch   make   take   move   fail   have |

1 Usually we don't have students under the age of sixteen here, but we'll _____ **an exception** in your case.
2 The new superhero books always _____ **my eye** when I'm in the bookshop.
3 Let's _____ **out of the way** of the people in the race.
4 If they _____ **the test**, they'll have to take it again next month.
5 I know your foot hurts, but please try to _____ **a step** towards me.
6 Drive more slowly, or you'll _____ **an accident**!

Compound words

2 **Match the two parts of the compound words and use them to complete the sentences. Then look back at the text on page 30 to check.**

| life   mid-   open-   pop   mid- |

| style   mouthed   air   sentence   corn |

1 My dog can jump really high and catch a ball in _____ .
2 I'd love to be an actor. They have such a cool _____ .
3 She looked at him, _____ . She couldn't believe what she was seeing!
4 '… and then they … ' He stopped _____ .
5 We always buy _____ to eat while we watch a film.

Stories (2)
Adverbs

3 **Complete the sentences with these adverbs.**

| safely   reluctantly   well   gently   lazily   badly   enthusiastically |

1 I didn't want to, but _____ I agreed.
2 She can sing really _____ . She should be a pop star!
3 I just hope that they all get back home _____ .
4 They lay in the sun _____ . What a relaxing day!
5 We lost the match 6–0. We played very _____ .
6 _____ , she picked up the sleeping boy without waking him up.
7 'I'd love to go on the trip!' she said _____ .

4 **What are the adjective forms of the adverbs in Exercise 3?**

5 **These words can be adjectives or adverbs. Complete the sentences and decide if the word is used as an adjective or adverb.**

| hard   far   early   fast   late |

1 'Have you walked _____ ?' 'No, only a couple of kilometres.'
2 I had a _____ night yesterday. I didn't get to bed until 1 a.m.
3 That test was _____ , but you got a good mark. Well done!
4 I always get up _____ so that I can see the sunrise.
5 You'll have to move _____ to get to the shop before it closes.

6 **Match the adverbs in bold with their meanings.**

1 I've been working **hard**.   a almost not
2 I've **hardly** done any work.   b recently
3 She always arrives **late**.   c not on time
4 She hasn't been here **lately**.   d with a lot of effort

Verbs
Ways of looking

7 **Read the sentences and write the verbs in bold next to the definitions below.**

1 They **stared** at me for several minutes without smiling. 'How rude!' I thought.
2 She **glared** at her sister. She was too angry to speak.
3 He **studied** the diamond carefully. 'Yes, it's real,' he said at last.
4 I **glanced** at my watch. I still had plenty of time.
5 She **peered** through the window. Someone was there, but it was too dark to see their face.

a looked carefully, because it was difficult to see _____
b looked at something or someone for a long time without moving the eyes _____
c looked at something carefully in order to find something out _____
d looked angrily at someone for a long time _____
e looked quickly at something or someone _____

Ways of speaking

8 Circle the correct option.

1 stammer **loudly / nervously**
2 whisper **softly / in terror**
3 scream **softly / in terror**
4 hiss **loudly / quietly but angrily**
5 yell **softly / loudly**

9 How are the people speaking? Listen and complete the sentences with verb phrases from Exercise 8. Use the past simple form.

1 'Help!' she _____.
2 'You stupid idiot!' he _____.
3 'I'm over here!' he _____.
4 'H-h-hello! N-n-nice to m-m-meet you,' she _____.
5 'You look beautiful tonight,' he _____.

Ways of walking

10 Match the verbs (a–e) and adverbs / adverbial phrases (i–v) with the pictures (1–5).

> **a** stroll **b** limp **c** creep **d** march **e** rush

> **i** painfully   **ii** like a soldier   **iii** quickly   **iv** quietly
> **v** in a slow and relaxed way

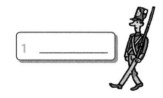
1 _____

2 _____

3 _____

4 _____

5 _____

Verbs + prepositions

11 Read the text and circle the correct preposition.

Do you believe ¹**in / at / for**

aliens?

Many people think that they have seen spaceships from other planets here on Earth. Many others laugh ²**for / to / at** these people and blame sci-fi writers ³**about / with / for** putting crazy ideas into their heads. 'It's easy to mistake a plane ⁴**for / with / by** an alien ship,' they say.

Of course, we shouldn't rely ⁵**in / on / of** the stories of a few individuals, but thousands of people around the world, including several astronauts, tell very similar stories of what they have seen. Four hundred years ago, scientists were punished ⁶**for / on / about** saying that the Earth was round, not flat. Now few people disagree ⁷**to / with / against** their ideas. Will an alien encounter be the next great event to change our beliefs for ever?

They have those silly communication boxes like our ancestors did!

CHATROOM

- Describe situations when you have walked, looked or spoken in a different way from normal. Use some of the ideas below or your own ideas.
  - an argument
  - a frightening situation
  - a difficult situation
  - being outside in the dark
  - an injury
  - a secret
  - being late

  e.g. *I had an argument with my brother last week, and I really yelled at him for the first time.*

More practice on pages 132–133.

Grammar
Present perfect simple and Present perfect continuous

1 Read the grammar notes and circle the correct options.

Present perfect simple
- states and completed actions at a(n) [1]**specified / unspecified** time in the past

I've heard that story before.

- states and actions that began in the past and [2]**continue / don't continue** up to now (often with *for* and *since*)

I haven't been interested in fairy tales since I was five years old!

- actions completed [3]**recently / long ago**

I've just finished reading it.

- repeated actions in the recent past

They've met their favourite writer three times.

- with expressions like *the first, the best, the worst*

It's the first biography I've ever bought.

Passive: *The film has been seen by millions of people.*

Present perfect continuous
- actions that began in the past and [4]**continue / don't continue** up to now (often with *for* and *since*)

She's been writing her autobiography since April.

- longer actions in the recent past, where the results [5]**can / can't** still be seen

You've been reading too many sci-fi stories, so now you're imagining aliens everywhere.

There is no passive form.

Past simple vs Present perfect

The past simple is used for a [6]**specified / unspecified** time in the past.

I saw that film last week.

Compare with the present perfect simple.

I've seen that film before.

Time expressions often used with the Present perfect:

for, since, just, already, yet, ever, never, before, this week/month/year, today, recently, lately

> See **Grammar File**, page 161.

---

2 Complete the sentences with the present perfect simple or continuous.

1 'Why has she got paint in her hair?'
   'Because she _____ (paint) the ceiling.'

2 'Is Charlotte a friend of yours?'
   'Yes, although we _____ (not know) each other for very long.'

3 '_____ (ever / you / be) on TV?'
   'No, but I'd like to one day.'

4 'Do you know London well?'
   'Not very, but I _____ (stroll) round the city centre a couple of times.'

5 'Where's Matt?'
   'In the park. He _____ (play) football there for hours.'

6 'So where's your new computer?'
   'It _____ (not be delivered) yet.'

7 'Can I speak to Cara, please?'
   'Sorry, I'm afraid she _____ (just go) out.'

8 'Is *New Moon* a good book?'
   'It's brilliant! It's one of the best books I _____ (ever read).'

3 Complete the text with the past simple, present perfect simple or present perfect continuous.

In Japan, mobile phone novels are big news. They [1]_____ (grow) in popularity in the last few years, and [2]_____ (be read) by millions of people.

Last week, we [3]_____ (speak) to mobile phone author Asuka.

'So, Asuka, can you explain how these novels work?'

'Well, readers download a story from a website onto their mobile and read it on the mobile screen. Some mobile phone novels [4]_____ (also be made) into traditional books, but most young people prefer reading them on their phones.'

'[5]_____ (you / want) to be an author for a long time?'

'No, not really. As a young child, I [6]_____ (never be) very interested in books. Then one day I [7]_____ (realise) that you could tell a story in more modern ways, and suddenly my interest in writing [8]_____ (begin). I [9]_____ (start) my first novel in 2009, and I [10]_____ (write) full time since then. Four of my novels [11]_____ (already be published).'

Past perfect simple and Past perfect continuous

4 **Read the grammar notes and match the uses with the examples.**

Past perfect simple	Past perfect continuous
• an action that was completed before another past action (example [1]_____) • an action that was completed before a specific time in the past. (example [2]_____)	• to say how long something continued, up to a time or event in the past (example [3]_____) • a longer action that was completed before a specific time in the past, where the results could still be seen (example [4]_____)
Examples *A Two months later, Megan **had found** a job.* *B The test wasn't difficult because she **had studied** for it.* *Passive: She realised that she **had been given** a special skill.*	**Examples** *C They were tired because they **had been shopping** all day.* *D Megan **had been delivering** newspapers for a year before she noticed her wrinkles.* There is no passive form.

See **Grammar File**, page 162.

5 **Complete the sentences with the past perfect simple or past perfect continuous form of the verb in brackets.**

1 At five o'clock yesterday, we still _____ (not have) our lunch.

2 How long _____ (Ben / learn) English before he went to stay in London?

3 Their favourite TV programme _____ (already finish) when they got home.

4 When I first met Peter, I _____ (not read) any of his novels.

5 We couldn't make the machine work because we _____ (not be sent) any instructions.

6 Her eyes were hurting because she _____ (study) things under a microscope all day.

7 By the time Saskia arrived, we _____ (wait) for almost an hour.

CHATROOM

Choose from the situations below and tell the story. Explain what had happened previously and what you'd been doing just before.

- you lost something important
- you found something surprising
- you saw an unusual event
- you were very frightened

Back up your grammar

6 **Read the text and choose the best option, A, B, C or D to complete each gap.**

STRANGE BUT TRUE – news just in

A crocodile [1]_____ flying through the air in Sarov, Russia.

Yesterday morning, the one-metre crocodile [2]_____ on a pavement after it [3]_____ out of the window of the twelfth-floor flat where it had been living for several years. Experts think that it [4]_____ out of the window to sunbathe.

When the crocodile was discovered, terrified locals [5]_____ the emergency services and rescuers [6]_____ to catch the animal. It [7]_____ given back to its owner. It [8]_____ one of its teeth, but apart from that it is unharmed.

1	A has been seen	C	has seen
	B had been seen	D	had been
2	A has landed	C	has been landing
	B had landed	D	landed
3	A has fallen	C	has been falling
	B is falling	D	had fallen
4	A had been leaning	C	has been leaning
	B had been	D	has leaned
5	A were called	C	had been called
	B called	D	had called
6	A managed	C	had been managing
	B have been managing	D	had managed
7	A has now been	C	has now
	B had now been	D	had now
8	A broken	C	had been breaking
	B has broken	D	has been broken

More practice on pages 134–135.

Listening

Logged in

SuperDan

I saw a Dracula film on TV last night. It made me laugh so much – it wasn't scary at all. My sister is terrified of monsters and vampires, though. She only lasted ten minutes and then she was too scared to watch. Do you like horror films? What's the scariest film you've ever seen?

More soon ... Watch this space.

Listening 1

🔊 **1** **You will hear a news item about Bran Castle in Romania. Listen and write what you hear. You will hear the recording twice.**

Bran Castle has ...

Listening Tip: dictation

If you have difficulty with a word or phrase, write down the sound you hear, even if it is not a real word.

When the recording has finished, go back to the difficult words and write down your best guess. Use the context to help you.

Check your text carefully for spelling mistakes.

Listening 2

🔊 **2** **Listen to part of a radio programme and choose the phrase that best completes each sentence.**

Listening Tip: multiple choice

Remember, an answer isn't correct just because you hear some of the same words on the recording. Think about general meaning, not individual words.

1 James Metcalf is on the radio because
  A he wrote a book.   C he is in a film.
  B he is a scientist.

2 The character Victor Frankenstein
  A becomes a monster.   C creates a new life.
  B brings his dead friends back to life.

3 When Victor sees the monster alive, he
  A leaves him on his own.   C looks after him.
  B teaches him about the world.

4 The monster kills people because
  A he's a very bad person.   C Victor asks him to.
  B he wants revenge on Victor.

5 The first version of the Frankenstein story was
  A written by a teenager.   C written by a poet.
  B a traditional fairy tale.

6 The idea for the Frankenstein story came to the writer while she was
  A reading a science book.   C walking in the rain.
  B staying with friends in Switzerland.

7 At the same time, John Polidori wrote
  A a story about vampires.   C a fairy tale.
  B a story about Dracula.

CHATROOM

Have you ever seen a film or TV show of the Frankenstein story, or about vampires? What did you think of them?

WebSearch

www.brancastlemuseum.ro

Speaking
Making a choice

1 Imagine you work for a film company and you have to choose a story to make into a film. In pairs, look at pictures 1 and 2. Student A: ask the questions below to find out about the stories. Student B: give answers, using the information on page 125.

- What type of story is it?
- Where is the story set?
- Who are the characters?
- What happens in the story?

2 Listen to the conversation. Which story has the speaker chosen to make into a film? Why? Which story has the speaker rejected? Why?

3 Do you agree or disagree with the speaker's choice?

4 Now do the speaking task below in your pairs. Use the Language Upload box to help you.

Situation

Imagine you work for a film company. Choose one of these stories to make into a film for teenagers.

Student B

Look at pictures 3 and 4 and ask:

- What type of story is it?
- Where is the story set?
- Who are the characters?
- What happens in the story?

Student A: give answers, using the information on page 125.

Student B

When you have all the information you need, explain which story you have chosen. Be ready to explain why you didn't choose the other story. Remember to use information you learn to explain your choice.

Speaking Tip: making a choice

Try to give several reasons for your choice, and explain why you've rejected the alternative.

5 Talk about these questions.

1 Do the pictures remind you of any films that you've seen? How are they similar or different?
2 Do you watch many films? Where and when do you usually watch them?
3 Do you prefer watching films in your own language or in English? Why?
4 Who are your favourite film actors at the moment? What good films have they been in recently?

Language Upload

Expressing a choice

This is an easy/hard choice to make.
I've chosen the sci-fi story.

Giving an opinion

In my opinion, you can't beat a good thriller.
Personally, I'm (not) a big fan of ….
I'm (not) very keen on …
I prefer …
The setting sounds good.
… sounds like an interesting character.
I (don't) think the plot sounds very exciting/ entertaining/interesting/scary.

Writing: A story
Before you write

1 Read the writing task and answer the questions below.

> Your teacher has asked you to write a story for your school's English magazine. The story must begin with the following words:
>
> *I continued to follow the path through the trees. I was exhausted, and completely lost.*
>
> Write a story of 120–180 words.

1 Who is going to read the story?
2 What situation is the person in the story in?
3 Which part of the story has already been written?

2 Read Sara's story. What scares the narrator?

I continued to follow the path through the trees. I was exhausted, and completely lost. I usually walked home from school through the park. ¹**That afternoon / After that**, however, the park gate had been locked, so reluctantly I had taken the path through Widden Woods. Dusk was now falling. I had been walking for hours.

The leaves moved gently in the wind ²**as / by now** I followed the path round a corner. ³**Meanwhile / At last**, some luck! There was a little cottage next to the path. Delighted, I peered in through the window.

I screamed in horror. A scary-looking witch was staring back at me! I turned and ran, but ⁴**immediately / the next day** my foot hit something hard. It hurt terribly but I limped on, wanting to get away from the cottage. ⁵**Suddenly / Finally**, I heard footsteps behind me. I froze, terrified.

'I hope I didn't scare you,' said a friendly voice. I glanced back and saw the witch there, smiling at me. 'I'm f-f-fine,' I stammered weakly. 'I'm going to a rehearsal of *The Witch's Cat* at the theatre,' said the woman. 'If you're lost, you can follow me to the bus stop.'

3 Read Sara's story again and circle the best time markers.

4 Complete Sara's plan for the story.

Writing Plan

Paragraph 1	Set the scene for the story	use story opener in task, then: • park gate was _____ • _____ was falling
Paragraphs 2 – 3	Main part of the story: say what happened	• saw a house • saw a _____ through the window • ran away • hurt _____ • heard footsteps – it was the _____!
Paragraph 4	End the story in a satisfying or surprising way	• witch explains that she's in a play, and offers to help find the _____

5 Find examples of these connecting words in the story.

Connecting words

Showing emotion and attitude

-ed adjective

I listened to his story, **amazed**.

adverb of manner

We said goodbye **sadly**.

in + noun

She glared at him **in anger**.

participle clause

I walked through the trees, **hoping to find a road**.

6 Complete the sentences with these words.

excitement   laughing   painfully   fascinated

1 He limped _____ to the door.
2 I screamed in _____ when I heard the good news.
3 They sat in the classroom, _____ at Ben's jokes.
4 We stared at the weird creature, _____ .

7 Expand these sentences to show the subject's emotions or attitude. Use the connecting words from Exercise 5.

1 She looked over her shoulder at the vampire
_____
2 The two brothers rushed towards each other
_____
3 I heard a voice coming from inside the cupboard _____
4 We decided to go home _____

Time to write

8 You are going to write a story. Read the writing task and answer the questions below.

You have seen this advert in an international magazine for learners of English. Write a story for the competition.

> ### Short Story Competition
> Write a story of 120–180 words. The story must begin with the following words:
> *I rushed along in panic. I was late again, and today was the one day that I really couldn't be late.*
> The best stories will be published in the magazine.

1 Who is going to read your story?
2 What situation is the person in the story in?
3 Which part of the story has already been written?

9 Decide the details of your story. Make notes about these questions.

1 Where was the narrator going?
2 Why was it so important to be on time?
3 Why was he/she late? What had happened before that?
4 Where was he/she?
5 Did the narrator arrive on time? If yes, how? If not, what were the consequences?
6 What happened in the end? Did the story have a happy ending, a sad ending or a surprising ending?

10 Make a plan for your story, similar to the writing plan in Exercise 4. Then write your story, using the Memory Flash and the Connecting words box to help you.

Writing Tip: a story

Make your writing sound more interesting by:
• using a mix of long and short sentences.
• starting your sentences in different ways.
• including some direct speech.

Memory Flash

Saying what had happened previously	Describing the background situation	Saying what happened	What people said
The park gate had been locked.	Dusk was falling.	Suddenly, I saw / heard …	'…' said a friendly voice.
I had taken the path through Widden Woods.	I was running along a crowded pavement.	There was …	'…' I stammered weakly.
I had been walking for hours.			

Vocabulary

1 **Complete the text with words from the box.**

> superhero   heroine   villain   alien   victim
> setting   plot   revenge   thriller   facts

Rain Cloud

Author:

Andy Taylor

☆☆☆☆☆

Andy Taylor is a successful comic book writer. His best known stories are about the ¹_____ AstroMan, who can turn into the shape of any ²_____ from any planet in the cosmos. He has also written some fascinating books with weird ³_____ about science, but his latest book is a ⁴_____.

The ⁵_____ of his new novel, Rain Cloud, is a likeable teenage girl called Liesel. Liesel's father was killed in an accident at work. Now, Liesel wants to find out exactly what happened. She gets in touch with Mick, the son of another ⁶_____ of the accident. At first Liesel and Mick work together, but after some time Liesel realises that, in ⁷_____ for his mother's death, Mick has been killing the people responsible. Liesel has to stop him before more people die!

Mick is the perfect ⁸_____ – a very unpleasant person indeed, and the ⁹_____ of the story, in small-town USA, makes an interesting change from the big city environment of most crime stories. The ¹⁰_____ moves quickly and is very exciting. If you're a fan of thrillers, you should definitely read this book!

2 **Circle the correct word.**

1 I don't **believe / rely** in ghosts.
2 'It's all your fault,' she **hissed / stammered** angrily at Natasha.
3 'You can't **blame / mistake** me for all your problems,' she replied.
4 He **marched / crept** up to him quickly and confidently and asked for an explanation.
5 Have you read any good books **late / lately**?
6 'That's the actor in *Transformers*,' he **screamed / whispered** quietly in my ear.
7 She **glanced / stared** at her watch for a second.
8 I've been studying very **hard / hardly** for the test.
9 We **strolled / rushed** slowly back from school.
10 I don't want my parents to **punish / disagree** me for coming home late.

Grammar

3 **Complete each sentence with a suitable word or phrase.**

1 I _____ never enjoyed detective stories before I read this one last week.
2 It's the first time she _____ ever been here.
3 Before she got ill, she'd _____ hoping to visit Romania.
4 'What's wrong?' 'My story _____ been chosen to appear in the magazine and I'm a bit disappointed about it.'
5 _____ you see that adventure film on Tuesday?
6 They _____ bought the DVD yet, but they're planning to get it tomorrow.
7 When the alien appeared, they _____ already been living in space for several months.
8 When the alien appeared, they _____ know what to do.

4 **Expand the prompts in blue to make sentences in your notebook.**

1 I can't believe it!
   I / just / see / a ghost

2 She was late for class.
   her alarm clock / not wake her up

3 I felt ready for the test.
   I / study / for days

4 He's very tired.
   he / not sleep / well / recently

5 His mum blamed him for the accident.
   he / be told / to stay away from the fire

6 I'm not used to my new school yet.
   I / only / go / there / since September

7 That TV show with the Scottish detective is good.
   you / ever / watch / it / ?

8 We can't have any fun this weekend.
   we / be given / too much homework

9 Jimmy's clothes are wet.
   what / he / do / ?

10 Her French wasn't very good.
   she / not learn / for very long

11 Don't worry about your school books.
   I / already / put them / in your bag

12 Why was she so angry with them?
   they / not do / anything wrong

The world's a big place. I'd love to have the time and money to explore it properly one day, but I can't decide where I'd go first. What about you? Where would you most like to go?

4 The World's Your Oyster

Vocabulary Starter
Transport (1)

1 **Look at the words in the box and answer the questions.**

> ferry sledge coach tram yacht
> cable car high-speed train speedboat
> spacecraft snowmobile van
> hot air balloon jet ski

1 Which can you see in the photos?
2 Which travel on land, which by air, and which by sea?
3 Which are forms of public transport, carrying lots of passengers?
4 Which do you think is the biggest, the smallest, the fastest, and the slowest?
5 Which would you most like to travel on?

2 **Complete the sentences with the words in the box.**

> guidebook landmark arrival return
> departure excursion guided tour
> backpack destination luggage

1 What's the most famous ☐ _ _ _ _ _ _ _ in your country?
2 Do you prefer exploring places on your own, or going on a _ _ _ _ _ _ _☐_ _ ?
3 Would you like to go on an _ _ _ _ _☐_ _ _ to see some beautiful caves?
4 Do you like carrying your stuff in a _☐_ _ _ _ _ _ _ when you travel?
5 Is it more expensive to buy two single tickets than a _ _ _ _ _☐?
6 Do you read a ☐_ _ _ _ _ _ _ _ about a place before you go there on holiday?
7 Have you ever had problems because of the late _☐_ _ _ _ _ _ _ _ of a plane, train or coach?
8 Would you prefer an _ _ _ _ _ _☐ time of 7 a.m. or 7 p.m.?
9 How many items of _ _ _ _ _ _☐ do you usually take with you on holiday?
10 Which _ _☐_ _ _ _ _ _ _ _ would you choose, Thailand, the UK or South Africa?

3 **Answer the quiz question by completing the missing word with the letters in the boxes in Exercise 2.**

Which city, now the second biggest in the USA, was part of Mexico before 1848?

_____ _____

CHATROOM

Ask and answer the questions in Exercise 2.

Reading

1 Read the information sheet quickly and tick the subjects it includes.

- hotel ☐
- transport ☐
- business travellers ☐
- things to do ☐
- things to bring ☐
- Internet access ☐

2 Read the information sheet again and choose the best answer, A, B, C or D.

Reading Tip: Information sheet

Use the headings to help you find the relevant information quickly.

1 Why has Felix been sent this information sheet?
A because he is trying to choose a holiday
B because he has reserved a place on the tour
C because he is going to be a guide on the tour
D because he has recently been on the tour

2 Which of these will Felix have to pay extra to do?
A go to the top of the Empire State Building
B see a live sporting event
C go ice skating
D take a ferry to the Statue of Liberty

3 What happened on Ellis Island eighty years ago?
A People built ships.
B People found out about their ancestors.
C People went on sightseeing tours.
D People from other countries were examined by doctors.

4 When can Felix check in at JFK Airport?
A 7.20   B 9.20   C 9.45   D 11.45

5 On which day is there a free afternoon?
A Day 1   B Day 2   C Day 3   D Day 4

6 Felix's friend Sophie is going on the Big Apple Tour in May. What should she pack?
A a sunhat   C a winter coat
B comfortable shoes D sunglasses

The Big Apple

1 New York's historic landmarks, fashionable shops and people-watching opportunities make it one of the world's most popular destinations. We guarantee that by the end of your trip you will have fallen in love with New York — the city that never sleeps.

7 Felix's surname is Lodge. What should he do?
A buy a new ticket
B get a new passport
C tell the airline what his surname is
D tell Top Tours what his surname is

8 What was a world record-holder until 1973?
A the New York Yankees baseball team
B the Statue of Liberty
C *Chicago*
D the Empire State Building

9 What is the first activity on the tour?
A rollerblading   C travelling on a boat
B eating out in the city D visiting the shops

2 ## Thank you for making your booking with TOP TOURS

Your booking reference: 1284792
Tour name: Big Apple Tour
Tour Reference: BATJAN13
Dates: JAN 3 – JAN 7
Passenger name: Felix Hodge

PLEASE NOTE:
You will be sent a ticket with your name spelled as above, unless you notify us of a correction. Some airlines will refuse to carry passengers whose name on the ticket does not match exactly the name on their passport.

3 ## Flight details

Outward journey
London Heathrow to New York JFK, Flight VG271, Economy Class
Departure: 09:20
Arrival: 12:20
Duration: 8 hours

Return journey
New York JFK to London Heathrow, Flight VG305, Economy Class
Departure: 11:45
Arrival: 23:55
Duration: 7 hours 10 mins

PLEASE NOTE:
- Check-in opens two hours before departure.
- Two hot meals will be provided on the plane.
- You are flying with Virgin Atlantic Airlines. Please see their website for more information.

4 ## Accommodation

During your holiday you will be staying at the Cube Hotel (www.cubehotelny.com), just ten minutes' walk from Times Square. This modern, two-star hotel is the perfect base for your visit to New York. The rooms offer TV, telephone and shared shower.

5 ## Itinerary

Day 1 – Fly London to New York. Coach transfer to your hotel accommodation. Welcome meal in a restaurant near Times Square.
Day 2 – Guided sightseeing tour of Manhattan, including an elevator ride to the top of the Empire State Building.
Day 3 – Free morning to explore the city's famous museums, art galleries and shops. Afternoon: ice-skating or rollerblading in Central Park.
Day 4 – Morning: guided tour of the Statue of Liberty and Ellis Island. Free afternoon to relax or to continue exploring the city.
Day 5 – Coach transfer to airport. Fly New York to London.

6 ## Highlights

The Empire State Building was designed to look like a pencil. It was the tallest building in the world for more than forty years after its completion in 1931 and, at 443 metres, is currently the tallest skyscraper in New York.

The Statue of Liberty was sent to the USA as a gift from the people of France in the late nineteenth century. For millions of people arriving on ships from Europe, the green lady's head was their first sight of America. The ferry from Manhattan sails past yachts and speedboats in New York Harbour to the island where the statue stands. From the ferry, enjoy an unforgettable view of the New York skyline.

Ellis Island was the arrival point for millions of immigrants entering the United States between 1892 and 1954. More than 100 million Americans can follow their family history back to this island, where their ancestors were given medical checks before starting new lives in the New World.

7 ## Optional extras

- Watch one of the top US baseball teams, the New York Yankees, in action at their home stadium.
- Go to a Broadway show and experience the world's most famous theatre district. The choice includes *Chicago*, *Mamma Mia* and *The Phantom of the Opera*.

PLEASE NOTE: Booking essential. Tickets not included in tour price – please enquire for details.

8 ## What to pack

- Suncream, sunhats and sunglasses are recommended from June to early September. Temperatures in July and August often reach 32°C.
- From December to March, snow is not uncommon, and temperatures can drop to -12°C. Warm winter clothes are essential.
- Our guided tours involve a lot of walking. Be sure to bring comfortable shoes.
- You'll want to take a lot of photos. Don't forget some extra memory cards for your camera.

3 **Match the words with their definitions.**

1	guarantee (section 1)	a	someone who comes from abroad to live permanently in another country
2	notify (section 2)		
3	duration (section 3)	b	particular area of a city or the countryside
4	itinerary (section 5)	c	very tall city building
5	skyscraper (section 6)	d	formally tell someone about something
6	immigrant (section 6)	e	the length of time that something continues
7	district (section 7)	f	plan or list of places you will visit on a journey
		g	promise something will happen

CHATROOM

What do you think of the New York holiday described in the text? What aspects of it would you like and/or dislike? Why?

WebSearch

www.newyork.com

Vocabulary
Words from the text
Word formation: verbs and nouns

1 Complete the table. You can find the words in the information sheet on page 43.

	Verb	Noun
1		enquiry
2	correct	
3	see	
4	book	
5		experience
6	give	
7		refusal
8	complete	

2 Complete the sentences with words from Exercise 1.

1 I've had an answer to my _____ about the holiday.
2 Remember to _____ that mistake with the booking.
3 This T-shirt was a _____ from my granny after her holiday in Greece.
4 They _____ to go on the trip unless we go too.
5 In Hawaii, you can _____ the excitement of surfing in the Pacific Ocean.
6 The _____ of the Alps as we flew over them is something I'll never forget.
7 Since the _____ of the bridge in 2003, a billion vehicles have driven across it.
8 In order to _____ a room, please fill in the form.

Adjectives

3 Circle the correct adjectives.

BARCELONA

❖ Visiting Barcelona is a(n)
  ¹**unforgettable / common** experience.
❖ The ²**modern / historic** district known as the Barri Gotic dates back to the Middle Ages.
❖ The city's famous street entertainers are especially ³**common / historic** on a street called Las Ramblas.
❖ The Sagrada Familia is an extraordinary, ⁴**modern / optional** church that is still being built.
❖ There is an ⁵**essential / optional** visit to the Picasso Museum, for those interested in art.
❖ It is not ⁶**unforgettable / essential** to learn Barcelona's official language, Catalan.

Transport (2)
Places

4 Complete the table with these words. You can use some words more than once. What happens at each place?

> passport control   deck   check-in desk
> departure gate   harbour   platform
> ticket office   cabin

Air	Sea	Rail

Phrasal verbs

5 Match the phrasal verbs with their definitions.

1 My friend can **put me up** for the night.
2 I'm leaving at eight. Can you **see me off**?
3 I hope the train doesn't **break down**.
4 Dad, can you **pick me up** in the car?
5 Please **queue up** here to buy tickets.
6 If we **set off** at six, we'll be there by seven.
7 Don't **hold me up** now. I've got to go!
8 When does the train from Bath **get in**?

a start to go somewhere
b arrive (used for a train, plane, etc.)
c stop working
d stand in a line
e make me late
f collect me
g let me stay in his/her home
h come to my place of departure to say goodbye

6 Complete the dialogue with phrasal verbs from Exercise 5.

A: When are you going on your surfing trip?
B: Tomorrow. The train leaves at nine.
A: How exciting! I'll come to the station and ¹_____ (you) if you want.
B: That would be nice. We should probably ²_____ for the station before eight because you sometimes have to ³_____ for ages at the ticket office.
A: Yes, I agree. Is it a high-speed train?
B: No! It doesn't ⁴_____ to Newquay until half past four – if it's on time. Something might ⁵_____ (it) and make us even later.
A: And is Aunt Meg planning to ⁶_____ (you) when you arrive?
B: Probably. Her car is causing her problems, but she's hoping it won't ⁷_____ tomorrow! It's really kind of her to ⁸_____ (me) at her house.

7 Complete the table with the words underlined in the texts below.

	UK	US
1	lift	
2		traffic circle
3	flat	
4		gas
5		freeway
6	cupboard	
7	underground	
8		parking lot

Tourist apartment in Washington D.C.

The <u>apartment</u> has two bedrooms, two bathrooms, and a huge <u>closet</u> in every room. It is only two minutes' walk from the nearest <u>subway</u> station.

Please Note: The apartment is on the fourth floor and there is no <u>elevator</u>, so it is unsuitable for wheelchair users.

Britain: The Pocket Guide   19

In Britain, teenagers have to pass a driving test before they can drive alone and on <u>motorways</u>. To pass the test, they must show that they can change direction, drive round a <u>roundabout</u>, and park at the edge of the road and in a <u>car park</u>. A good teacher will also discuss how to drive without wasting <u>petrol</u>.

Motoring

CHATROOM

Talk about a long journey that you've made. Say where and when you started and give details of all the places you went to before reaching your destination.

Holidays
Accommodation

8 Explain the difference between the following:

1 a **campsite** and a **hostel**
2 a **budget hotel** and a **luxury hotel**
3 **self-catering** and **bed and breakfast**
4 an **ensuite bathroom** and a **shared bathroom**
5 a **single room**, a **double room** and a **twin room**

Activities

9 Look at the pictures of film star Gloria Goody on holiday. Which four of these activities did she do?

a go on a cruise
b sunbathe
c hitchhike
d shop for souvenirs
e go white-water rafting
f go scuba diving
g go sightseeing
h taste the local specialities
i go snorkelling

10 Complete the sentences with activities from Exercise 9.

1 When the car broke down, I had to _____ home.
2 I want to _____ to help me remember our holiday.
3 When you _____, you have a tank of air on your back so you can stay underwater.
4 You should definitely _____ while you're in Athens. It's got the world's most famous ancient buildings.
5 I don't think I'd like to _____. I always feel sick when I'm on ships.

CHATROOM

Talk about what you like to do and where you like to stay on holiday.

More practice on pages 132–133.

Grammar
The future

1 Read the grammar notes and match the examples (a–f) to the uses.

a I'**m going to** buy lots of souvenirs.

b Check-in **opens** two hours before departure.

c You'**ll want** to take a lot of photos.

d You **are flying** with Virgin Atlantic Airlines.

e During your holiday, you **will be staying** at the Cube Hotel.

f By the end of your trip you **will have fallen** in love with New York.

Future simple (*will*)
- facts about the future

*It **will be** early afternoon when the plane gets in.*
- spontaneous decisions, offers, promises and requests

*I'**ll come** and see you off at the airport if you want.*
- predictions
1 _____

going to
- plans and intentions
2 _____

- predictions based on present evidence

*It's eight o'clock! You'**re going to be** late for check-in.*

Present simple
- timetabled events
3 _____

Present continuous
- fixed or personal arrangements
4 _____

Future continuous
- actions that will be in progress at a certain time in the future
5 _____

Future perfect simple
- actions that will be completed before a certain time in the future
6 _____

Passive forms

*Meals **will be provided** on the plane.*

*I **am going to be given** a guided tour of the city.*

*By January, the new art gallery **will have been completed**.*

There is no passive form of the future continuous.

See **Grammar File**, page 163.

---

2 Circle the correct option.

1 Look at those clouds! It **is going to rain** / **is raining** later.

2 **Will anyone have invented** / **Does anyone invent** flying cars by the end of the century?

3 It **isn't being** / **won't be** summer in Argentina in July.

4 The first cable car of the morning **goes** / **will have gone** at eight o'clock tomorrow.

5 This time next week, we **will lie** / **will be lying** on a beach, sunbathing.

6 She **is being picked up** / **is picked up** at the airport at half past five.

7 **Will you get** / **Do you get** my passport out of the bag, please?

3 Complete the text with the correct future form. Use the verb in brackets in one of the tenses given (see key).

Predicting the future isn't easy. 'In fifty years, people 1 _____ (travel PS / FC) to work by hot air balloon,' predicted a scientist just before the invention of the plane. 'Astronauts 2 _____ (visit PS / FP) Mars before the end of the twentieth century,' many people involved in early space travel believed. 'By the year 2010, cars 3 _____ (be powered FS / GT) by the sun,' said environmental campaigners two decades ago. They were all wrong.

Some visions of the future, however, seem to be coming true. Next month, Steve Buckley 4 _____ (become GT / PS) the tenth tourist to travel into space. I asked him a few questions.

'How 5 _____ (you get PC / PS) into space, Steve?'

'I've booked a trip on a Russian spacecraft, the Soyuz. We 6 _____ (set off PS / FP) at 2 a.m. on 5 March, and reach the International Space Station fifty-one hours later.'

'You're going to be on the space station for two weeks. What 7 _____ (you do GT / FP) there?'

'I 8 _____ (be given PS / GT) lots of science experiments to do. I 9 _____ (not have FS / FP) time to get bored!'

Key:

PS	present simple
PC	present continuous
FS	future simple
FC	future continuous
FP	future perfect
GT	*going to*

Soyuz spacecraft

WebSearch

www.spaceadventures.com

Future time clauses

4 **Read the grammar notes.**

> **Present tenses for future**
> We use present tenses after these time words:
> *when, while, before, after, as soon as, by the time, until, the moment*
> *I won't phone you **until I arrive**.*
> *No one will be able to take photos **while this work is going on**.*
> Remember! Don't use *will* or *going to* in future time clauses.

See **Grammar File**, page 163.

5 **Complete the sentences with the correct form of the verbs in brackets.**

1 There'll be lots of exams before school _____ (finish) for the summer.
2 The moment our last exam _____ (end), my friends and I are going to go camping.
3 By the time we _____ (get) to the campsite, the sun will have set.
4 We'll have to put up our tent in the dark before we _____ (go) to bed.
5 My friend Kate is going to cook our supper while we _____ (get) the tent ready.
6 As soon as we _____ (wake up) in the morning, we're going to have a swim in the campsite pool.

6 **Complete these sentences about your plans, intentions and predictions for the future.**

1 When I go on my next holiday, _____ .
2 _____ stay at school until _____ .
3 After I leave school, _____ .
4 As soon as I get a job, _____ .
5 _____ while I'm still young.
6 _____ get married before _____ .

CHATROOM

How do you think the world will be different at various times in the future (next year, by 2030, in the twenty-second century, when you're fifty, etc.)? Talk about travel and transport, education, entertainment, celebrities, homes and the environment.

"IT MAKES NO SENSE TO WORRY ABOUT THE FUTURE. BY THE TIME YOU GET THERE, IT'S THE PAST!"

Back up your grammar

7 **Choose the best answer, A, B, C or D.**

1 Don't take the motorway! You _____ for ages because of the accident.
   A will hold up   C will be held up
   B are held up   D are being held up

2 By ten o'clock tonight, the plane _____ 5000 kilometres.
   A flies   C will be flying
   B will have flown   D is flying

3 When I'm older, I _____ an airline pilot.
   A will have been   C am
   B am being   D am going to be

4 Please _____ with my luggage?
   A will you help   C are you going to help
   B are you helping   D do you help

5 Before I _____ a room at a bed and breakfast, I'm going to ask Liz if she can put us up.
   A will be booking   C am going to book
   B book   D will book

6 Don't worry. I _____ for the tickets in the morning.
   A will have queued up   C will queue up
   B am queuing up   D queue up

7 At three o'clock this afternoon, she _____ on the deck of Liam's yacht. Why aren't I there, too?
   A will have sunbathed   C will be sunbathing
   B is sunbathing   D sunbathes

8 We're running out of petrol! We _____ to a petrol station in time.
   A aren't going to get   C won't have got
   B won't be getting   D aren't getting

Listening

GlobalGiraffe

I've just got back from a holiday with my friend Nick. What a nightmare! I love waking up early and being active. For him, a holiday isn't a holiday unless he can stay in bed most of the morning. Do you prefer being active or lazy on holiday? Have you ever been away with anyone who has very different ideas about holidays from you?

More soon ...Watch this space.

Listening 1

 1 You will hear five different people talking about travel. Match the descriptions (A–F) with the speakers. There is one extra letter which you do not need to use.

Listening Tip: multiple matching

You will hear the recording twice. If you are unsure of an answer, wait for the second listening before making your choice.

This person:

A can't often visit the destinations he/she flies to.
B loves budget travel.
C is worried about the insects he/she might see.
D doesn't enjoy travelling very much.
E isn't looking forward to his/her journey.
F likes travelling, but not too fast.

Speaker 1	
Speaker 2	
Speaker 3	

| Speaker 4 | |
| Speaker 5 | |

Listening 2

2 Listen to an Australian travel agent's recorded message about their excursions and complete the gaps.

Listening Tip: gap completion

Look very carefully at the table before you listen, and think about the information you need. Is it a day, a time, a place, a noun, a verb?

AUSTRALIA TRAVEL EXCURSIONS FROM CAIRNS			
	Excursion 1	**Excursion 2**	**Excursion 3**
Activity	Ride in a 1_____	Three-day 6_____	11_____ _____
Location	Daintree Rainforest	the Great Barrier Reef	the Tully River
Day/Date	Every 2_____ _____	Wednesday 7_____	Every day except 12_____
Start time	3_____	8_____	13_____
Meeting point	Office at 22 4_____, Cairns	9_____, Cairns	14_____ of the Sea View Hotel, Cairns
Price	$101 for adults, 5_____ for children	$520 per person. Scuba diving: 10_____ per day	€195 including 15_____ _____

CHATROOM

Would you like to go on any of the excursions in Exercise 2? Why/Why not?

WebSearch

www.tourstogo.com.au

Speaking
Making a decision

1 What kind of holidays do these photos show?

4 With a partner, talk about the following questions.

1 What's the best holiday you've ever been on? What made it so good?
2 Do you like to know a lot about your holiday before you go, or do you prefer to just go and see what happens?
3 Which area of your country would you like to get to know better? Why?
4 In your experience, do people of different ages usually prefer different types of holiday? Give examples.
5 Many experts think that it will soon be possible to wear a helmet and a special suit and experience a virtual world as if it's real. Do you think virtual travel will become more popular than real travel in the future? Why / Why not?

2 Two students are doing the task below. Listen to part of their conversation and answer the questions.

> Imagine that you have won a free holiday to go on together. You can choose any of the holidays in the photos. First, talk to each other about how much fun each holiday would be. Then decide which holiday to go on.

1 Which holiday are they talking about?
2 Who is more enthusiastic about it, the boy or the girl?

3 Work with a partner and do the task in Exercise 2. Use the Language Upload box to help you.

Speaking Tip:

Try to share the conversation equally between the two of you. Say something, then ask your partner a question.

Language Upload

Managing a discussion

Shall we start with this one?
What do you think?
How do you feel about …?
Shall we move on to … ?

Expressing and justifying opinions

I think … looks fantastic.
I (don't) think we'd have fun at … because we could …
In my opinion, … would be a good choice because there would be …

Agreeing and disagreeing

I agree, but I also think …
Yes, that's true.
I don't feel quite the same way. I think …
I'm not so sure. Perhaps we should …

Making a decision

Do you agree that the best choice is …?
Let's go for …
We've chosen …

Writing: Informal email
Before you write

1 **Read the writing task and answer the questions.**

> Your family has invited your English-speaking friend Melissa to stay with you. Read Melissa's email and the notes you have made. Then write an email to Melissa using all your notes.
>
> Write your email in 120-150 words.

Thursday — say why

No, hotel — describe it

Hi Cara,

Thank you so much for inviting me to stay with you. My mum says I can come. I'm so excited!

Will it be better to arrive on Thursday 11 April or Friday 12? Both flights get in at 17.10.

You mentioned that you're planning to visit your grandparents' village in the mountains that week. That sounds nice. Will we be staying in their house? And will we be able to do some mountain activities?

Yes — give details

One last question: what clothes should I bring with me?

I'm really looking forward to seeing you again. Write soon!

Bye for now, Melissa

Describe weather in April and suggest suitable clothes.

1	Who is Melissa?	3	When Cara replies, how many points should she cover?
2	Why has she written to Cara?	4	Should she use formal or informal language?

2 **Read Cara's reply. Then complete each gap with a suitable word.**

◯◯◯

Dear Melissa,

I'm so glad you can come and stay. That's great news!

You asked about your flight. The Thursday flight will probably be better because Mum won't be able to pick you up from the ¹_____ until eight p.m. on Friday.

In my grandparents' village, we'll be staying in a hotel because their house is too small. You and I will be in a twin ²_____ together, and we'll even have an ensuite ³_____! We'll be able to do some cool ⁴_____ like white-water rafting, horse riding and rock climbing.

To answer your last question, you ⁵_____ definitely need some summer clothes because it is usually quite hot in April. I suggest you bring some warm ⁶_____ too, though – a coat and a thick jumper, for example – because it's a lot colder in the mountains in the evenings.

Let me know if you think of any other questions.

Love, Cara ☺

3 **Complete Cara's plan for her email.**

Writing Plan

Paragraph 1	Introduction and react to Melissa's news in a friendly way	I'm so glad you can come and stay.	
Paragraphs 2–4	Cover the four points in the notes	**Flight** • better on _____ • earliest pick-up on Friday: _____ p.m. **Accommodation** • _____ • twin room with ensuite bathroom	**Activities** • _____, horse riding, _____ **Clothes** • summer clothes and warm clothes • weather: hot, but _____ in the mountains
Paragraph 5	End in a helpful and friendly way	Let me know if you think of any more questions.	

4 Look at the Connecting words box. Find examples in Cara's letter.

5 Complete the sentences with connecting words from Exercise 4.

1 Active holidays _____ ski trips and treks are much more fun than beach holidays.
2 A lot of celebrities have stayed here, _____ Brad Pitt and Angelina Jolie.
3 I'd love to live in another country – Australia, _____ .
4 There are some interesting landmarks in the town. You should definitely visit the Temple of Apollo, _____ .
5 Local specialities _____ Thailand's fried insects are delicious.

Time to write

6 Read the writing task below. Then make a plan for your letter, using the writing plan opposite to help you.

> Your family has invited your English-speaking friend Edward to stay with you during the school holidays. Read Edward's email and the notes you have made. Then write an email to Edward using all your notes.

Connecting words

Giving examples

Let's go somewhere fun **like** the beach.

There are lots of ski resorts in countries **such as** Switzerland.

Let's invite some other people too – Milly and Jack, **for instance**.

Dress for hot weather. A sunhat would be useful, **for example**.

Wear warm clothes, **for example** a coat.

There are lots of interesting landmarks, **including** a statue in the harbour.

Hi there,

My parents have booked my flight! It's flight HG104 from Manchester, and it gets in at 15.20 on 21 July. Will you be able to pick me up at the airport, or should I get a taxi to your house?

 *Taxi, because …*

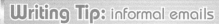 *Give details*

I'm so excited about the weekend on the island that you mentioned. What sort of accommodation will we be staying in? And what activities are we going to do there?

 *Describe it*

Is there anything in particular that I should pack?

Describe weather in July and give suggestions.

I can't wait to see you on the 21st. Write soon!

Bye for now,

Edward

Writing Tip: informal emails

Read the instructions, the original letter and the notes very carefully before you start. Use all the notes in your reply.

7 Now write your letter (120–150 words). Use the Memory Flash and Connecting words box to help you.

Memory Flash

Reacting to good news	Describing a future holiday	Introducing the answer to a question	Saying what to bring
I'm so glad that …	We'll be able to …	You asked about … .	You will definitely need …
That's great news!	We'll be staying at …	To answer your last question, …	I suggest you bring …

Vocabulary

1 Match the words in the two boxes, and use them to complete the sentences.

> self- sun camp scuba
> land back hitch hot air

> balloon bathing diving pack
> catering site hike mark

1 We're going to stay in a _____ cottage.
2 I'd love to fly in a _____ .
3 I can't pay for a coach ticket, so I'll _____ .
4 I love _____ on the beach in the summer.
5 We are staying in a tent at the _____ .
6 The Statue of Liberty is the only _____ in New York I know about.
7 I've never been _____ because I'm scared of going underwater.
8 She doesn't take much with her when she's travelling – just a few clothes in her _____ .

2 Complete each sentence with the correct form of the word in capitals.

1 What time is your _____? DEPART
2 His _____ to learn a foreign language makes it difficult for him to travel. REFUSE
3 Thank you for your _____ about our scuba diving holidays. ENQUIRE
4 Visiting Russia was _____! FORGET
5 We should get to the airport in time for the plane's _____ . ARRIVE
6 We made a _____ for a double room. BOOK
7 It's essential to bring a passport, but a camera is _____ . OPTION
8 Seville is an attractive, _____ city in Spain. HISTORY

3 Complete each sentence with the correct verb.

> queue put see set hold pick get

1 If you can _____ me up, I won't have to pay for a taxi.
2 Let's buy our tickets online, so we don't have to _____ up.
3 The first ferry doesn't _____ in until nine a.m.
4 Let's go to the airport to _____ Kitty off.
5 Don't worry. We can _____ you up at our house tonight.
6 Josie will _____ me up because she walks so slowly.
7 _____ off soon, or you won't arrive until really late.

Grammar

4 Expand the prompts to make sentences about the future. Write them in your notebook.

1 while / you / pack / I / make a picnic
2 the plane / not leave / before / you / get on it
3 by the time / we / find our hostel / it / be closed for the night
4 they / have a great time / when / they / visit Berlin
5 the moment / I / reach the island / I / go snorkelling

5 Read the text and choose the best answer, A, B, C or D to complete the gaps.

At the moment, Sweden's famous Ice Hotel doesn't exist. The building work [1]_____ until the temperature drops below 0°C. When this [2]_____, we are going to cut ice from the river and the sixty-two bedrooms of this winter's Ice Hotel [3]_____. During November and December, artists from around the world [4]_____ hard, creating works of art from ice. [5]_____ our first guests arrive, the hotel will have been [6]_____.

From December to April, we [7]_____ a wide choice of excursions and activities to our guests. In February, when the sun [8]_____ after 100 days of darkness, the ski resort of Björkliden opens. A coach [9]_____ from the hotel at eight a.m. every morning to take you there.

The moment spring arrives, the Ice Hotel will start to disappear. But don't worry – it [10]_____ back again next winter.

1 A will start   C won't start
  B is starting   D starts
2 A will happen   C is going to happen
  B happens   D will have happened
3 A will be building   C will build
  B will be built   D is being built
4 A will be working   C will have worked
  B are working   D work
5 A Until   C While
  B By the time   D After
6 A complete   C completes
  B completing   D completed
7 A are offered   C are being offered
  B will have been offered D are offering
8 A is returning   C returns
  B will return   D will be returning
9 A is setting off   C sets off
  B will have set off   D is set off
10 A won't be   C will be
  B is going   D isn't going

I haven't got a best friend. I prefer having lots of mates that I can hang out with on different days. What do you think? Is a best friend cool, or does a group of mates rule?

5 Best Mates

Vocabulary
Relationships (1)

1 Answer the questions below with words from the box.

> classmates   a coach   an ex   colleagues
> a gang   flatmates   a headteacher
> teammates   neighbours   a bully

1 Which people can you see in the pictures?
2 Who might you live with when you leave your family home?
3 Who is in charge of your school?
4 Who was once a person's boyfriend, girlfriend, husband or wife?
5 What do you call a group of friends?
6 Who is often mean to someone?
7 Which people live very near you?

2 Complete the sentences with words from the box.

> makes (x 2)   spreads   has   tells (x 2)
> gets   keeps   hurts   calls

1 This person often _____ **lies**.
2 This person _____ you **names**.
3 This person always _____ **the truth**.
4 This person often _____ you **into trouble**.
5 This person _____ **rumours about** you.
6 This person often _____ **your feelings**.
7 This person always _____ **a good impression on** adults.
8 This person _____ **a crush on** you.
9 This person always _____ **excuses** instead of helping you.
10 This person always _____ **a secret** for a friend.

3 Which people in Exercise 2 would you want as friends? Which would you not want?

CHATROOM

What are the two most important qualities, and the two worst faults in a friend? Use ideas from Exercise 2 or ideas of your own.

Reading

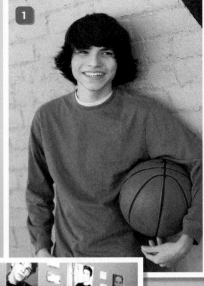

1 You are going to read part of an online problem page. Read the texts quickly and match the people (A–D) with the photos (1–4).

2 Choose one of the people (A–D) for each question. The people may be chosen more than once.

Reading Tip: multiple matching

Read the question carefully and underline key words and phrases. Look for words and phrases in the text that mean the same thing.

Which person:

is advised to give up a bad habit?	1
is worried about the behaviour of people he/she likes?	2
is taking advantage of someone else's hard work?	3
is losing interest in a hobby?	4
should do more jobs around the house?	5
enjoys different things from his/her friends?	6
is advised to take more exercise?	7
thinks that he/she has to follow unfair rules?	8
is told to stop keeping secrets from his/her friends?	9
is advised to be friendly to someone who isn't his/her friend?	10
has been given praise that he/she didn't deserve?	11
should be careful not to say everything he/she is thinking?	12
feels that he/she is more talented than someone else	13
ought to be ready to change friends?	14
would like to be trusted more?	15

3 Underline words or phrases in the article that match these meanings.

1 support him (A, 2 phrases)
2 behaving dishonestly or against the rules (B, 2 phrases)
3 feel sorry about something you've done (B)
4 chooses (C)
5 hard work and loyalty (C)
6 power to choose what to do (D)
7 make something less strict (D)

A

http://www.ask_alice.com

Ask Alice ...

My best friends are great ... most of the time. It's fun being in their gang, but the problem is, they're bullies. They keep picking on a boy in our class called Michael. They're always calling him horrible names. They trip him up and throw things at him as well. It's all a laugh to them, but I hate it. How can they enjoy being so mean? I'm never mean to Michael myself, but I never stick up for him either because I don't want to lose my friends.   *Tom, Manchester*

You say that your best friends are fun to be with, but it doesn't sound as though you're having much fun with them. Do they really deserve your friendship? You should tell them clearly and calmly that you think what they're doing to Michael is wrong. They might listen to you, but if they don't, it's time to find some new friends. It's also important to let Michael know that you are on his side. Bullying can cause terrible psychological damage, and some kind words from you could make a big difference.   **Alice**

B

http://www.ask_alice.com

Ask Alice ...

I've been copying my sister's History coursework for ages. One night last year, I was in a panic about homework, so my big sister gave me her old work to copy ... and my teacher loved it. He told the whole class that he was really proud of me. After that, I copied more and more, and now my teacher wants me to take my exam early. Help! I'll get terrible marks if that happens. What should I do?   *Maddy, Cornwall*

As you've already realised, cheating is never a good idea. It's easy to start, but you'll always regret it in the long run. What should you do? First of all, stop cheating. From now on, only hand in work that is truly yours. If your teacher still wants you to take the exam early, tell him that you don't feel ready. If he doesn't listen, perhaps you'll have to do what you should have done a long time ago – be honest.   **Alice**

C

http://www.ask_alice.com

Ask Alice ...

I'm in a basketball club and I used to really enjoy it. Recently, though, things have changed. We've got a new coach and he never picks me for the team, even though all my teammates say I'm easily good enough. Instead he picks his own son, who's useless at basketball. It's so unfair! It's the only team in my neighbourhood, so I can't play for a different one. I'm thinking of giving up basketball altogether, but it seems a shame when I used to love it so much.   *Connor, Kent*

Your basketball club has been great for you in the past, so don't give it up without a fight. I think you ought to try showing your commitment to the team by working hard on your fitness and ball skills in your spare time. Then tell the coach how hard you've been practising and ask him to give you another chance on the team. If that doesn't work, perhaps your friends could talk to him on your behalf. A word of warning, though: don't say anything against his son. That might make your problem worse. Good luck!   **Alice**

D

http://www.ask_alice.com

Ask Alice ...

I've got lots of great mates at school, but they do fun stuff together at the weekend and I'm starting to feel really left out. You see, I have to stay at home because I'm not allowed out without an adult, even though I'm sixteen years old! I'm too embarrassed to tell my friends that my parents treat me like a little kid, but I'm starting to run out of excuses for not going out with them. How can I persuade my parents that I'm old enough to go out on my own?   *Amy, Hull*

It must be hard living with parents with such strict rules, but remember that they're only being strict because they care about you. You might have done some things in the past that make them feel anxious about giving you more freedom, but now it's time to show them how mature and responsible you are. I suggest you start helping out more at home. This may persuade them to relax their rules. Even if it doesn't, you mustn't keep on lying to your friends. Tell them the truth and I'm sure they'll understand.   **Alice**

CHATROOM

Do you agree with Alice's advice for each person? What other advice would you give them?

WebSearch

www.friendship.com.au

Vocabulary

Words from the text
Useful phrases

1 Choose the correct prepositions to complete these phrases from the text on page 55.

1 from now **on / up / off**
2 **from / in / at** the long run
3 a word **in / for / of** warning
4 **on / in / at** your spare time
5 **for / on / at** your behalf
6 feel left **up / out / off**

2 Complete the sentences with phrases from Exercise 1.

1 Do you do any sport _____ ?
2 I've done some silly things in the past, but _____ I'm going to be really sensible.
3 Shall I talk to him _____ and tell him how you feel?
4 I should give you _____ about Amy. She gets upset very easily.
5 When people go to parties without me, I _____ .
6 He doesn't like staying in at the weekend to study, but it will help him _____ .

Phrasal verbs

3 Complete the text with the words from the box.

> trips   given   picks   hands   run   sticks

---

http://www.ask_eric.com

Ask **Eric** …

My sister Beth used to be really nice, but she's changed. She ¹_____ **on** our little brother for no reason, and sometimes she ²_____ him **up** just for a laugh. Until recently she studied hard, but now she ³_____ **in** her homework late – or doesn't do it at all. She always seems to have ⁴_____ **out of** pocket money, too, and keeps asking to borrow mine. I've tried speaking to Mum about her, but I've ⁵_____ **up** now. Mum always ⁶_____ **up** for her and doesn't really listen to what I'm saying. What should I do?

CHATROOM

What advice would you give in response to the email in Exercise 3?

Word formation
Suffixes -*ship* and -*hood*

4 Read the text below and complete the table.

Leonardo DiCaprio and Tobey Maguire have been friends for decades. DiCaprio's childhood was similar to Maguire's. They both grew up without a father at home, and lived in poor neighbourhoods of Los Angeles. Their relationship started in the early 1990s, when they were trying to get the same acting jobs. A close friendship soon developed.

As adults, they are both members of the famous Academy of Motion Picture Arts and Sciences which awards the Oscars. They love going to basketball matches together, and there are rumours that an acting partnership will be coming to our screens soon.

	Person	Person + suffix
1	friend	
2	relation	
3	child	
4		membership
5	neighbour	
6		adulthood
7	partner	
8		fatherhood

5 Complete the sentences with words from Exercise 4.

1 'Where's your new home?' 'In a nice, friendly _____ just east of the city centre.'
2 I can't wait for _____ , so I can get a job and live on my own.
3 Rachel and I have a great dance _____ . We've won lots of competitions together.
4 I want to join the Fitness Club, but _____ costs £100 a year.
5 I have a very good _____ with my brother, but I don't get on as well with my sister.
6 Tom and Rob have been best mates since they were three. They're lucky to have a _____ like that!

Relationships (2)
Adjectives + prepositions

6 **Complete the sentences with these adjectives.**

> proud bored jealous guilty popular
> mean interested anxious pleased

1 I'm a bit _____ of him because he's much better-looking than I am!
2 I feel really _____ about cheating in the race.
3 You were brilliant in the play. I'm so _____ of you!
4 She's feeling very _____ about the competition. She's worried she'll make a mistake.
5 The bully is always being _____ to the little kids at school.
6 I'm _____ of doing the same thing every day.
7 He's attractive, outgoing, funny – very _____ with the girls in his class.
8 Tina's _____ with the lovely presents her friends gave her.
9 They're _____ in science because they have a very motivating teacher.

Verb antonyms

7 **Match the opposites. Then complete the sentences below with a verb in the correct form.**

1	ignore		a	deny
2	admit		b	discourage
3	praise		c	reject
4	encourage		d	criticise
5	accept		e	pay attention to

1 Tonia's parents have always _____ her to dance. They'd be delighted if she became a professional dancer.
2 I _____ I made a mistake, but I promise I won't do it again.
3 Why did you _____ Lucy's offer of help? Now there'll be no one to help you.
4 My grandparents are always _____ me. They're unhappy about my friends, my clothes, my music, … everything!
5 When my little sister gets angry, we don't even look at her. We just _____ her, and she soon calms down.
6 His parents have always _____ his interest in horseriding because it's such an expensive hobby, and can be dangerous too.
7 Everyone _____ her for her fantastic performance in the concert last week.
8 'Are you going to _____ their invitation?' 'Yes, I can't wait to go.'
9 Everyone says he did it, but he _____ it. He says he's not the person responsible.
10 _____ the teacher, so that you know what to do.

Verbs + prepositions

8 **Complete the text with the correct prepositions from the box.**

> about (x3) like for of in (x3) on

TV Week Highlights

Showdown

This week's exciting episode starts with a huge argument between Kate and Jade. Kate has found out [1]_____ Jade's relationship with Micky and is accusing Jade [2]_____ being disloyal. Jade replies that Kate doesn't care [3]_____ anyone except herself and treats her friends [4]_____ dirt. All the boys tease Micky [5]_____ the trouble he's caused, but Micky confides [6]_____ Sam and tells him that he's no longer interested in Jade. Sam thinks he should apologise to both girls [7]_____ his behaviour but Micky doesn't want to. In the end, Sam decides to interfere [8]_____ the girls' argument, and this results [9]_____ disaster. We can always depend [10]_____ Sam to make things worse! Don't miss this episode!

→ **Wednesday, 8.30 p.m., Channel 5**

CHATROOM

What TV series do you like? Describe the problems that characters in the series have in their relationships.

More practice on pages 136–137.

Grammar
Modal verbs

1 Read the grammar notes and match the examples to the uses.

a He **can't** be ill, because I saw him shopping in town a few minutes ago.

b That **might** make your problem worse.

c You **mustn't** lie to your friends.

d You **should** tell them to stop being bullies.

e I **can't** do anything to stop them.

f I **have to** stay at home because I'm not allowed out without an adult.

---

ability   *can, be able to*
1 _____

advice   *should, ought to*
2 _____

asking permission   *can, could, may*
May I have another biscuit?

obligation or necessity   *must, have to, need to*
3 _____

lack of necessity   *don't have to, don't need to, needn't*
You needn't pick me up from school – I'll walk home.

prohibition   *mustn't*
4 _____

present and future possibility   *might, may, could*
5 _____

present certainty   *must*
It must be hard living with parents with such strict rules.

present impossibility   *can't*
6 _____

See **Grammar File**, page 164.

2 Use the modals in the box to complete these rules. Where two options are possible, write them both.

---

mustn't   don't have to   has to
must   have to   needn't

Rules For Using The School Computer Room

1 A teacher _____ / _____ be in the room before you can enter.

2 You _____ / _____ listen carefully to your teacher's instructions.

3 You _____ play computer games or download software.

4 Students _____ give their password to anyone else.

5 You _____ / _____ switch off the computer at the end of the lesson; the computers can be left on until the end of the school day.

3 Circle the correct option.

A: Hey! Look at this photo of all of us at the park … but who's that boy with red hair?

B: It [1] **can't / must** be Dom's brother. He's got red hair.

A: No, it [2] **can't / might** be Dom's brother. Dom's emailed me to ask who he is!

B: Katerina's boyfriend [3] **can / might** have red hair.

A: No, I think he's blond. Let's show Becky the photo tomorrow. She [4] **can't / may** know him.

B: Good idea … although I suppose he [5] **could / must** be someone who was just walking through the park.

4 Choose the correct word or phrase, A, B or C to complete each gap.

Logged in 🔵

Facebook is a great way to keep in touch with friends online. How does it work?

- You [1]_____ to ask people if you can be their friend on Facebook.
- When someone gets a message saying '[2]_____ be your friend?', they [3]_____ say yes. They [4]_____ choose to reject your friendship request.
- You can put up pictures on your Facebook page. However, you [5]_____ put up any pictures that [6]_____ upset people.
- You [7]_____ be very careful about meeting up with friends that you've got to know online.

1	A must	B have	C can
2	A can I	B I should	C Ought I
3	A haven't	B mustn't	C don't have to
4	A mustn't	B don't need	C might
5	A shouldn't	B can	C ought not
6	A should	B needs	C could
7	A can	B must	C ought

I've got 12 million Facebook friends, and none of them know I'm an alien.

5 Complete the grammar notes with these headings.

   a past certainty   b past ability   c past obligation or necessity

---

1 _____

could / was/were able to + infinitive
*I **wasn't able to ride** a bike until I was eight years old.*

regret or criticism about the past
should have / ought to have + past participle
*You **should have stopped** them from bullying Michael.*

2 _____

had to + infinitive
*Last month we **had to study** very hard for our exams.*

past possibility
might have / may have / could have + past participle
'Why don't my parents trust me?'
*'You **might have done** some naughty things in the past.'*

lack of necessity in the past
didn't have to / didn't need to + infinitive
*We **didn't have to** do the washing up on holiday because there was a dishwasher.*

needn't have + past participle
(Note: You can only use this structure if the action happened.)
*Thanks for doing the washing up, but you **needn't have done** it. We've got a dishwasher!*

3 _____

must have + past participle
*His parents died when he was young, so he **must have had** a difficult childhood.*

past impossibility
can't have + past participle
*They **can't have finished** their homework yet. They only started five minutes ago.*

> See **Grammar File**, page 165.

---

6 Look at the pictures and choose the most suitable modal to make sentences.

  1 ignore the sign (shouldn't have / might have)
     She shouldn't have ignored the sign.

  2 leave home on time (could have / can't have)
     _____

  3 accuse him of lying (may have / ought to have)
     _____

  4 tease him about his hair (shouldn't have / could have)
     _____

  5 have some good news (must have / can't have)
     _____

Back up your grammar

7 Complete the second sentence so that it has a similar meaning to the first sentence, using the word given.

  1 We were wrong to pick on her.
     shouldn't
     We _____ on her.

  2 Perhaps he has decided not to come.
     may
     He _____ not to come.

  3 It's important that you don't tell a lie.
     mustn't
     You _____ a lie.

  4 It wasn't necessary to apologise for their mistake.
     needn't
     They _____ for their mistake.

  5 It's time for me to admit I was wrong.
     ought
     I _____ I was wrong.

  6 It was my duty to give him the news.
     had
     I _____ him the news.

CHATROOM

Talk about your actions last week: things it was necessary to do, things that you regret doing, and things that were impossible to do.

Listening

Logged in

BlogChick

My friends are great, but with each one I have a slightly different relationship. Some are great for a good time but with others, I love having a quiet night in. Do *your* friendships work in a similar way?

More soon ... Watch this space.

Listening 1

1 A TV company is looking for teenagers to take part in their new show, *With Friends Like These*. Listen to a phone interview with someone who wants to be on the show and complete the form.

Listening Tip: taking notes

Before you listen, think of other words associated with the categories in the left column of the form. Listen out for these words as you hear the recording.

APPLICANTS FOR
With Friends Like These

Name of applicant: [1]

Age: [2]

Name of best friend: [3]

When they first met: when they were [4]

How they first met: their [5] were friends

Best memory: our [6] at school

Worst argument: about a [7]

Friend's best quality: [8]

Friend's worst fault: [9]

Availability in April: free after [10]

CHATROOM

Imagine you and your partner work for a TV company. Think of an idea for a new TV show about teenage friendships.

Listening 2

2 You will hear ten short conversations. After each conversation, you will be asked a question. Choose the correct picture, A, B or C.

Listening Tip: choosing the correct picture

Before you listen, think of the English words for the pictures and any connected words.

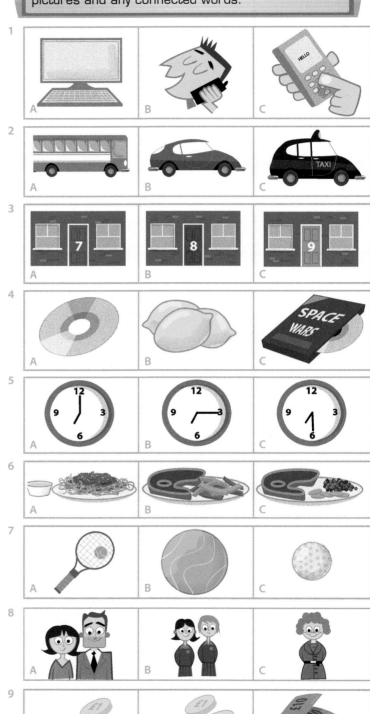

Speaking
Roleplay

1 Listen and decide which situation the students are roleplaying.

1   You are friends. Student A starts:
    'Do you want to come round to my house tonight?'

2   You are neighbours. Student A starts:
    'We've got lots of friends coming round for a meal today. Could we borrow some knives and forks, please?'

3   You are classmates. Student B starts:
    'Do you think you're ready for the exam tomorrow?'

4   You are teammates. Student B starts:
    'How did we lose that match? We were winning 2-0 at half-time.'

2 Work with a partner. Roleplay the other conversations in Exercise 1. Add two or three lines for each.

3 Read the role card. Then listen to the dialogue and answer the questions below.

> **The situation**
>
> You can't play in the football match next Saturday because you have to go to your grandfather's seventieth birthday celebration. You speak to your football coach.

> **Your goal**
>
> Explain the problem and apologise.

1   Why is it a problem that the girl can't play in the match?

2   What solution does the coach suggest?

3   Is the coach's suggested solution going to work? Why/Why not?

4   Do they finally agree that the girl is going to play in the match, go to her grandfather's celebration, or both?

4 Listen again and tick the expressions in the Language Upload box that you hear.

5 Roleplay the conversation below. The English teacher's role card is on page 125.

> **The situation**
>
> You are late for your after-school English class, and may be late for other classes in the future because the bus timetable has changed. You speak to your English teacher.

> **Your goal**
>
> Explain the problem and apologise. Try to find a solution to the problem.

Speaking Tip: roleplay

Think about useful language before you start speaking, but don't plan what you're going to say too carefully. Make sure that you respond correctly to your partner's words.

Language Upload

Apologising

I'm so sorry I'm late.
I'm sorry, but I can't …
I'm afraid I can't …

Responding to an apology

Don't worry.
Oh well – never mind.
Oh dear. That's a bit of a problem.

Explaining a problem

You see, …
The problem is, …

Discussing a solution

Is there any way you could …?
I might be able to …
Perhaps we should …

> We're having a surprise party for William's birthday.

> We're having a surprise party for William's birthday.

> Hey, Will! We're having a surprise party for your birthday.

Writing: An Essay
Before you write

1 Read the writing task and answer the questions opposite.

> Your teacher has asked you to write an essay giving your opinion on the following statement:
>
> *'A good friend always keeps your secrets.'*
>
> Write your essay in 120–180 words.

1 What must you write?
2 What must you give your opinion about?
3 Should you use formal or informal language for the task?

2 Read Jonah's essay. Do you agree with his arguments and conclusion?

> Most of us like to confide ¹_____ a friend from time to time. Is it possible to have a good friend who tells other people our secrets?
>
> Most people would agree that they can't trust a friend who doesn't keep their secrets. Without trust, there's no friendship. Moreover, secrets are usually secret for a reason. When the wrong people find out ²_____ them, there can be big problems.
>
> However, perhaps sometimes secrets are unfair. If someone keeps a secret about something bad that their friend has done, they might get into trouble themselves when the truth is discovered. Their friend shouldn't ³_____ told them the secret in the first place. Furthermore, if someone knows that their friend is in danger, they ought ⁴_____ help their friend however they can. Imagine they know their friend is stealing or taking drugs. They should do all they can to stop this behaviour, if necessary by telling other people.
>
> In conclusion, while I agree that in most circumstances a good friend ⁵_____ your secrets, there are a few situations when that isn't true.

3 Now complete the gaps in the essay with suitable words.

4 Complete Jonah's plan for the essay.

Writing Plan

Paragraph 1	introduce the issue	• it's nice to _____ in a friend
Paragraph 2	arguments agreeing with the statement	• can't _____ someone who doesn't keep secrets • problems when the _____ people find out about secrets
Paragraph 3	arguments disagreeing with the statement	• a secret is _____ if a friend might get in trouble for keeping it • important to help if you know a friend is in _____
Paragraph 4	conclusion	• in a few situations, the statement isn't true

5 Find some examples of these connecting words in Jonah's essay.

Connecting words

Adding a similar argument

Furthermore, Moreover, In addition

Furthermore, you might lose your friend's trust for ever.

Also

Secrets can **also** be very difficult to keep.

Too, As well

People should think of their friend's safety **as well**.

6 Complete the sentences with the connecting words from Exercise 5.

1 A good friend knows how to listen, and might be able to help you _____ .

2 Keeping a diary is fun. _____ , it can be helpful to write about your problems.

3 Sometimes teachers give good advice about bullying. _____ , the headteacher can speak to the bully about his or her behaviour.

4 My parents don't understand my problems. They're _____ too busy to listen properly when I want to talk.

5 Discussing your problems with parents can make your relationship stronger. _____ , their advice will be useful because they have a lot of life experience.

6 I often confide in my big sister. I sometimes confide in my twin brother _____ .

Time to write

7 You are going to write the following essay. With a partner, discuss ideas that support and disagree with the statement.

> Your teacher has asked you to write an essay giving your opinion on the following statement.
>
> *'A good friend is always honest.'*
>
> Write your essay in 120–180 words.

8 Read these questions and say if a good friend would give honest replies.

> Do you like my new trousers?

> Am I a good singer?

> What do Jack and Eliza say about me?

> Was I wrong when I told him he'd upset me?

9 Make a plan for your essay using the writing plan opposite to help you.

10 Now write your essay, using the Memory Flash and the Connecting words box to help you.

Writing Tip: essays

Don't forget to include suitable connecting words.

Memory Flash

Opening the essay	Starting an argument	Giving examples	Describing responsibilities	Giving an opinion
Most of us like to …, Is it possible to have a good friend who …?	Most people would agree that …	For example, … Imagine …	They should … A friend ought to … There are times when … is important.	While I agree that in most circumstances …, there are a few situations when …

Vocabulary

1 Complete each gap with ONE suitable word.

My sister Saffy has a best friend called Rachel, and I must admit, I don't understand their ¹_____ at all. One moment they're getting on well, and the next they're being really mean ²_____ each other. Last week, for example, Saffy got jealous ³_____ Rachel because she had a new iPod. She started spreading ⁴_____ that Rachel had stolen it, and lots of people believed them. When Rachel ⁵_____ out about this, she didn't speak to Saffy for days. She completely ⁶_____ her. Saffy started to feel guilty ⁷_____ what she'd done, and she apologised to Rachel ⁸_____ her unkindness. Rachel didn't ⁹_____ her apology, though. Instead, she ¹⁰_____ the teachers lies about Saffy in order to ¹¹_____ Saffy into trouble at school. Finally, a boy called Tyson started teasing them ¹²_____ their silly behaviour. They both have a crush ¹³_____ Tyson, so they really ¹⁴_____ about what he thinks of them. Soon, they'd decided to be best friends again!

2 Circle the correct word in these sentences.

1 Our school's got a new **headteacher / colleague / neighbour**.
2 We live in the same **membership / neighbourhood / gang**.
3 He **denied / interfered / confided** breaking the window.
4 I'm **pleased / anxious / bored** of hanging out with the same people every day.
5 The argument **resulted / depended / rejected** in the end of their friendship.
6 Her coach **criticised / discouraged / praised** her for her fantastic goal.

3 Match the sentence halves.

1 You made a really good   a   for me.
2 This is important, so pay   b   my feelings.
3 I don't know why you make   c   impression.
4 Her parents treat her   d   secrets.
5 I'm terrible at keeping   e   like an adult.
6 No one ever sticks up   f   excuses for her.
7 We want to live together as   g   attention.
8 He really hurt   h   flatmates.

Grammar

4 Circle the correct options.

A: You ¹ **don't have to / mustn't** forget to phone Charlie.
B: Oh yes. I'll phone him now … No answer!
A: He ² **may / needn't** have left his phone at home. Or he ³ **can't / could** be somewhere noisy where he can't hear it ringing.
B: Well, I ⁴ **can't / needn't** keep phoning him. I ⁵ **should / should have** charged my phone last night, but I forgot. The battery's almost dead.
A: You ⁶ **can / might** use my phone if you want.
B: Thanks. In fact, ⁷ **might / may** I use it now?
A: Sure. Here you are.
B: He's still not answering. Oh dear! Next time we ⁸ **should / ought** to arrange everything before we go out.
A: Hey, look! There's Charlie!
B: Oh good! Someone ⁹ **must have told / had to tell** him we were here.
A: Yes. We ¹⁰ **mustn't / needn't** have worried about him.

5 Rewrite the first sentence so that it refers to the time in brackets. Replace the underlined word(s).

1 I can't dance in the show <u>tonight</u>. (last week)
   <u>I couldn't dance in the show last week.</u>

2 We don't have to buy any milk <u>this morning</u>. (yesterday)
   _____

3 They needn't have done their homework <u>last Tuesday</u>. (tomorrow)
   _____

4 You must be tired <u>now</u>. (earlier)
   _____

5 He could be on the way to school <u>at the moment</u>. (an hour ago)
   _____

6 They must remember to take some money with them <u>today</u>. (yesterday)
   _____

7 It might have resulted in disaster <u>last weekend</u>. (next weekend)
   _____

8 She shouldn't say that <u>all the time</u>. (last night)
   _____

> Some people say hobbies are a waste of time, but I think they're so wrong! I learn just as much from my hobbies as I do at school, and they keep me fit too. What do you think? Are *your* hobbies a waste of time? Why/Why not?

6 Do Something Different!

Vocabulary Starter
Free time

1 Read the sentences and match the words and phrases in bold with the definitions below.

1 Chess often **appeals to** people who like Maths.
2 You shouldn't do skydiving **casually**, without thinking about the dangers.
3 Cameron Diaz campaigns on green issues, and **takes** this work very **seriously**.
4 **Experts** say that playing video games is good for your eyes.
5 If you **have a passion for** adventure, you'll love sailing.
6 Johnny Depp can play the guitar **to a high standard**.
7 I'm absolutely **hooked on** this book. I can't put it down!
8 She **is** really **enthusiastic about** her new art classes.
9 This cookery course aims to **attract** people who've never cooked before.

a seems interesting to _____
b people with special knowledge of a subject _____
c love _____
d not seriously _____
e addicted to _____
f make someone want to participate _____
g believes that something is important _____
h enjoys and is very interested in _____
i very well _____

2 Complete the list of reasons for doing a hobby with words from the box.

> instructors   techniques   productive
> demanding   express yourself   fresh air

Why do a hobby? Because you can ...

a learn new skills and _____ . ☐
b be taught by _____ that you like. ☐
c _____ creatively. ☐
d do something physically _____ . ☐
e go outside and get some _____ . ☐
f do something _____ with your time. ☐

3 Put the list in Exercise 2 in order of importance. Explain your reasons.

CHATROOM

Talk about the hobbies in the photos, and other hobbies you know about. What do they involve? What kind of people do they appeal to? Use expressions from Exercises 1 and 2.

Reading

1 Read the adverts below and on page 67 quickly. Talk about each one. Would you be interested in doing the activities offered? Why/Why not?

2 Choose the correct answers, A, B, C or D.

1 You want to have a birthday party for ten friends. Where could you have it?

   A 1   B 2   C 3   D 5

2 You like checking out activities on the Internet first. Which activity could you look at?

   A 1   B 2   C 3   D 4

3 You want to try something new, but Dunton is too far away from your home. Which activity might be possible?

   A 1   B 3   C 4   D 5

4 Which do you have to get organised a long time in advance?

   A 1   B 2   C 3   D 4

1 It's Time to Rock

Come and take part in the Wellington Rock School this half-term!

Rock School allows guitarists, keyboard players, drummers and singers to play together in a band. Spend the week rehearsing, then invite your family and friends to enjoy a spectacular performance on the last day.

You'll discover talents you never knew you had, and you'll even have the chance to jam and perform with world-class musicians.

Young musicians of all levels are welcome, from beginners through to experienced performers. Please bring your own instrument. Microphones and other equipment are provided in our rehearsal rooms at Green Tiger Recording Studio in Wellington.

21–25 February

Morning, afternoon and all-day sessions available.

To participate, ☎ 03285 385392 or visit our website www.timetorock.org.uk for more details.

2 Your Local Ultimate Frisbee Club needs YOU!

Whether you are new to the sport of Ultimate Frisbee, have played it casually with friends, or are already an experienced player, you're welcome to come and join in here at Dunton Ultimate. Ultimate Frisbee is catching on in a big way, and there's always plenty going on at our club: indoor and outdoor practice sessions, matches against other clubs, and plenty of social events too. We compete in all divisions (Men's, Women's, Mixed Adult, Boys', Girls' and Mixed Junior), so we're sure to have a team that's just right for you!

Practice Times
(term time only)

Wednesday
Great Field (Outdoors)
Juniors: 4–6p.m.
Adults: 6–8p.m.

Saturday
Parker Sports Hall (Indoors)
Juniors: 10a.m.–1p.m.
Adults: 1–4p.m.

5 Your friend Nessa has very strict parents who only let her do free-time activities with other girls. Which activity can they be sure is OK for her?

A 2   B 3   C 4   D 5

6 You are eighteen years old. Which activity or activities are you unable to do?

A 1   B 2 and 5   C 4   D 4 and 5

7 You want to do something that no one in your area has done before. Which activities interest you?

A 1 and 2   B 2 and 5   C 1 and 4   D 4 and 5

8 You are interested in trying a new activity during the week of half-term. Which activities could you do?

A 1 and 2   B 2 and 4   C 1 and 4   D 3 and 5

9 Which adverts say they want to attract both beginners and people with more experience?

A 1 and 2   B 2 and 3   C 1 and 4   D 4 and 5

10 You are looking for something that will get you fit. Which activities appeal to you?

A 1 and 2   B 3 and 4   C 2 and 5   D 1 and 5

3 Find words or phrases in the adverts that match these meanings.

1 natural abilities or skills (advert 1) _____
2 play music with others without practising first (advert 1) _____
3 opportunities for meeting friends (advert 2) _____
4 not adult (advert 2) _____
5 people who are invited (advert 3) _____
6 in the future (advert 4) _____

CHATROOM

With a partner, choose another activity to advertise. Decide what to include in the advert.

3

Jewellery making at Silver Heart Studio

❖ Express yourself creatively
❖ Create the jewellery to suit your individual style
❖ Make beautiful gifts for family and friends
❖ Learn all the essential techniques for this fabulous art form

Classes every Saturday, 10–12

Looking for something different to do for your birthday party? Making jewellery is the perfect activity, either here at the studio or in your own home. (maximum fifteen guests)

Silver Heart Studio, 17 Reach Lane, Dunton

4

Don't Just Play Video Games. Create Your Own!

If you have a passion for video games, you'd better sign up for this brand-new course today! You'll be amazed to find out how easy game programming can be. Explore the world of video game creation and, no matter where your imagination takes you, you'll have your very own game to bring home with you at the end of the week.
Courses run during every half-term and school holiday.

Forthcoming dates in Dunton: 21–25 February, 4–8 April, 11–15 April
10a.m.–4p.m.   Age 12–17

Limited availability. Book early to avoid disappointment!

WebSearch

www.findmeahobby.com

5

The Parkour training area in Dunton Park opens next week!

You've seen it on TV. Now come and try it out. Parkour involves running, jumping and climbing – fantastic for fitness, and fantastic fun! In celebration of Dunton's wonderful new training area, instructors from *Jump Dunton* will be getting people to try some parkour moves at informal training sessions throughout January. There is also a three-week course on offer for those who are interested in taking up the sport.

Free sessions
Every Saturday in January, 10–3, Dunton Park

Course for beginners
Monday 7th, 14th and 21st March, 6–7.30p.m., Dunton Leisure Centre, £15

Unfortunately, under 13s are not allowed to participate in Jump Dunton's training sessions.

Vocabulary

Words from the text
Word formation: verbs and nouns

1 Complete the table. You can find the words in the adverts on pages 66–67.

	verb	noun
1	create	
2	imagine	
3		participation
4	disappoint	
5		competition
6	celebrate	
7		invitation
8	equip	

2 Complete the sentences with words from Exercise 1.

1 It was a _____ when the show was cancelled. Everyone had been looking forward to it.
2 Anyone who can write novels must have a fantastic _____ .
3 Have you received an _____ to the sports club party?
4 We've got all the _____ we need to cut stones for the jewellery.
5 If he enters the dancing _____ , he'll probably win.
6 The _____ of so many pop stars in the campaign helped to get the issues discussed on TV.
7 We're having a big _____ on Friday, because our team has won all its matches this year.
8 The _____ of a new skate park in town would be very popular with local teenagers.

Phrasal verbs

3 Circle the correct options. Then match the infinitive form of the phrasal verbs to the definitions below.

1 What's **going on** / **in** / **up** after school this week?
2 Please **sign on** / **up** / **over** by Thursday if you want to be in the show.
3 We often kick a ball around in the park, but Chris never **joins up** / **off** / **in**.
4 Have you **tried up** / **off** / **out** your new video game?
5 My dad invented a new sport called Hodball, but it didn't **catch up** / **out** / **on**.
6 Did you take **place in** / **part in** / **point in** the competition?

a participate in
b use or do something to see what it's like
c become popular
d put your name on a list to do something
e happen
f do something with people who are already doing it

Hobbies
Music

4 Match some of the words with the picture.

> audience   composer   drummer   guitarist
> keyboard player   lead singer   microphone
> musical instrument   rehearsal

1 _____   2 _____   3 _____
4 _____   5 _____

5 Complete the sentences with the remaining words from Exercise 4.

1 A _____ is a person who writes music.
2 The _____ are the people watching a concert.
3 You can play a _____ to make music.
4 You have a _____ before a performance, to practise.

Visual arts and crafts

6 What activities do you do to make these things? Complete the table with the activities in the box.

> jewellery making   sketching   sculpture   pottery
> carpentry   animation   fashion design
> web design   digital photography   filmmaking

things to wear	
useful things for the home	
moving images	
still images in 2D	
works of art in 3D	

CHATROOM

What musical hobbies do you have, or would you like to have? What are the advantages and disadvantages of learning a musical instrument?

7 Which sports involve the places and verbs below? Choose from the sports in the box, or use ideas of your own.

> golf   baseball   football   tennis   horseracing
> running   hockey   cricket   boxing
> motor racing   basketball   volleyball

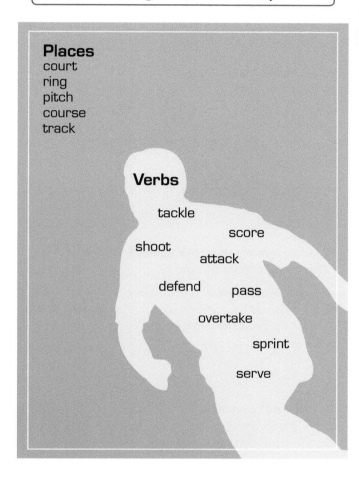

Places
court
ring
pitch
course
track

Verbs

tackle

score

shoot

attack

defend

pass

overtake

sprint

serve

8 Match the speech bubbles with the same meaning.

How did the match go?

1 We were in the lead at half-time.

a Victory!

2 We lost.

b We drew.

3 We beat the other team.

c We were defeated.

4 It was a tie.

d We were winning at half-time.

9 Choose the correct words, A, B, C or D to complete the gaps.

http://www.jedborofc.org.uk

Jedborough Football Club

Under 16s

The season began with a 7–1 ¹_____ against Ruxton. Liam Telson ²_____ six of our goals!

A week later, however, we played on a very wet ³_____ . We ⁴_____ badly and lost 2–1: a disappointing performance.

In our third match, we managed to win 3–2 against Sunderton who were in the ⁵_____ until the final ten minutes, and in our fourth we ⁶_____ 2–2. Then, in a terrible fifth match, Liam Telson was injured when he was dangerously ⁷_____ , and we were ⁸_____ 9–0.

Luckily we weren't ⁹_____ during the rest of the season, and we finished in seventh place. Well done to everyone in the team for their hard work and commitment!

1	A tie		C track	
	B draw		D victory	
2	A passed		C scored	
	B tackled		D sprinted	
3	A course		C ring	
	B pitch		D court	
4	A defended		C served	
	B beat		D scored	
5	A tie		C winning	
	B lead		D victory	
6	A drew		C served	
	B won		D passed	
7	A overtaken		C served	
	B tackled		D shot	
8	A defended		C won	
	B defeated		D lost	
9	A scored		C won	
	B beaten		D lost	

CHATROOM

What sports have you tried? Which aspects of the sports are/were you good at? Which aspects would you like to get better at?

Grammar

-ing form vs *to* + infinitive

1 Read the grammar notes and match the examples (a–f) with the uses.

-ing form	**to + infinitive**
• the subject of a sentence	• after certain verbs (without object)
Making jewellery is the perfect activity.	*e.g. agree, arrange, choose, continue, decide, deserve, expect, forget, hope, manage, plan, pretend, seem, tend, want, would like, would prefer*
• after prepositions	*I'm hoping to be given a new mountain bike for my birthday.*
Are you interested in taking up the sport?	4_____
1_____	• after certain verbs (with object)
• after certain verbs	*e.g. allow, encourage, expect, help, want, would like*
e.g. avoid, dislike, enjoy, finish, involve, keep, suggest	5_____
He dislikes playing team sports.	• after certain adjectives
2_____	*e.g. first, last, happy, sad, surprised, excited, amazed, easy, difficult, likely*
• after certain expressions	6_____
it's (not) worth, don't mind, can't help, can't stand, there's no point, look forward to	
3_____	

See **Grammar File**, page 166.

a I've **arranged to learn** more about it.

b He apologised **for being** late for the match.

c You'll be **amazed to find** out how easy game programming can be.

d I **can't stand playing** hockey in the rain.

e Rock School **allows musicians to play** together in a band.

f I **enjoy being** taught new skills.

2 Complete the text with *-ing* or *to* + infinitive.

Logged in

In Switzerland, we tend ¹_____ (get) a lot of snow in winter. My friends and I always look forward to ²_____ (go) snowboarding. Between December and April, we manage ³_____ (spend) most of our Sundays in the mountains. We usually arrange ⁴_____ (meet) early to avoid ⁵_____ (travel) when the roads are busiest. We don't mind ⁶_____ (get up) early for snowboarding!

3 Read the grammar notes and match the forms (1 and 2) with explanations (a and b).

verbs followed by *-ing* form and *to* + infinitive
• with the same meaning
e.g. begin, like, prefer, start
I started skiing when I was three.
= I started to ski when I was three.

• with a different meaning
e.g. regret, remember, stop, try
Halfway through the race, I stopped to drink some water.
I've stopped drinking cola because it's bad for my teeth.

| 1 | stop + *-ing* | a | the activity of drinking finishes |
| 2 | stop + *to* + infinitive | b | something else finishes so the activity of drinking can start |

See **Grammar File**, page 166.

4 Complete the sentences with the correct form of the verb.

1 After an hour, they **stopped** _____ (have) a rest.

2 They **stopped** _____ (swim) at 5 o'clock.

3 I **remember** _____ (hear) that song.

4 I **didn't remember** _____ (bring) my gloves.

5 She **tried** _____ (play) golf but she found it boring.

6 She **tried** _____ (hit) the ball straight but she couldn't.

7 I **regret** _____ (go) skiing yesterday.

8 I **regret** _____ (tell) you that you haven't been chosen.

Infinitive without to

5 Read the grammar notes and match the verbs (1–4) with their meanings (a–d).

> *My mum **makes me learn** the violin, but I hate it.*
> *Her parents only **let her do** spare-time activities with other girls.*
> *They'**d rather go** home to bed than play football.*
> *You'd **better sign up** for this course today.*

1	make		a	should
2	let		b	allow to
3	would rather		c	oblige to
4	had better		d	would prefer to

See **Grammar File**, page 167.

6 Choose the best word, A, B, C or D to complete the sentences.

1 I'd _____ go. I've got an art class in a few minutes.
   A should   B better   C like   D prefer

2 I can't _____ you learn golf if you don't want to.
   A like   B must   C let   D make

3 He'd _____ to take up windsurfing rather than sailing.
   A rather   B better   C prefer   D enjoy

4 Leah isn't _____ to go skiing, as it's expensive.
   A allowed   B allow   C let   D better

5 They don't _____ us dive into the pool.
   A allowed   B allow   C let   D better

6 They'd _____ not play in the match, but they don't have any choice.
   A like   B choose   C prefer   D rather

The causative

7 Read the grammar notes and complete the gaps.

> We use the causative for things that we've arranged for someone else to do for us.
>
> *have / get* + object + past participle (+ *by* + agent)
> *I **had** my portrait **painted** by a local artist.*
> *I got a ring _____ (make) for Sophie's birthday.*
>
> *get* + agent + *to* + infinitive
> *Instructors will be getting people _____ (try) some parkour moves.*

See **Grammar File**, page 167.

More practice on pages 138–139.

CHATROOM

What things do your parents make you do?
What things do they not let you do?

8 Complete the sentences using the causative.

1 When I was seven, I _____ (get / my dad / lend) me his digital camera.

2 I managed _____ (get / my dad / make) some very silly faces for the camera!

3 My friends soon wanted _____ (have / their photos / take) too.

4 They've _____ (have / their photos / frame) and hung them on their walls.

5 I _____ (not get / all my photos / print) yet, because prints are so expensive.

6 I must _____ (get / my parents / give) me more pocket money!

Back up your grammar

9 Complete the second sentence so that it has a similar meaning to the first sentence, using the word given.

1 I'm not allowed to do watersports on my own. **let**
   My parents _____ watersports on my own.

2 They made arrangements for Max to take me surfing. **got**
   They _____ me surfing.

3 Balancing on the surfboard was very difficult. **balance**
   It was very difficult _____ on the surfboard.

4 After a lot of practice, I succeeded in standing for about a second! **managed**
   After a lot of practice, _____ for about a second!

5 The waves continued to throw me off the board. **kept**
   The waves _____ off the board.

6 I'd prefer not to go surfing again! **rather**
   I _____ surfing again!

Listening

Logged in

My friend sent me a great ecard the other day, with a cartoon dog on a surfboard. Do you ever send or receive ecards?

Mad4It

More soon ... Watch this space.

Listening 1

1 You will hear a radio interview with a teenager called Natasha. Listen and tick *True, False* or *Not stated* for each statement.

> **Listening Tip: true/false statements**
>
> You will hear many words on the recording that appear in the statements. Be careful! That doesn't always mean the statement is true.

1 Natasha creates cartoon characters.
□ TRUE □ FALSE □ NOT STATED

2 She has a passion for computers.
□ TRUE □ FALSE □ NOT STATED

3 As a child, she loved cartoons on television.
□ TRUE □ FALSE □ NOT STATED

4 She was good at doing magic tricks.
□ TRUE □ FALSE □ NOT STATED

5 The flick book that she made when she was five was brilliant.
□ TRUE □ FALSE □ NOT STATED

6 She was given her first animation computer program by her brother.
□ TRUE □ FALSE □ NOT STATED

7 Her business partner helped her start the business.
□ TRUE □ FALSE □ NOT STATED

8 She is very rich because of her business.
□ TRUE □ FALSE □ NOT STATED

Send eCards
FREE!

Jokes

Birthdays

Christmas

New Year

Animals

Listening 2

2 You will hear people talking in eight different situations. Choose the best answer, A, B or C.

1 You hear two people talking about a friend's hobby of collecting spoons. What do they think of the hobby?
A It's strange.
B It's fascinating.
C It costs too much money.

2 You hear a mum talking to her son. What is she trying to persuade him to do?
A return to an old hobby
B start a new hobby
C give up his hobbies and study harder

3 You hear a girl talking about her voluntary work at an animal rescue centre. How does she feel when she's working there?
A useful
B sad
C angry

4 You hear a news report about an international texting competition. What are the winner's plans for the future?
A to win more texting competitions
B to become a professional musician
C to work for a mobile phone company

5 You hear two people talking about a sculpture. Who has made it?
A an artist
B the girl who is speaking
C a four-year-old child

6 You hear two people talking about a forthcoming concert. Who's giving the concert?
A the speakers' favourite band
B a band that the speakers don't like
C people that one of the speakers knows

7 You hear two people doing a hobby together. What's the hobby?
A cookery
B fashion design
C carpentry

8 You hear a coach talking to some players. When is this conversation taking place?
A just before a match
B at half time
C at the end of the match

> **CHATROOM**
>
> Do you think it's a good idea for teenagers to have a job or do voluntary work? Why/Why not?

Speaking
A presentation

1 Listen to a student called Oscar answering this question. Choose the correct options in the table.

> Can you tell me about something you enjoy doing in your free time?

1	What's the activity?	**kite / bike** buggying
2	What does it involve?	**sitting in / standing on** a buggy attached to a kite
3	What does he like most about it?	the **fresh air / jumps**
4	Where does he do it?	the **park / beach**
5	How long has he been doing it?	two **months / years**
6	How did he get into it?	His **friend / brother** persuaded him to try it.
7	When does he do it?	windy **evenings / weekends**
8	What are his plans for the future?	to go to the **USA / France**

2 Listen to two different speakers saying these sentences. Circle the speaker who sounds enthusiastic.

1	I just love it!	**girl / boy**
2	It's a fantastic feeling.	**girl / boy**
3	There are some brilliant beaches.	**girl / boy**

3 You are going to give a presentation to your partner, answering the task question in Exercise 1. Think of a hobby and answer the questions in the table.

What's the activity?	
What does it involve?	
Where do you do it?	
What do you like most about it?	
How long have you been doing it?	
How did you get into it?	
When do you do it?	
What are your plans for the future?	

4 Write two more questions about your hobby in the table, and write in your answers. Then number them in a logical order for your presentation.

5 Look at the Language Upload box. Then give your presentation.

Speaking Tip: presentation

Try to speak for at least a minute and a half. Look at your partner as you speak and try to express your enthusiasm in your face and voice.

6 With a partner, ask and answer the follow-up questions below.

1 Do your friends have the same hobbies as you?
2 How has your choice of hobbies changed over the years?
3 What new hobby would you most like to take up?
4 Would you like to have a job that involved a favourite hobby?

Language Upload

Describing an activity

It involves …
It (almost) feels like flying.
It's important to …

Expressing enthusiasm

I just love it!
It's a fantastic feeling!
What I love most about it is that you …
It's great to be able to …

Talking about abilities

I've managed to learn …
I'm pretty good at …
I'd love to be able to …

Writing: Report
Before you write

PERHAPS YOU'D BETTER TAKE UP A NEW HOBBY!

1 What musical activities are on offer at your school and in your local area? Should there be more?

2 Read the writing task and answer the questions below.

> You are a member of a youth club. The leader of the club wants to encourage more interest in music among young people. He has asked you to write a report on the musical activities available to young people in your area, and to suggest how the youth club could improve the music scene in the area.
>
> Write your report in 120–180 words.

1 What are you going to write?
2 Who are you going to give your written work to?
3 What is the purpose of the task?

3 Read Robert's report. What recommendation(s) does he make? Think of at least one alternative recommendation.

Introduction
The purpose of this report is to outline the musical opportunities for young people in Lexbridge and to recommend a way for the youth club [1] **encouraging / to encourage** more participation in music.

Music at school
All schools offer individual classes in a variety of musical instruments. School music teachers also organise groups that rehearse and perform together. These groups tend [2] **being / to be** very well equipped but are popular only with people who take their music very seriously.

Music outside school
A lot of young people play in bands, either casually or more seriously. It is difficult for these bands [3] **buying / to buy** the equipment they need, and there is often no one to give them advice. [4] **Organising / To organise** performances can also be a problem.

Recommendation
I suggest [5] **having / to have** band nights at the youth club where local bands could perform. This would help musicians to build up their confidence and would also create more interest in the local music scene. Professional musicians could come to the events and give advice.

4 Now circle the correct options in the report.

5 Complete Robert's plan for the report.

Writing Plan

Paragraph 1	Introduction: write the purpose of the report and who it's for	• outline musical opportunities • recommend a way to encourage more participation
Paragraph 2	Music at school	• can learn musical _____ • groups organised by teachers
Paragraph 3	Music outside school	• bands • problems with buying _____ no one _____
Paragraph 4	Recommendation	• band nights • build up _____ • more interest in the local music scene • professional _____ to give advice

6 Find some examples of these connecting words in the report.

Connecting words

Making a recommendation

I **recommend/suggest having** band nights at the youth club.

I **recommend/suggest that** the youth club organises equipment hire for local bands.

In my opinion, we should create a recording studio at the youth club.

Justifying a recommendation

This would mean that young people could give more performances.

This would help young people **to** build up their confidence.

More young people **would then be able to** participate in music.

7 Use the prompts to make and justify recommendations.

1 recommend / schools / provide / more cookery lessons
2 this / mean / young people / know more / about the food that they eat
3 opinion / schools / should / stop / selling crisps and fizzy drinks
4 young people / then / unable / buy unhealthy food during the school day
5 suggest / put up / healthy food posters
6 this / help / us / remember / eat healthily

Time to write

8 You are going to write the following report. Read the writing task.

Your headteacher is worried about the low fitness levels of pupils at your school. He has asked you to write a report on the sporting activities that young people can do in your area, both at school and elsewhere, and to suggest something that would help to improve pupils' fitness.

Write your report in 120–180 words.

What do you mean, I'm not fit? I've got the fittest thumbs in the school.

9 Tick the notes that are true for your school and local area.

At school		Outside school	
1 three PE lessons per week	☐	5 many activities available to young people	☐
2 PE teachers organise sports teams	☐	6 clubs encourage less sporty people to take part	☐
3 teams practise after school – not enough time for homework!	☐	7 expensive	☐
4 only best sportspeople in teams	☐	8 transport to activities a problem	☐

10 Make a plan for your report, using the writing plan opposite to help you. Then write your report. Use the Memory Flash and the Connecting words box to help you.

Memory Flash

Writing Tip: reports

Use headings to organise your report.

Always include an introduction at the start and a recommendation at the end.

Introducing a report	Outlining opportunities	Outlining problems	Making generalisations
The purpose of this report is to outline the opportunities for … / recommend a way to …	There are a lot of … available to young people. Most of the activities are …	It is difficult/impossible for people to … There is often no one to … … can also be a problem.	All/A lot of schools … These groups tend to … There is/are often …

Vocabulary

1 Complete the texts with words from the box.

| sprinting | serving | shoots | win | beat | track |
| victory | overtake | tie | court | passes | lead |

What an exciting tennis match! Murray is
¹_____ well, and Federer is ²_____ from one
side of the ³_____ to the other, reaching every
ball. He's a hard player to ⁴_____ .

The cars are racing round the ⁵_____ , with Alonso
in the ⁶_____ . Hamilton keeps trying to ⁷_____ ,
but he can't get past the driver in front. ⁸_____ is
going to go to Alonso in this race.

He ⁹_____ the ball to Papaloukas, who
¹⁰_____ . Yes! The ball goes in the basket! It's a
¹¹_____ , 55 all. Either team could ¹²_____ !

2 Choose the best word A, B, C or D to complete the sentences.

1 I'm so tired. It's the most physically _____ sport I've ever tried!
   A demanding   C productive
   B disappointing   D enthusiastic

2 We're hooked _____ the game *Lava World* at the moment.
   A in   B at   C onto   D on

3 He's an _____ golfer. He's beaten lots of professional players.
   A easy   C expert
   B express   D equipped

4 Speak into the _____ so that your voice is loud enough for everyone to hear.
   A sculpture   C audience
   B microphone   D instrument

5 I made a table at school once, but I can't do carpentry to a very high _____ .
   A standard   C passion
   B creation   D technique

6 Are you planning to _____ the competition?
   A sign up   C catch on
   B take part in D participate

7 The boxers are in the _____ , waiting for the match to start.
   A track   B course   C ring   D pitch

8 I've always loved clothes, so a course in _____ really appeals to me.
   A fashion design   C pottery
   B web design   D sketching

3 Complete the sentences with the correct form of the words in capitals.

1 I'm the _____ in a band.   GUITAR
2 Why don't you use your _____ more?   IMAGINE
3 I'd really like to learn a _____ instrument. MUSIC
4 The _____ starts at eight. Don't be late!   REHEARSE
5 They need to buy some new _____ .   EQUIP
6 We should have a _____ if we pass.   CELEBRATE

Grammar

4 Complete each gap with ONE suitable word.

1 We _____ better ask the instructor for some help.
2 'Does your sister _____ you borrow her clothes?'
3 The audience got the band _____ play some more songs.
4 I'm going to _____ my photo taken.
5 Please don't _____ me go into the cold water!
6 I'd _____ go skydiving than make jewellery.
7 I'm looking forward _____ going scuba diving.

5 Circle the correct option.

I've been interested in ¹**to dance / dancing** since I was about three years old, but I wasn't allowed ²**to have / have** lessons until I was five. After that I was hooked, and I seemed ³**spending / to spend** all my spare time at the dance studio. I was the first person in my family ⁴**to be / being** in a show in a proper theatre. ⁵**Being chosen / To be chosen** for that show was brilliant. I had a pretty little dress ⁶**to make / made** for me. I remember ⁷**standing / to stand** in front of the audience, feeling so excited. At one moment, I kept ⁸**dance / dancing** after everyone else had stopped because I was enjoying ⁹**to perform / performing** so much!
I really wanted ¹⁰**to go / going** to a special secondary school for dancers when I was eleven, but my parents made me ¹¹**to go / go** to my local school instead. They'd prefer me ¹²**to learn / learning** all the ordinary subjects properly, and they don't think it's easy ¹³**to do / doing** that at a dance school. They've agreed ¹⁴**letting / to let** me ¹⁵**to study / study** dance when I've left school, though. I'm hoping ¹⁶**to become / becoming** a professional dancer. It will be difficult, but I don't mind ¹⁷**working / to work** when I'm doing something that I love.

> I love gadget websites. It's amazing what you can buy these days! What do you reckon is the greatest gadget ever invented?

7 I Want One of Those!

Vocabulary Starter
Gadgets and gadget adjectives

1 Complete the sentences with words from the box.

transparent waterproof environmentally-friendly
portable lightweight high-tech wind-powered
solar-powered remote-controlled touch-sensitive

1 I always cycle to school because I prefer to use _____ transport.

2 I wear a _____ watch when I'm scuba diving.

3 I've got a _____ umbrella, so I can put it right over my head and still see where I'm walking.

4 My brother's _____ car needs new batteries.

5 Sailing boats are _____ and don't need petrol.

6 My uncle spends a lot of money on the latest _____ gadgets.

7 My latest mobile doesn't have number keys. The numbers appear on a _____ screen.

8 My MP3 player is so _____ I can hardly feel it in my pocket.

9 You can carry a _____ computer in a bag.

10 The electric light in the garden is _____ – great in the summer but more of a problem on rainy days.

2 Find pictures of the words in bold, either on this page or later in this unit. Do the quiz. Then check your answers at the bottom of the page.

Trivia Quiz

1 The first known **nail varnish** dates from around 3000 BC. `True False`

2 **Solar panels** can be made out of human hair. `True False`

3 **Velcro**® was used to stop soldiers falling off their horses in the nineteenth century. `True False`

4 A girl in the USA can pop seventy-one bubbles in a sheet of **Bubble Wrap**® in fifteen seconds, using only her hands. `True False`

5 Children's **roundabouts** were invented by the Italian artist Leonardo da Vinci. `True False`

6 Human-shaped **robots** existed in the thirteenth century. `True False`

7 The world's first **games console**, which came out in 1972, was American. `True False`

8 A coin-sized area of the world's strongest **glue** can stick an adult elephant to the ceiling. `True False`

CHATROOM

Describe some gadgets that you use. Use words from Exercise 1.

Answers: 1T, 2F, 3F, (only invented in the 1950s) 4T, 5 F, (only invented in the nineteenth century) 6 T, (a robotic clock was created in 1206) 7 T, 8 F, (however, a substance produced by bacteria found in rivers has the potential to do this)

Reading

Technofreak

I'd love to be an inventor. I'm OK at carpentry – I've made a table and a toy lorry for my little cousin. But I'd really like to learn electronics and invent cool, hi-tech gadgets. That would be brilliant! What about you? Do you enjoy making things? What have you made?

More soon ... Watch this space.

1 Read this article about inventions and match the headings (A–H) with the sections of the article (1–6). There are TWO headings that you do not need.

A Bending the rules
B The digital age
C That eureka moment
D Life in the fast lane
E Shaping the future
F Unusual results
G In a spin
H A big mistake

2 Read the article again and answer the questions.

Reading Tip: open questions

When you've written your answer, read the question again to check that you've answered it fully and accurately.

1 How did plant seeds attach themselves to George de Mestral's dog?

_____

2 What was Bubble Wrap® originally supposed to be?

_____

3 In what way does vanishing nail varnish change when it isn't in sunlight?

_____

4 What problem did one of the inventors of the nail varnish have at school in the past?

_____

5 What annoying habit does Elvis have?

_____

6 What two benefits has Peter Ash got from his invention?

_____

7 How did Rishi Bhat make money as a teenager?

_____

8 Why was Shawn Fanning unpopular with many business people?

_____

'I wish there was a gadget that could do that!' We all think this from time to time, but few of us have the skills and determination to invent the gadgets we dream of. For inventors, however, these passing thoughts can provide vital inspiration.

1

It was a boring, everyday event that triggered George de Mestral's most famous invention. On a Swiss summer's day in 1948, he took his dog for a walk. Returning home, he discovered that his dog's fur and his own clothes were covered in little sticky plant seeds. The tiny hooks on these seeds made them very difficult to remove. As de Mestral carefully cleaned his dog, the idea for Velcro® was born.

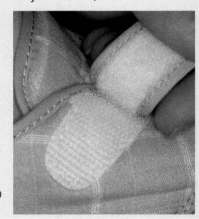

3 Find words or phrases in the article that match these meanings.

1 essential (introduction) _____
2 made something happen suddenly (section 1) _____
3 animal hair (section 1) _____
4 take away (section 1) _____
5 the material used to cover and protect something (section 2) _____
6 something that disappears (section 3) _____
7 saying that something isn't allowed (section 3) _____
8 make people feel shocked and frightened (section 5) _____

CHATROOM

Do you think young people in your country are interested in becoming inventors? Why/Why not?

WebSearch

www.ideafinder.com
www.yankodesign.com

Great ideas, great inventions!

2

One thing essential to an inventor is an open mind. Take Bubble Wrap®, for example. In the 1950s, Alfred W. Fielding and Marc Chavannes worked hard to invent some modern-looking plastic wallpaper. All their efforts came to nothing, however, until Fielding realised that their bubbly creation, useless as wallpaper, could be used for another purpose. Packaging has never been the same since.

Those sticky yellow Post-it® notes have a similar story. They were the result of an experiment to create a new glue, thought to be a failure until it was realised that a weak glue could have good uses too.

3

Middle-aged scientists aren't the only ones with good ideas for inventions. The recent successes of some girls at secondary school in the UK have shown that it's not about age or experience, but about knowing the people you're inventing for. While working on a business project at school, they came up with a great new idea: vanishing nail varnish.

The nail varnish is bright red in natural sunlight, but indoors it transforms into a much paler colour that is almost transparent.

'If your school has strict rules banning nail varnish, you'll love this product,' explained one of its young inventors.

'If only this product had been around last year!' laughed another. 'I got into loads of trouble for wearing nail varnish at school. It was awful. But I'd never have been caught if I'd been wearing vanishing nail varnish.'

The nail varnish is already being made in China and will soon be available in the shops, in a choice of thirty-two different colours. Go girls!

4

Sixteen-year-old Peter Ash from Somerset is another young inventor. He came up with his bright idea, an environmentally-friendly mobile phone charger, when his sister complained about getting too little sleep. Her problem? The family hamster, Elvis, who spent his nights running around noisily in his exercise wheel.

'Elvis is in his wheel for four or five hours a night, keeping my sister awake,' said Peter. 'I thought, if he's feeling energetic, he should do something useful!'

Peter started to wonder if Elvis's favourite activity could be used to make electricity, and for the next thirteen months he worked on the project. The resulting invention helped him to pass his electronics exam with flying colours. Even better, he can now charge his mobile for free, getting thirty minutes of talk time for every two minutes that Elvis goes for a spin.

5

When it comes to computer technology, teenagers rule. Many successful computer programs have been the work of people who were still at school. Some teens, like Rishi Bhat, invent things that the adult world is grateful for. Rishi wrote his software *SiegeSoft* at the age of fifteen, and sold it a year later for $1.6 million. Others, like Shawn Fanning, create things that horrify the adult world. Shawn's software Napster®, written in the very early days of MP3, upset the business community as it helped people around the world to download their favourite music for free. Napster changed the music industry for ever.

6

It is impossible to guess the future of this planet, but one thing is certain: it will rely on the inventive minds of today's young people. What world will you invent?

Vocabulary
Words from the text
Word formation

1 Complete the table. You can find the words in the article on pages 78–79.

	Verb	Noun	Adjective
1	invent	a invention	
		b inventor	
2	succeed		successful
3	use	use	a useful
			b
4	determine		determined
5	fail		failed
6	experiment		experimental

2 Read the text below. Use the word in capitals at the end of some of the lines to form a word that fits the gap in the same line.

I don't believe it!

In 1770, the Hungarian ¹_____ Wolfgang von Kempelen created an incredible machine — a chess-playing robot called the Turk. It seemed to play with great ²_____ and skill. Some of the best chess players in Europe ³_____ in beating it, but many more were embarrassed by their ⁴_____ to defeat this mindless machine. The French leader, Napoleon Bonaparte, tried several times. He ⁵_____ on it by covering its eyes, and by putting a magnet on the chess board to make its machinery ⁶_____. Nothing worked, and he lost every time. After von Kempelen's death, people found out that the Turk's movements had really been controlled by a human chess player hidden under its seat!

INVENT

DETERMINE

SUCCESS
FAIL

EXPERIMENT

USE

Useful phrases

3 Choose the correct option A, B, C or D to complete the sentences.

1 She passed the exam with flying _____ .
  A numbers B colours C pigs D birds
2 Don't decide too soon. Keep an _____ mind.
  A even B air C open D other
3 We were really disappointed that all our hard work came to _____ .
  A not B nowhere C nil D nothing
4 You don't have to pay for water. You can get it _____ free.
  A of B for C with D at
5 That's a _____ idea. In fact, it's brilliant!
  A light B quick C bright D fast

Machines, gadgets and inventions
Verbs

4 Complete the text with words from the box. Then, with a partner, decide which of the inventions described are likely to exist in the next 100 years.

> mend   vanish   transform   spin
> charge   store   steer   bend

Logged in ☒

It would be fascinating if we could see the most important inventions of the next hundred years! Here are some possibilities:

- A mobile phone that can ¹_____, so you can wrap it round your wrist.
- A machine that makes people ²_____, and then appear again in a different place.
- A car that can ³_____ itself through traffic without the driver's help.
- A computer the size of a coin that can ⁴_____ every novel ever written.
- A machine that can ⁵_____ rubbish into healthy food.
- Sunglasses made of solar panels that can ⁶_____ all your electrical gadgets.
- A machine that can ⁷_____ people round and round very fast to make them lose weight.
- A watch that you never have to ⁸_____ because it stays in perfect condition for ever.

5 Match the words with the picture. Can you think of any other words for parts of machines or computers?

> pedal   pump   handle   engine   switch
> hook   wire   controls   button

9 _____

1 _____

2 _____

8 _____

7 _____

3 _____

6 _____

4 _____

5 _____

Phrasal verbs

6 Complete the phrasal verbs with prepositions from the box.

> out (x2)   up (x2)   in   up with

1 **A:** I can't **figure** _____ how this clock works.
   B: It's an old-fashioned one. It won't work unless you **wind** it _____ .
2 **A:** I'm trying to **come** _____ a good idea for a new invention.
   B: How about a robot that'll **fold** _____ all these clothes for me!
3 **A:** Apparently, they're **bringing** _____ a new type of solar heating.
   B: But I'm cold *now*. Can you **plug** _____ the electric heater for me?

Adjectives
Adjectives ending in -y

7 Match the sentence halves.

1	Silver and gold are	a	fizzy.
2	A tennis ball is	b	shiny.
3	Glue and honey are	c	bendy.
4	Elastic is	d	sticky.
5	Wire is	e	stretchy.
6	Soda water is very	f	bouncy.

Extreme adjectives

8 Match the normal adjectives (a–h) with their stronger equivalents (1–8). Then write sentences in your notebook, using each of the extreme adjectives.

> **a** clean   **b** dirty   **c** big   **d** small   **e** old
> **f** good   **g** beautiful   **h** ugly

1 ☐ fabulous   5 ☐ filthy
2 ☐ ancient   6 ☐ tiny
3 ☐ spotless   7 ☐ hideous
4 ☐ gorgeous   8 ☐ enormous

Order of adjectives

9 Read the information then order the adjectives in the sentences below.

> Adjectives usually go in this order in a sentence:
> *opinion, size, age, shape, colour, origin, material, type*
> We rarely use more than four adjectives in a row.

1 If I were you, I'd buy one of those **black / tiny / portable / Japanese** computers.
2 She's got a **plastic / square / useful** thing for carrying her paintings in.
3 Thomas Edison was a **nineteenth-century / successful / American** inventor.
4 Her **lovely / digital / new** camera will be perfect for her holiday.
5 You should read this **science / little / fascinating** book about space travel.
6 Whose is that **purple / hideous / environmentally-friendly** car?

10 Complete the sentences with two or more adjectives from the box in the correct order.

> long   modern   useful   small   flat
> sharp   round   cool   metal   portable

1 A kitchen knife is a _____ tool for cutting vegetables.
2 A mobile phone is a _____ gadget for communicating with friends.
3 A coin is a _____ object that you use to pay for things.
4 A watch is a _____ thing that tells you the time.

CHATROOM

> Describe objects for your partner to guess. Use three adjectives for each.

Grammar
Conditionals

1 **Read the grammar notes and complete the examples with the clauses (a–d) below.**

Zero conditional
- general truths

if + present simple // present simple
*If water **gets** colder than 0°C, [1]_____ .*

First conditional
- events that we expect to happen in the future

if + present simple // will
*If your school **has** strict rules banning nail varnish,
[2]_____ .*

Second conditional
- imaginary, hypothetical or unlikely situations

if + past // *would*
*[3]_____ if we **could** see the inventions of the future.*

Third conditional
- possible events in the past that did not actually happen

if + past perfect // *would have* + past participle
*[4]_____ if **I'd been wearing** vanishing nail varnish.*

Notes

Modal verbs can be used instead of *will* and *would*, e.g. *can, could, might* and *should*.
*If he's feeling energetic, he **should** do something useful.*

- We sometimes use *were* instead of *was* in second conditional sentences.
*If I **were** you, I'd buy one of those cameras.*

> See **Grammar File**, page 168. »»»»»

a I'd never **have been caught**
b you**'ll love** this product
c it **freezes**
d It **would be** fascinating

2 **Complete the sentences with the correct form of the verb in brackets.**

1 If you get one of those, you _____ (not use) it very much.
2 Who would be able to mend it if it _____ (break)?
3 Why _____ (anyone / want) a waterproof watch if they didn't like swimming?
4 If I _____ (hear) my mobile ringing, I'd have answered it.
5 The machine always _____ (make) a noise if that button is pressed.
6 We _____ (can try out) his new remote-controlled plane if we'd been there.
7 If they _____ (bring out) a better games console, I'll definitely buy it.
8 He shouldn't work in the garden if it _____ (rain).

CHATROOM

- How do you feel if your gadgets go wrong? How would you feel if you lost or broke your favourite gadget?
- Talk about something bad that happened to you recently and how you could have avoided it.

---

3 **Read the grammar notes and circle the correct word in the example sentences.**

Unless means *if not.*
*It [1] **won't** / **wouldn't** work unless you wind it up.*

As long as and **provided/providing** have a similar meaning to *if.*
*It'll last for years provided you [2] **look** / **will look** after it properly.*

Supposing means *imagining the situation that.*
*Supposing you were offered a job designing motorbikes, [3] **would** / **did** you take it?*

In case means *because it's possible that.*
*[4] **I'll** / **I'd** bring my charger in case the battery runs out.*

See **Grammar File**, page 169. »»

4 **Circle the correct option.**

1 You won't be able to become an inventor **unless** / **as long as** you study hard in science.
2 We could spend the day at the robot museum, **provided** / **in case** it's open.
3 **Supposing** / **Unless** his invention had been successful, would he have become a millionaire?
4 Bring a normal battery for your solar-powered laptop, **provided** / **in case** you want to use it at night.
5 I think it'll work **supposing** / **as long as** it's lightweight enough.

wish / if only

5 Complete the grammar notes with the following:

  a past perfect   b past simple   c *would*

---

wish / if only + ¹_____
regrets about the present
I **wish** there **was** a gadget that could do that.

wish / if only + ²_____
complaints about the present and/or desire for
something to change in the future
I **wish** he **would** help us more.

wish / if only + ³_____
regrets about the past
If only this product **had been** around last year.

See **Grammar File**, page 169. »»

6 Complete the thought bubbles. Use *I wish* or *If only*.

  1 I / can / fly

> I wish I could fly.

  2 the engine / not break down / here

  3 he / think of / a different way up

  4 I / use / glue / instead

  5 I / have / a new mobile

  6 someone / invent / the wheel / soon

Back up your grammar

7 Read the text and think of the word which best fits each gap. Use only <u>one</u> word in each gap.

TV Highlights
Week

Rubbish Race

If you like crazy machines, you ¹_____ love *The Rubbish Race*! Don't miss the latest episode (at 7 p.m. on Sunday night), ²_____ of course you're too busy building your own crazy machine …

Each week, two teams have to design a machine to do an unusual task and build it out of rubbish. If your team ³_____ the best machine, you compete again the following week.

Mike Davis recently took part in the show. 'You only have two days to build your machine,' he told me. 'It ⁴_____ be a lot easier if you had more time. It was great fun though. As long ⁵_____ you get on well with your team, you can have a brilliant time.'

And did their machine win? 'Well, no. If it ⁶_____ not crashed ten metres before the end of the race, we might have had a better chance. If ⁷_____ that wheel hadn't fallen off! I wish we ⁸_____ won. And I wish we ⁹_____ take part in other episodes. I learnt so many useful things on the show.'

➜ **Sunday, 7 p.m., Channel 6**

CHATROOM

• Talk about the aspects of your life now and in the past that you wish you could change.

More practice on pages 142–143. »»

Listening

Logged in ⊗

Technofreak

I had a bad day yesterday. First I sent a very personal text message to the wrong person – how embarrassing! Next I lost my MP3 player on the way home from school and it took me ages to find it. Then my computer didn't work. Grrr! Sometimes I wonder whether technology causes more problems than it solves! What do you think? Does technology make the world a better place?

More soon … Watch this space.

Listening 1

 1 You will hear six short unfinished conversations. Choose the best reply to continue the conversation.

Listening Tip: dialogue completion

Try to get the gist of the conversation. Don't panic if you don't understand every word.

1. A No, not really. This one's just right.
   B Oh no! Now the handle's broken too.
   C Just in case it rains.
   D OK, I'll help if you want.

2. A She can't find it.
   B The pedals don't spin round.
   C Maybe we could mend it tomorrow.
   D Wow! That's gorgeous!

3. A Maybe I need something stretchy.
   B I'd steer more carefully if I were you.
   C I love old-fashioned photos.
   D Yes, it does, next to the on/off switch.

4. A Well, I hope it's waterproof.
   B The shiny ones are so cool.
   C If it's bendy, it'll be useless.
   D And try not to miss the bus!

5. A I won't unless I'm really late.
   B Don't forget to phone!
   C I'd go if you came with me.
   D Yeah, but the music sounds great!

6. A It's so tiny I can hardly see it.
   B I can't believe you just did that!
   C And how much does that cost?
   D It would be awful if you fell.

Listening 2

 2 You will hear an interview about the Clean Green Machine Competition. For questions 1–10, complete the sentences.

Listening Tip: sentence completion

Read the text before and after listening to make sure the words you have chosen make sense.

The Clean Green Machine Competition

It's a competition for [_____1] of all ages.

You can enter as an individual or as a [_____2].

The winner of each category will get [_____3].

The overall winner will be given a week in [_____4].

The PlayPump was invented in [_____5].

Many people in South Africa walk a long way to get [_____6].

Trevor Field liked the idea of a PlayPump because it was [_____7], and fun too.

The first PlayPump design didn't work because it wasn't [_____8] to play on.

There are now PlayPumps in thousands of [_____9] in Africa.

Where there's a PlayPump, families don't get as many [_____10].

CHATROOM

In groups, try to come up with an idea for an invention that you could enter in the Clean Green Machine Competition.

WebSearch

www.stepin.org

Speaking
Information gap

1 With a partner, decide which of the factors below are most important in choosing a new gadget.

1 sensible price   4 no one else has it
2 high quality   5 very hi-tech
3 all my friends have it   6 cool features

2 In your pairs, read the speaking task below.
Student A: your information card is A on this page.
Student B: your information card is B on page 126.

> You work for a hi-tech online product shop and are looking for a new product to sell. Work with a partner. Each of you has been sent information about a different product. Read your own information card. Then ask questions about your partner's card and decide which product to choose.

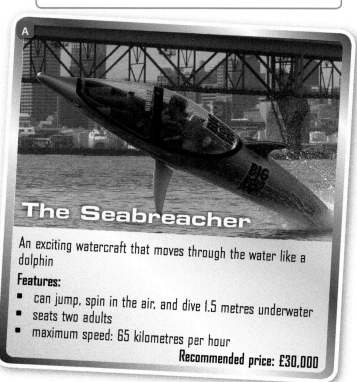

The Seabreacher

An exciting watercraft that moves through the water like a dolphin

Features:
- can jump, spin in the air, and dive 1.5 metres underwater
- seats two adults
- maximum speed: 65 kilometres per hour

Recommended price: £30,000

3 Complete the gaps in these questions.

1 _____ is it called?
2 What does it look _____?
3 _____ is it described?
4 What features _____ it have?
5 _____ much is it?

4 Now ask and answer the questions in Exercise 3 about the products on the cards. Then decide which product to choose.

Speaking Tip: information gap
Remember to ask the person you are talking to for their opinion. You have to reach a <u>joint</u> decision.

 5 Listen to two people doing the last part of the task in Exercise 2. Do they make the same choice as you?

6 Listen again and tick the expressions in the Language Upload box that you hear.

7 Now do the task in Exercise 2 about two gadgets.
Student A: your information card is D on page 127.
Student B: your information card is C on this page.

C

Rocket alarm clock

The alarm clock that will *really* get you up in the morning.

Features:
- a rocket which shoots into your bedroom when the alarm starts
- the alarm can only be switched off if you get up and find the rocket

Recommended price: £15

Language Upload

Asking for opinion

What do you think of the ...?
Does the ... look cool / attractive?

Stating opinion

The ... looks / sounds fabulous.
If we put the ... on the website, it would be really popular.
I think it's a great product.
It's quite good value.

Reaching a decision

Shall we choose the ...?
Are you happy with that decision?
Yes, I think so.

Writing: A review
Before you write

1 People write reviews of many different things: films, books, concerts, video games, hotels, restaurants, products. Do you ever read reviews? Of what? How often do you agree with the review writer?

2 Read the writing task and answer the questions below.

> You recently saw this notice in an English language magazine called *Gadgets Galore*.
>
> ## Reviews needed!
>
> Have you bought or been given an environmentally-friendly gadget recently? If so, could you write us a review of it? Include information on its appearance, features, strong points and drawbacks, and give your overall opinion.
>
> Write your review in 120–180 words.

1 What sort of text are you going to write?
2 What should your text be about?
3 What information should it include?
4 Who is going to read it?

3 Read Tamsin's review. Would you like to own the product described? Why/Why not?

The EMP Revolution is an environmentally-friendly MP3 player. You don't charge it by plugging it in. Instead, you turn a little handle to wind it up.

Its shiny black and silver design ¹_____ attractive and it has lots of useful features. It can play music (MP3 and radio), play video, take photos, record sound ... and you can even ²_____ a mobile phone with it! What's great about this gadget is that you can ³_____ all its features without feeling guilty about global warming.

However, it does have a few drawbacks. It is 2.5cm thick, so it doesn't fit into a pocket as easily as most MP3 players. Personally, I ⁴_____ its controls were easier to use and that it had more memory. With four gigabytes, it can only ⁵_____ about 1,000 songs, whereas most MP3 players at a similar price can store 2,000 or more.

In my opinion, the pros outweigh the cons, however. If you have more than £100 to spend on an MP3 player and you care about the environment, you should definitely ⁶_____ it.

4 Now complete the gaps in the review with these words.

> enjoy   charge   consider   store   looks   wish

5 Complete Tamsin's plan for the review.

Writing Plan

Paragraph 1	write a basic description	• environmentally-friendly _____ • turn a _____ to wind it up
Paragraph 2	give the strong points	• attractive design • a lot of useful _____ (play music, play video, take photos, record sound, charge a phone) • don't have to feel guilty about global _____
Paragraph 3	explain the drawbacks	• thicker than most MP3 players • _____ not easy to use • not enough _____
Paragraph 4	write an overall opinion	• a good choice if you care about the _____ and have more than £100

6 Find some examples of these connecting words in the review.

Connecting words

Contrast

but, whereas, although, despite, in spite of, however

Although it can store a lot of songs, the sound quality isn't great.

I like listening to MP3s, **whereas** my sister prefers the radio.

It looks fabulous, **but** it's too expensive.

He managed to buy one, **despite** the queues at the shop.

In spite of its attractive appearance, it doesn't appeal to me.

It has some good features. **However**, it isn't very popular.

It has a camera. The photos it takes are not very good, **however.**

7 Complete the sentences with connecting words from Exercise 6.

1 It is selling well, _____ its limited features.

2 _____ it's expensive, it's useful.

3 I think it's a fantastic gadget, _____ few people agree with me.

4 I like its touch-sensitive screen. It's very heavy, _____ .

5 I want one, _____ I won't use it very often.

6 _____ having no Internet connection, they found out the information they needed.

7 Films take up a lot of memory. _____ , it's worth downloading one or two.

Time to write

8 Read the writing task for the review which you are going to write.

> You recently saw this notice in an English language magazine called *Gadgets Galore*.
>
> **Reviews needed!**
> The next issue of our magazine is going to have a section on the top ten gadgets of the twenty-first century. Please write us a review of a gadget that you think should be included. Provide information on its appearance, features, strong points and drawbacks, and give your overall opinion.
>
> Write your review in 120–180 words.

9 A student has written some notes in preparation for the writing task, but some ideas are unsuitable in a review. Write S (strong point), D (drawback), or U (unsuitable).

1 friend got one ☐   5 possible birthday gift ☐
2 easy to use ☐   6 wide choice of colours ☐
3 expensive ☐   7 120 gigabytes memory ☐
4 can use anywhere ☐   8 matches my bag ☐

10 Make notes about the gadget you will write about and then make a plan for your review, using the writing plan opposite to help you. Write your review. Use the Memory Flash and the Connecting words box to help you.

> **Writing Tip:** reviews
>
> Try to use a variety of adjectives to make your review sound interesting.

Memory Flash

Describing the object's appearance	Talking about strong points	Talking about drawbacks	Giving an overall opinion
It's about … cm long/ wide/thick.	Its … design is attractive.	However, it does have a few drawbacks.	In my opinion, …
	It has a lot of useful features.	I wish it was … / could … / had …	The pros outweigh the cons.
	You can …, and you can even … with it.	It would be better if it was … / could … / had …	If you want a … , you should definitely consider the …
	… is easy to use.		
	What's great about this gadget is that …		

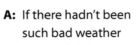
Vocabulary

1 Match to make words and phrases to describe gadgets.

1	water	a	weight
2	environmentally-	b	proof
3	solar-	c	controlled
4	remote-	d	powered
5	hi-	e	friendly
6	touch-	f	tech
7	light	g	sensitive

2 Complete the sentences with words from the box.

> spotless vanished shiny panels bent
> varnish figure pedal plug glue

1 I wish I could _____ out how to make this gadget work.

2 I love the colour of your nail _____ . It's gorgeous!

3 If you push that _____ down with your foot, the car will start moving.

4 You have to _____ the radio in somewhere – it hasn't got batteries.

5 'Why are your hands so sticky?'
   'I've been using _____.'

6 If you have solar _____ near the swimming pool, you can heat the water for free.

7 Who's _____ my knife? It's useless now!

8 'What's that _____ thing on the ground? Is it a coin?'
   'No. It's a little round mirror.'

9 'Wow! Your bedroom's _____!'
   'Yes. I've been tidying it all day.'

10 Where's Sam? He was here a minute ago, but now he's _____ .

3 Complete the sentences with *a/an* where necessary and the words in brackets in the correct order.

1 Archimedes was _____ (inventor / ancient / Greek).

2 Her TV has got _____ (flat / screen / enormous).

3 He's got _____ (digital / square / watch / hideous).

4 Wind it up with _____ (long / handle / metal / black).

5 For the show, he's been transformed into _____ (king / British / middle-aged / fat).

6 She made me some _____ (round / tiny / biscuits / chocolate).

Grammar

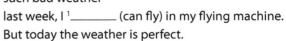

4 Complete the dialogue with the correct form of the verbs in brackets.

A: If there hadn't been such bad weather last week, I [1]_____ (can fly) in my flying machine. But today the weather is perfect.

B: If it doesn't work, you [2]_____ (be killed)!

A: I wouldn't jump if I [3]_____ (not be) sure about it.

B: You were sure about your last machine, and you would have died in it if it [4]_____ (not land) in the lake.

A: Oh yes! If only you [5]_____ (have) a camera that day! It was very funny!

B: You almost died! And the same thing [6]_____ (happen) again today unless you're really lucky.

A: I wish you [7]_____ (stop) taking things so seriously.

B: Well, I wish I [8]_____ (not worry) about you so much. If I were you, I [9]_____ (forget) about flying machines and invent something safer.

5 Complete the second sentence so that it has a similar meaning to the first sentence, using the word given. Use between two and five words, including the word given.

1 The machine won't fly if it hasn't got wings. **unless**
   The machine won't fly _____ wings.

2 I didn't mend my bike so I couldn't cycle to school. **if**
   _____ my bike, I could have cycled to school.

3 I'd like to have more memory on my computer. **wish**
   I _____ more memory on my computer.

4 You should bring your MP3 player, because you might want to listen to music. **case**
   You should bring your MP3 player _____ listen to music.

5 No one is interested in his inventions because they aren't useful. **if**
   People might be interested in his inventions _____ useful.

6 A camera will be useful, provided it's a lightweight one. **long**
   A camera will be useful, _____ a lightweight one.

7 Imagine living somewhere without electricity. Would you get bored? **supposing**
   _____ somewhere without electricity, would you get bored?

> I love going shopping, but I never spend very much. What about you? Do you save your money, or shop until you drop?

8 Spend, Spend, Spend!

Vocabulary Starter
Shopping

1 Look at the words in the box and answer the questions.

> newsagent's   post office   shopping mall
> butcher's   department store   baker's
> online seller   chemist's   jeweller's
> auction house   supermarket   market stall
> fashion boutique   greengrocer's   hypermarket

1 Which can you see in the photos?

2 From which can you buy the following?
designer clothes   cheap clothes
second-hand clothes   food   medicine
magazines   antiques

3 Which do you go to regularly? What do you do there?

2 Complete the sentences with these words. With the letters in the boxes, spell out the names of two cities famous for their fashion boutiques.

> receipt   dishonest
> bargain   shop assistant
>   traders
>   customers   offer
>   samples   complaint

P_____ and _____

1 I like shopping at that boutique because the
_ _ _ [P] _ _ _ _ _ _ [ ] _ _ is very helpful.

2 There's a special _ _ _ _ [ ] on MP3 players this month. They're half price!

3 Clothes are very cheap at the hypermarket, so you can always find a _ _ _ _ _ [ ] _ there.

4 The market opens at six a.m., so the _ _ _ _ _ _ [ ] there have to start work very early.

5 The mall is never busy in the morning. Most _ _ _ _ _ [ ] _ _ _ don't start shopping until lunchtime.

6 I bought a new watch but I wasn't given a _ _ _ _ [ ] _ _ . Now I can't return it if it stops working.

7 They were giving away free _ _ _ _ [ ] _ _ of a new chocolate bar in town today.

8 I want to make a _ _ _ _ _ [ ] _ _ _ . I bought this bag here last week and it's already broken.

9 Don't believe everything that he tells you. He can be very _ _ _ _ _ [ ] _ _ _ when he's trying to sell something.

Reading

Logged in

Ollz99

I love shopping for clothes on the Internet because there's so much choice, but sometimes the clothes look very different from the pictures online. My new green trousers have just arrived, but they aren't green – they're a horrible brown colour. What a disaster! What's your favourite place to go shopping? Why do you like it? Have you ever shopped on the Internet, or abroad? What was it like?

More soon ... Watch this space.

1 You are going to read an article about four places where you can go shopping. Read the article quickly and match the places (A–D) with the photos (1–4).

2 Choose one of the places (A–D) for each question. The places may be chosen more than once.

Reading Tip: multiple matching

Read the question carefully and underline key words and phrases.

Look for words and phrases in the text that mean the same thing.

Read the question again before *choosing* your answer.

In which place …

do shoppers never see the people that they are buying from?	1
were the bones of an extinct animal sold?	2
is there a very international range of shops?	3
can you buy turtles?	4
are the shop assistants unwelcoming to ordinary people?	5
is the food very expensive?	6
are there people who want to see celebrities?	7
can you eat the traditional food of the local area?	8
can you do a sport as well as shopping?	9
are there people who try to trick you?	10
do traders start selling before the sun is up?	11
are there good opportunities for taking photos?	12
do you have to walk a long way when you shop?	13
is it often possible to buy things very cheaply?	14
do you have to book ahead before entering a shop?	15

1

A

Vietnam is famous for its floating markets, and one of the best is at Phung Hiep.

Trading begins as early as 4 a.m., and by sunrise the water is packed tight with the long, narrow boats of both traders and customers. On a typical day you might see coconuts, mangoes, a pile of turtles or even a box of snakes being sold at the busy market. People selling small items put samples on long sticks and wave them around in the air so that everyone can see them.

Shoppers arrive by land and water, and climb from boat to boat to discuss prices. Their shopping is often interrupted to enjoy a bowl of noodles, a favourite in this part of Vietnam. The noodles are cooked on an open fire in one of the market's many 'fast food' boats.

Be sure to bring a camera to this colourful market. With the beautiful landscape, the houses on the river, the traditional boats and the local people, the photographic possibilities are endless.

3 Find words or phrases in the article that match these meanings.

1 staying on top of the water
   (A) _____
2 stopped in the middle (A) _____
3 an answer to a problem (B) _____
4 unusual (B) _____
5 a long, narrow route under something
   (C) _____
6 look at things in the shops without planning to buy anything
   (D) _____
7 notice or see something
   (D) _____

CHATROOM

• Which place would you most like to visit as a tourist?
• At which place would you spend the most money?
  Give reasons for your answers.

A World of Shopping

C

The Dubai Mall in United Arab Emirates is one of the world's biggest shopping malls. It covers an area as big as fifty football fields, so wear comfortable shoes – shopping here will involve lots of walking! With more than 1,200 shops, there's something for everyone. You can visit the French department store Galeries Lafayette, do your weekly food shopping at the British supermarket Waitrose, or choose from half a million books in six different languages at the Japanese bookshop Kinokuniya. And when you've done your shopping, put on some skates for a turn on the mall's ice rink, or walk along a glass tunnel under its giant aquarium – home to 33,000 species of sea creature including sharks and giant turtles. With a twenty-two-screen cinema and an indoor theme park inside the mall, too, you will never get bored.

B

For those who don't like to leave home to go shopping, eBay is the perfect solution. You can buy just about anything on this online auction website: a stylish second-hand dress, a signed photo of your favourite celebrity, or a DVD of an old film. There are lots of bargains to be found, but not everything comes cheap. A date with Scarlett Johannsen was sold (for charity) for £20,000, a mammoth skeleton for £61,000, and a cornflake in the shape of the US state of Illinois for $1,350!

You have to be careful of dishonest traders, of course. One item described as 'PlayStation2 – Original Box and Receipt' was sold for around $425. The buyer then received exactly what the seller had described ... a PlayStation2 box and receipt, with no games console in the box!

These problems are rare, however. On a website where an MP3 player is sold every minute and a mobile phone every twenty-one seconds, there are very few complaints and millions of happy customers.

D Rodeo Drive in Beverly Hills is probably the most expensive shopping area in the world. It is here that the rich and famous buy their clothes, and tourists window-shop while trying to spot a star.

All the world's most famous fashion and jewellery designers have shops on the street: Armani, Gucci, Valentino, Cartier, Tiffany ... The most expensive shop in the world is here. It's a men's boutique called Bijan. You must have an appointment just to go inside, and the average customer spends about $100,000 at each visit.

The shop assistants on Rodeo Drive are famous for being friendly only to those who look rich. Film star Jennifer Love Hewitt went shopping recently at Valentino's. No one recognised her in her casual clothes, and she was asked to leave the shop. We can only imagine the shop assistants' embarrassment when they realised that she was actually a wealthy actress!

Bargains will be impossible to find here. Even a quick bite to eat will cost a fortune. For people-watching in one of the world's most glamorous locations, however, Rodeo Drive is fantastic!

WebSearch

http://en.wikipedia.org/wiki/Shopping
www.worldreviewer.com
http://thejokes.co.uk/jokes-about-shopping.php

Vocabulary

Words from the text
Word formation: nouns and adjectives

1 Complete the table. You can find the words in the article on pages 90–91.

	noun	adjective
1	colour	
2	tradition	
3		possible
4	comfort	
5	style	
6	friend	
7		embarrassed
8	wealth	

2 Complete the sentences with the correct form of the word in capitals.

1 The fruit stall at the market always looks so _____ . COLOUR
2 We discussed the _____ of opening a shop together. POSSIBLE
3 When I broke the necklace in the jeweller's, I almost died of _____ . EMBARRASSED
4 The people in Vietnam are incredibly _____ . FRIEND
5 I love the _____ clothes that Vietnamese people wear on special occasions. TRADITION
6 He always looks _____ , even when he's only wearing jeans and a jumper. STYLE
7 Are all their friends as _____ as they are? WEALTH
8 Those shorts really suit you, but are they _____? COMFORT

Collocations

3 Choose the best word, A, B, C or D to complete the sentences. Then look back at the text on pages 90–91 to check.

1 I'm hungry. Shall we get a _____ to eat?
  A bit   C bite
  B plate   D food
2 The meal was delicious, but it cost a _____ .
  A luxury   C money
  B fortune   D height
3 You have to make an _____ if you want to meet her.
  A advantage   C attitude
  B appointment D arrangement
4 Some of the most expensive hotels in the _____ are in Dubai.
  A earth   C planet
  B world   D existence
5 'What are you wearing to the party?'
  'Just _____ clothes – shorts and a T-shirt.'
  A casual   C living
  B general   D generous

Money
Verbs

4 Complete the text with words from the box.

> afford   borrow   save   waste
> lend   earn   pay   buy

Some people prefer to [1]_____ all their money and keep it in the bank until they need it. Others like to [2]_____ something nice for themselves every week. But what about the ones who spend money on things that they can't [3]_____? The ones who think 'want' is the same as 'need'? There is a word for people like this. They are called 'shopaholics'.

Do you [4]_____ money on clothes that you never wear, or gadgets that you never use? Do you [5]_____ money from your friends and family until no one will [6]_____ any more to you? Then, like an estimated five percent of the population, you are probably a shopaholic. Let's hope you get a good job in the future and [7]_____ lots of money so that you can [8]_____ for your expensive tastes!

Prepositions

5 Circle the correct option.

1 I never lend money **to / for** my friends.
2 How much did you pay **on / for** that DVD?
3 If you haven't got any cash, you can pay **by / on** cheque or credit card.
4 Maybe we could borrow some money **by / from** Mum.
5 Don't waste your money **on / with** that rubbish!
6 I spend a lot of money **on / for** presents for my family.

CHATROOM

- What do you spend your money on? Do you ever waste money? How?
- Are you good at saving money? Where do you keep your savings?
- Do you ever borrow or lend money? Who do you borrow from or lend to?

Clothes

Accessories

6 Match the words with accessories 1–9.

belt   scarf   baseball cap   necklace   ring   earrings   sandals   bracelet   gloves

Parts of clothes

7 Complete the text with words from the box.

hood   pockets   collar
sleeves   zip   buttons

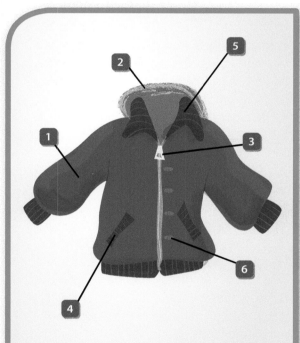

This is the perfect jacket for British summers! The jacket has long ¹_____ , so you won't get cold. It has a ²_____ to keep the rain off your head. This great jacket has a ³_____ , so you can take it off easily when the sun comes out. There are two useful ⁴_____ at the front, big enough to carry your mobile phone. The ⁵_____ is made of fleece so it feels wonderfully comfortable around your neck. And with smart metal ⁶_____ down the front, you will always look stylish!

Adjectives

8 Complete the table with these words.

stripy   baggy   leather   tight   trendy   plain
cotton   spotty   denim   silk   checked   woollen
fleece   glamorous

Opinion	Shape	Pattern	Material
trendy	baggy	stripy	leather

Phrasal verbs

9 Circle the correct words so that the meaning of the phrasal verb is similar to the meaning of the word in brackets.

1   It's cold today. Do **on / up** your coat! (close)
2   I can't wear those trousers. I've grown **up / out of** them. (they're too small)
3   She doesn't look **for / after** her clothes. (take care of)
4   I want to dress **up / out** for tonight's party. (wear special clothes)
5   Don't buy it without trying it **on / up**. (putting it on to see if it fits)
6   I can't get **out of / off** my dress. It's too tight. (take off)

CHATROOM

Tell a partner about your favourite clothes:
• for an ordinary day.
• for the beach.
• for a party.
Remember to use the correct order for adjectives (see page 81).

Grammar
The passive

1 Complete the grammar notes.

> *be* + past participle (+ *by*)
>
> **present simple**
> *The collar **is made** (make) of fleece.*
>
> **present continuous**
> *More money **is being** ¹_____ (spend) on mobile phones every year.*
>
> **present perfect simple**
> *The photo **has been** ²_____ (sign) by Scarlett Johannsen.*
>
> **past simple**
> *It **was** ³_____ (sell) for £20,000.*
>
> **past continuous**
> *A box of snakes **was being** ⁴_____ (carry) to the market.*
>
> **past perfect**
> *He found out that a famous film star **had been** ⁵_____ (ask) to leave the shop.*
>
> **future simple**
> *A big new mall **will be** ⁶_____ (build) here next year.*
>
> **modal**
> *It **can be** ⁷_____ (buy) very cheaply on eBay.*
>
> **impersonal**
> ***It is said that** Paris has got the best clothes shops.*

See **Grammar File**, page 170.

2 Circle the correct option.

1 Traditional jeans **make / are made** of a strong, blue material called denim.
2 Levi Strauss first **designed / was designed** his jeans in the 1850s for Californian gold miners.
3 Before this, denim trousers **had often worn / had often been worn** by American slaves.
4 Jeans **didn't start / weren't started** to become popular outside the USA until the 1950s.
5 They usually have several pockets, and can **be done up / been done up** with buttons or a zip.
6 The average American **is said to own / is said that he owns** eight pairs of jeans.

3 Rewrite the sentences in the passive.

1 They hold London Fashion Week every September.
London Fashion Week _____ .
2 It is thought to be one of the most important fashion events in the world.
It is thought that _____ .
3 We have created some gorgeous jeans for the event.
Some gorgeous jeans _____ .
4 Is a famous model going to wear them?
Are they _____?
5 You can buy the stripy dress for £10,000.
It _____ .
6 Have you decorated it with real diamonds?
Has it _____?

4 Complete the text with the correct passive forms.

The world's first shopping trolley

The shopping trolley ¹_____ (invent) in 1940 by American shop owner Sylvan Goldman. Before that, people's shopping ²_____ (carry) in baskets. At first, customers hated Goldman's new invention. 'Does Goldman think that we aren't strong enough to carry our own shopping?' said the male customers. 'We have ³_____ (never, insult) like this before!'

'Babies ⁴_____ (push) around town in things like this,' said the female customers. 'We don't want to push our shopping around too!'

Goldman had an idea. 'Maybe models could ⁵_____ (hire) to push trolleys around my shops,' he thought. 'Then people will ⁶_____ (persuade) that trolleys are useful.' The idea was a great success. Soon trolleys ⁷_____ (use), not only at Goldman's shops but around the world, and Goldman became a multimillionaire.

Comparatives and superlatives

5 Read the grammar notes.

as + adjective + (*as*) to compare two things that are equal *It's **as big as** the Dubai Mall.*	*the* + superlative to compare three or more things that are not equal *They're **the best** games I've ever played.* *It's **the most expensive** shop in the world.* *She's **the least friendly** shop assistant I've ever met.*
comparative (+ *than*) OR *not as* + adjective + *as* to compare two things that are not equal *The gloves are **cheaper than** the earrings.* *Woollen scarves are **less comfortable than** silk ones.* *Denim **isn't as strong as** leather.*	*the* + comparative, *the* + comparative to talk about two changes which happen together ***The bigger** the mall, **the further** you have to walk.*

See **Grammar File**, page 171. ⟫⟫⟫

6 Complete the sentences. Use the correct form of the words in brackets.

1 Ice cream is the world's <u>most popular</u> (popular) summer treat.

2 Buying ice cream is _____ (easy) than making it yourself!

3 Women are not _____ (likely) to eat ice cream for dessert as men.

4 Ice cream is _____ (little) healthy than fruit.

5 Expensive ice cream is usually _____ (good) for you than cheap ice cream.

6 In Italy, the _____ (big) ice cream queues are late at night.

7 The world's _____ (fast) ice cream eater can eat 1.53 kg of ice cream in 31.67 seconds!

8 Garlic ice cream is very popular in Japan, but in Britain it is one of the _____ (little) popular flavours.

9 Ice cream should not be kept at a temperature _____ (high) than –18°C.

10 The _____ (hot) the weather, the _____ (interested) people are in buying ice cream.

Back up your grammar

7 Choose the correct answer.

1 It _____ pizzas were invented in Naples, Italy.
A is thought to be
B is thought that
C is thought by
D is thought to

2 In the first pizza restaurant in Naples, the pizzas _____ in ovens heated by hot rocks from the volcano Vesuvius.
A were cooked
B were cooking
C were being cooked
D have cooked

3 Tomatoes were unknown in Europe before the 16th century, and for many years they were believed _____ poisonous.
A that they were
B they were
C to be
D be

4 The _____ type of pizza, cheese and tomato, was created for Queen Margherita of Italy in 1889.
A cheap
B cheaper
C cheapest
D cheap as

5 No other cheese tastes _____ on pizzas as mozzarella.
A better
B best
C as good
D better than

6 The biggest pizza that _____ made was 37.4 metres wide.
A has ever been
B can have
C is being
D has

7 Burgers are bought by _____ people than pizzas.
A the most
B many
C more
D as many

8 Macdonald's burger restaurants can _____ in at least 121 countries.
A been found
B have been found
C find
D be found

CHATROOM

Work in groups of three. Each person chooses a snack food. Make comparisons. Which snack is the healthiest? The most delicious? The cheapest?

More practice on pages 142–143. ⟫⟫⟫

Listening

Ollz99

There's an advert that I really like on TV. I love the music, but it's for a drink that I don't like, so it'll never persuade me to buy the drink!

What are your favourite adverts – on TV, on the radio, on billboards …? Which adverts annoy you? How often do adverts make you want to buy things?

More soon … Watch this space.

Listening 1

 1 You will hear five different people talking about an advert they've seen or heard. Match the descriptions (A–F) with the speakers. There is one extra letter which you do not need to use.

> **Listening Tip:** multiple matching
>
> Read the options carefully and think of some other ways to say the same thing.
> Listen carefully for any relevant information.

A an advert that makes me give in to temptation
B an advert that gives me a place to dream about
C an advert that I find confusing
D an advert with irritating music
E an advert that encourages me to spend too much money
F an advert that I like because of the actor in it

Speaker 1		Speaker 4	
Speaker 2		Speaker 5	
Speaker 3			

Listening 2

2 You are going to hear a radio interview with a film maker who specialises in adverts. You will hear the interview in several parts. After each part you will hear some questions. Choose the correct answers.

> **Listening Tip:** multiple choice
>
> Note down key information as you listen.
> Listen to the questions very carefully.

1 A He made a film.
  B He worked in advertising.
  C He wrote stories.

2 A when the client is looking for ideas
  B when the client has decided on an idea
  C when a product is successful

3 A The length varies from country to country.
  B The length varies because of the actors.
  C thirty seconds

4 A a day
  B a week
  C Some adverts take longer than others.

5 A making adverts with big crowds of people in them
  B getting people to do things for you
  C using computers

6 A An actor was ill.
  B A helicopter crashed.
  C A camera wasn't working.

7 A an advert for clothes
  B an advert for an airline
  C an advert for a movie

8 A dance
  B use a computer
  C take photos

9 A actors
  B clients
  C sports stars

10 A He changes the plan for an advert.
   B He forgets what to say.
   C He makes sports stars say silly lines.

> **CHATROOM**
>
> Do famous sportspeople ever appear in TV adverts in your country? Are they good at acting? Describe some adverts you remember.

Speaking
Comparing two pictures

1 What is important for a successful advert in a city centre? Work with a partner and discuss this list. Decide on a number from 1 (the most important) to 8 (the least important) for each item.

a It is funny. ☐

b It has big, clear writing. ☐

c It is in a place that lots of people see. ☐

d It is colourful. ☐

e People know immediately what it is advertising. ☐

f It shows something unusual or surprising. ☐

g It has a celebrity on it. ☐

h It is very big. ☐

2 Look at these photos of unusual adverts or billboards. With a partner, compare photos 1 and 2, thinking about these points:

• their similarities and differences

• what they might advertise

• which you prefer and why

3 Now read the task and talk about photos 3 and 4. Use the Language Upload box to help you.

> Compare the photos. Which would you look at and why? Which do you think is cleverer? Do you think they might make you buy or use the products?

Speaking Tip: comparing photos

Don't panic if you don't know the word for something. You don't have to describe the picture in detail.

Use linking words like *however* and *whereas* to help you sound more confident.

Language Upload

Talking about similarities

Both the pictures are …

They both show …

I think they're both …

Talking about differences

The advert / billboard in picture 1 is …, whereas the advert in picture 2 is …

The first advert is definitely more / less / -er … than the second advert.

However, I think the second one is better because …

Vocabulary

eye-catching   impressive   advertiser   product

Writing: Informal Letter

Before you write

1 Read this letter from your family's English-speaking friend, Callum, who owns a shop. You have made some notes on the letter. Answer the questions below.

> There are a lot of teenage students from your country here in the summer, and it would be great if we could sell things in our shop that would interest them. I'm hoping you can give me some ideas.
>
> First of all, can you tell me what styles of clothes are popular in your country at the moment?
>
> Apart from clothes, what do teenagers like to buy when they're abroad? Have you got any ideas of cool things to sell?
>
> We're going to need some teenage shop assistants in the summer holidays. Would you like to come and stay at our house and work in the shop? We can afford to pay you a fair salary, and I think you'd have fun.
>
> Best wishes,
>
> Callum

Describe some popular styles.

Make some suggestions.

Yes, but ...

Ask for details.

1 Why has Callum written to you?
2 When you reply, how many points should you cover?
3 Should you use formal or informal language?

2 Read Kikki's reply. Complete each gap with a suitable word.

> Dear Callum,
>
> It's great to hear from you. Of course I'm happy to give you some ideas for your shop.
>
> First of all, you asked about fashion. The ¹_____ popular styles here are checked cotton shirts with big black belts for girls, and baggier jeans, trainers and sweatshirts with hoods for boys.
>
> As for other things to sell in the shop, you could try video games. Teenagers here spend a lot of money ²_____ them and they are often cheaper abroad ³_____ at home. Bracelets and bags are always popular too.
>
> As far as working in the shop is concerned, I'd love to do it, but I can't come until August because I've got to do a Maths course before that. You mentioned that you could ⁴_____ me something. Please could you let me know how much?
>
> Good luck with the shop, and I hope to hear from you soon.
>
> Best wishes,
>
> Kikki

3 Complete Kikki's plan for her letter.

Writing Plan

Paragraph 1	Introduction	• Say I received the letter and am happy to help
Paragraphs 2–4	Cover the four points in the notes	Popular styles of clothes • girls: checked cotton shirts, big black _____, tight jeans • boys: baggier jeans, trainers, sweatshirts with _____ Suggestions of other things to sell • video games, bracelets, _____ Reply to invitation • Yes, but not until _____ Ask for details about payment • How much?
Paragraph 5	Closing	• End in a friendly way

4 Look at the Connecting words box. Which phrases does Kikki use in her letter?

Connecting words

Referring to points in a letter...

First of all, you asked about my favourite shops.

As for jewellery, I haven't bought any rings or necklaces for six months.

As far as saving money **is concerned**, I've got more than €100 in the bank.

You mentioned that there were a lot of students in the summer.

5 Complete the sentences with a phrase from the Connecting words box.

1 As _____ as shoes are concerned, sandals are very trendy this summer.

2 First _____ , you asked about the shops in town.

3 _____ for the newsagent's, it's a great place to buy magazines.

4 You _____ that you want to open a new shop.

Writing Tip: informal letter

When you've finished writing, read your work and check the grammar, spelling and punctuation.

Time to write

6 Read the writing task below. Then make a plan for your letter using the writing plan opposite to help you.

Your English-speaking friend Trudy is thinking of starting an online fashion business. Read Trudy's letter and the notes you have made. Then write a letter to Trudy using all your notes.

I'm thinking of starting my own online fashion business! I'm very excited about it, but I'm a bit worried too. Online shopping is quite new here. In your country, are many clothes bought online, or do people prefer traditional clothes shops? • ——— Tell Trudy.

I'm looking for fashion ideas from around the world. What styles are popular with teenagers in your country at the moment? • ——— Describe some popular styles.

I'm going to need photos of teenagers wearing my clothes. Would you like to be a model for me? You could stay at my • ——— Yes, but... house for a week, and you'd be paid for it, of course. • ——— Ask for details.

Best wishes,

Trudy

7 Now write your letter (120–150 words). Use the Memory Flash and the Connecting words box to help you.

Memory Flash

Opening an informal letter	Comparing	Responding to an invitation	Closing an informal letter
Dear	The most popular styles here are ...	I'd love to come and work as a ...	Good luck with the ...
It's great to hear from you.	... is more/less popular than ...	I can't ... because ...	I hope to hear from you soon.
Of course I'm happy to ...		Please could you let me know ...?	Best wishes, ...
Your idea for ... sounds very interesting/unusual/exciting.			

Vocabulary

1 Circle the odd one out.

1 baker's   collar   hypermarket   greengrocer's
2 silk   woollen   belt   cotton
3 auction   hood   pocket   zip
4 customer   leather   trader   shop assistant
5 necklace   earring   bracelet   offer
6 afford   borrow   sandals   save
7 trendy   stylish   glamorous   sleeve
8 gloves   scarf   baggy   cap
9 stripy   checked   plain   fleece

2 Choose the best word to complete the sentences.

1 I need to buy some stamps at the _____ office.
   A post   B letter   C sending   D mail
2 My new jacket _____ a fortune.
   A paid   B cost   C spent   D tried on
3 If you buy them in the smaller size, you'll soon grow _____ them.
   A up to   B out of   C up   D for
4 He _____ £10 an hour in his new job at the butcher's.
   A earns   B pays   C affords   D buys
5 She always buys her clothes in department _____ .
   A malls   B shops   C stores   D stalls
6 My neck gets hot if I do _____ the top button on my shirt.
   A up   B after   C out   D off
7 You shouldn't waste all your money _____ sweets.
   A in   B for   C with   D on
8 My new sandals were very cheap – a real _____ .
   A sample   C complaint
   B bargain   D receipt

3 Complete the text with the correct form of the words in capitals.

Waterproof, ¹ _____ and warm, these   COMFORT
winter jackets are the ² _____ clothing   TRADITION
of the Sami people of Scandinavia.
Until now, only the ³ _____ could   WEALTH
afford one of these ⁴ _____ jackets,   COLOUR
but they are now available for only
£20 – and not from a ⁵ _____   HONEST
online ⁶ _____ , either, but from   SELL
StreetSmart, the ⁷ _____ fashion   FRIEND
boutique on West Street.

Grammar

4 Look at the information and complete the sentences. Include the correct form of the word in brackets.

	Superzooms	V10s	Tektraks
Sports	running	tennis, volleyball	running
Price	£12	£40	£28
Quality	*	*****	***
Country	India	China	China
Designer	Evie Smith	Chad Harper	Su Lin

1 Superzooms are not *as expensive as* Tektraks. (expensive)
2 V10s should _____ for running. (not wear)
3 Tektraks and V10s _____ in China. (make)
4 Superzooms are _____ of the three. (cheap)
5 Superzooms can _____ for running. (use)
6 Tektraks are _____ V10s. (bad quality)
7 The more you spend, the _____ the shoes. (good)
8 V10s _____ by Su Lin. (not design)

5 Complete each gap with one suitable word.

In 1985, the Coca-Cola® Company was in trouble. People were drinking ¹_____ Coke every year, and Pepsi was now more popular than Coke in America.
²_____ was thought that this was because Pepsi was sweeter ³_____ Coke, so the decision ⁴_____ made to change the recipe of Coke. 'New Coke' was born.
When Americans heard about New Coke, they were not ⁵_____ pleased as the Coca-Cola® Company had hoped. Thousands of angry letters were ⁶_____ to the company. The last few bottles of original Coke were ⁷_____ expensive than usual, because they ⁸_____ now seen as collector's items.
The boss of the Coca-Cola® Company realised that New Coke was the ⁹_____ mistake of his career. He acted fast. Within three months, original Coke had ¹⁰_____ put back on the supermarket shelves.
This was the ¹¹_____ embarrassing moment in the history of the Coca-Cola® Company, but it was the right decision. Coca-Cola® is now one of ¹²_____ most successful companies in the world.

I live in the city but whenever I can, I escape to the wilderness: fresh air, great views and healthy exercise. I love it! What about you? What do you like or dislike about the great outdoors?

9 Rising to the Challenge

Vocabulary Starter
The great outdoors

1 What do these pairs have in common? How are they different?

1. a **glacier** and an **iceberg**
2. a **puddle** and a **stream**
3. a **cave** and a **cliff**
4. an **oasis** and a **sand dune**

2 Complete the instructions below with words and phrases from the box.

> a search party   a shelter   the water   an SOS
> the weather forecast   on an expedition
> a compass   a flare   ordeal   medical attention
> risks   a positive attitude   a fire

How to survive in the wilderness

◆ Learn the basics first, especially how to read a map and navigate with ¹_____ .
◆ When you go ²_____ , plan carefully and don't take unnecessary ³_____ .
◆ Check ⁴_____ before setting off, and bring everything you might need in the predicted weather conditions.
◆ Always tell other people your plans. That way they'll be able to send out ⁵_____ if you get lost.
◆ Your most important survival tool is your brain. Always use it well, and keep ⁶_____ .

In an emergency situation, follow these instructions, in this order, to survive your ⁷_____ :

a S.T.O.P. (Stop, Think, Observe, Plan)
b Do what you can to help anyone who needs ⁸_____ .
c Find a building or cave. Alternatively, build ⁹_____ out of tree branches, leaves, or even snow.
d Light ¹⁰_____ to keep yourself warm. Make sure it's not near any trees.
e Send ¹¹_____ to ask for help. One way to do this, especially at sea, is to set off ¹²_____ .
f Drink plenty. If you drink from a stream, lake or puddle, purify ¹³_____ first, for example by boiling it over a fire.
g Last on the list, think about food. Remember – you can survive for weeks without eating.

CHATROOM

Which aspects of the advice in Exercise 2 would be easy for you? Which would be hard? Why?

Reading

Logged in

Joe2Go

I've never run a marathon, but I'd like to one day. What I *never* want to do is run an ultramarathon – several days of marathon running in a row. The guys who do those races are crazy! What about you? What's the furthest you've run in a day? Does long-distance running appeal to you? Why/Why not?

More soon ... Watch this space.

1 You are going to read a true story about a man who got lost in the desert. Read the story quickly and find out:

1 his name
2 his age
3 how long he was lost

2 Read the story again and choose the answer, A, B, C or D which you think fits best according to the text.

Reading Tip: multiple choice

Read the relevant parts of the text very carefully! Be sure the option you choose does not just give correct information. It must answer the <u>question</u> correctly.

1 What was the biggest challenge for the marathon runners?
  A carrying enough water to survive a week in the desert
  B building their own shelters to sleep in at night
  C finding the right route
  D running a long way with equipment in hot weather
2 Why did Prosperi stop running?
  A Because a sandstorm started.
  B Because he wasn't winning the race.
  C Because the sand was causing him pain.
  D Because he was too tired to continue.
3 After the sandstorm, why didn't Prosperi start walking immediately?
  A Because he wanted to enjoy the beauty of the desert.
  B Because he could see rescue planes in the distance.
  C Because he didn't know which way to go.
  D Because he had been told not to.

4 When Prosperi finally realised that he was lost, what did he think about first?
  A his chances of success in the race
  B his water supply
  C the weather
  D how to let people know where he was
5 Which sentence is true of Prosperi's journey through the desert?
  A He walked at night and slept in the day.
  B He ate whatever plants and animals he could find.
  C It was difficult to sleep at night because it was so hot.
  D He did nothing to tell people where he was going.
6 What happened when Prosperi arrived at the oasis?
  A He saw a footprint there.
  B He immediately started feeling better.
  C He felt worse before he felt better.
  D He found a beautiful lake full of water.
7 How did the girl react when she first saw Prosperi?
  A She was scared of him.
  B She gave him medical attention.
  C She decided that he didn't need any help.
  D She thought he was funny.
8 Which sentence is true of Prosperi?
  A He's avoided running in ultramarathons since 1994.
  B He was in good health after his ordeal in the desert.
  C The desert environment doesn't appeal to him now.
  D He travelled a huge distance while he was lost.

3 Find words or phrases in the article that match these meanings.

1 making little holes in (paragraph 3) _____
2 find out where he was (paragraph 5) _____
3 people in a responsible position (paragraph 6) _____
4 insects with a round, hard back (paragraph 7) _____
5 with excitement (paragraph 8) _____
6 group of animals (paragraph 9) _____
7 unable to understand (paragraph 9) _____
8 bones of the head (paragraph 9) _____

CHATROOM

- Do you think you would survive in a situation like Prosperi's? Why/Why not?
- What makes some people more likely to survive than others?

WebSearch

http://wildernesssurvivalstories.com

Fighting for survival

1 Mauro Prosperi's feet kicked up the sand as he ran through the desert. Although facing a run of eighty-four kilometres that day in temperatures of 46°C, his confidence was high. He was in seventh place in the world's most challenging running race.

2 It was April 1994 and thirty-nine-year-old Prosperi was taking part in the famous *Marathon des Sables* ('Marathon of the Sands') – an ultramarathon, almost 250 kilometres long, run over one week in the sand dunes and rocky emptiness of the Moroccan Sahara Desert. The organisers gave the competitors water and shelter for each night, but they had to carry their own clothes, food, camping stove, first aid kit and sleeping bag in a backpack. It was a race for the very fit, the very brave … or the mad.

3 It was about one o'clock when the sandstorm blew up. Prosperi soon lost sight of the other competitors but, reluctant to let anyone overtake him, he decided to keep on running. The sand felt like needles piercing his skin, however, and he was forced to reconsider his decision. He tied a towel round his face and found shelter behind a bush.

4 When the sandstorm finally died down, it was almost dark. Prosperi looked for the path, but found no sign of it. He was lost. He was absolutely furious with himself, because now he had no chance of winning the race. He got into his sleeping bag for the night, telling himself that a search party would be sent out for him the next day.

5 In the morning he climbed to the top of the nearest sand dune to get his bearings. His heart sank. In every direction stretched an endless ocean of sand. No runners, no buildings, no race markers. He had no idea where he was, and in the baking heat of the desert he had almost no water.

6 Officials had advised competitors to stay put if they got lost. Prosperi did just that at first. In the next couple of days, two rescue planes flew by, but despite setting off a flare, lighting a fire with the contents of his bag and writing an enormous SOS in the sand, Prosperi failed to attract their attention. He decided that his only hope of surviving this ordeal was to walk to safety.

7 He headed for a range of mountains on the distant horizon. He walked only in the early morning and the evening, leaving behind him a piece of shiny metal at the top of each dune to show the route he was taking. In the heat of the day, he rested in the shadow of cliffs and caves. He drank almost nothing – just the tiny drops of water that formed on rocks at night. He ate beetles and plants, and he once managed to kill and eat a snake. Every evening he dug a hole in the sand and slept inside it. This kept him warm during the cold desert nights.

8 After four days like this, he came to an oasis with a small puddle of water. He threw himself into it eagerly and drank, but was immediately sick. He drank again, more slowly this time – a small sip of water every ten minutes. All night he lay by the pool drinking, and by morning he had regained some of his strength. He decided to continue his journey.

9 After walking non-stop for twenty-four hours, his luck finally changed. He found a child's footprint in the sand. Soon he saw a young girl with a herd of goats. Prosperi limped towards her, but she ran away screaming. Puzzled by this reaction, he glanced at himself in the little mirror in his bag. His skin was like that of a tortoise, his eyes had almost disappeared inside his skull, and he had lost fifteen kilos since the start of the race. He was a horrifying sight.

10 The girl soon reappeared, this time with her grandmother, and led Prosperi to their home. Their family took him to the nearest town to get medical attention. When Prosperi asked where he was, he was told that he was in Algeria, almost 200 kilometres away from the race in Morocco!

11 After recovering in hospital for several months, Prosperi went home to Italy. Astonishingly, he returned to the *Marathon des Sables* four years later, and he has now completed the race six times. Despite those terrible nine days lost in the Sahara, he still loves the desert.

Vocabulary

Words from the text
Verbs with the prefix *re-*

1 Match the words with their definitions.

1	reconsider	a	get something back
2	reappear	b	be seen again
3	react	c	get better after ill health
4	recover	d	think again about something
5	regain		you've decided
		e	behave in a certain way because of something that has happened

2 Complete the sentences with the verbs in Exercise 1.

1 I think you've made the wrong choice. Please _____ .

2 It'll take him several months to _____ from the accident.

3 His success today has helped him to _____ the confidence that he lost last week.

4 He vanished under the water, and didn't _____ for a few moments.

5 No one knows how they'll _____ in an emergency until it actually happens.

Useful phrases

3 Choose the correct option, A, B, C or D, to complete the sentences.

1 We lost _____ of the campsite when we climbed down the other side of the mountain.
   A look   B seeing   C sight   D eyes

2 On the last day, a storm blew _____ suddenly and we couldn't finish the race.
   A up   B off   C out   D over

3 Don't go anywhere. Just stay _____ until I get back.
   A set   B put   C got   D had

4 Head _____ the hill with the tower on the top and you can't get lost.
   A for   B onto   C of   D off

5 One little _____ of water isn't enough when you're as thirsty as I am!
   A piece   B sip   C lump   D bite

6 I swam _____-stop for three hours.
   A not   B no   C never   D non

Survival
Equipment

4 Match the words with the pictures.

> blanket   camping stove   first aid kit
> fishing rod   GPS device   insect repellent
> matches   mosquito net   parachute
> raft   rope   sleeping bag   sunscreen
> torch   whistle

1 _____   2 _____   3 _____

4 _____   5 _____   6 _____

7 _____   8 _____   9 _____

10 _____   11 _____   12 _____

13 _____   14 _____   15 _____

5 Make sentences to explain why the objects in Exercise 4 are useful in dangerous situations.

You can stay warm at night in a sleeping bag.

6 Complete the table with the words in the box.

> blizzard fog hail lightning gale
> flood mist thunder downpour

Wind	Snow and ice	Water	Electric storms	Visibility

7 Complete the factfile with the words from Exercise 6.

FACTFILE

Weather

⚙ Roy Sullivan from the USA was often outside in a storm, and ignored the loud noise of the [1]_____ . He was hit by [2]_____ seven times and, amazingly, survived each time.

⚙ [3]_____ can be dangerous too. In 1986, balls of ice almost as big as footballs fell to earth in Bangladesh and killed ninety-two people.

⚙ The world's windiest place is Commonwealth Bay in Antarctica. A [4]_____ there often blows at 200 km per hour. When snow falls during wind like this, the [5]_____ makes it impossible to see things only a metre in front of you.

⚙ It is thought that there was a big [6]_____ 7500 years ago, when the Black Sea first became joined to the Mediterranean. Perhaps this explains the story of Noah and his boat full of animals.

⚙ Forks, home of Bella and Edward in the *Twilight* books, is a real town in the USA, and it's a great place for people who don't like sunlight. There's often a [7]_____ of rain, and it can be unsafe to drive because of the poor visibility due to [8]_____ and [9]_____ .

CHATROOM

- Order the weather conditions in Exercise 6 from the most dangerous to the least dangerous.
- What would be the three most important things to take with you on expeditions to the following environments?
  a) a mountain with glaciers   b) a hot desert
  c) a jungle   d) the Mediterranean Sea

Extreme adjectives (2)

8 Match the extreme adjectives (1–10) with their weaker equivalents (a–j).

1	baking	a	angry
2	soaking	b	unhappy
3	freezing	c	tired
4	starving	d	hot
5	astonished	e	surprised
6	terrified	f	wet
7	delighted	g	hungry
8	furious	h	happy
9	exhausted	i	cold
10	miserable	j	scared

9 Circle the correct word.

1 I felt really **miserable / starving** when my friends went on the expedition without me.
2 We're **exhausted / astonished** that there's been a flood, because it hardly ever rains here.
3 My sister always cries during a storm because she's **terrified / furious** of thunder.
4 She was **soaking / baking** because she'd fallen into the stream.
5 They were **delighted / freezing** when they heard your good news.
6 After a night sleeping without a blanket, I was **freezing / terrified**.
7 We were **furious / miserable** with Katie for forgetting the camping stove.
8 I was **delighted / exhausted** after working hard all day.
9 We've eaten nothing since breakfast, so we're absolutely **soaking / starving**.
10 It was a hot day, and he was **baking / astonished** inside his jumper.

Expressions with *heart*

10 Match the sentence halves.

1	Her **heart sank**	a	when her dog had an accident.
2	She's very **hard-hearted.**	b	Even now, she's refusing to help us.
3	She was **heartbroken**	c	She's decided to come on the expedition after all.
4	She's **had a change of heart**.	d	She helps whenever she can.
5	Her **heart's in the right place**.	e	when she realised she was lost.

CHATROOM

Talk about a challenging situation that you've been in.

More practice on pages 144–145.

Grammar
Reported speech

1 Read and complete the grammar notes.

Reported statements	Reported questions
• The verb moves one tense back from the direct speech tense.	• The verb moves one tense back from the direct speech tense.
• Pronouns and time and place words are often different from those used in direct speech.	• The subject and verb change position after question words.
• We mention the person spoken to after the verb *tell*.	• We use *if* or *whether* to introduce *yes/no* questions.

Reported statements
- The verb moves one tense back from the direct speech tense.
- Pronouns and time and place words are often different from those used in direct speech.
- We mention the person spoken to after the verb *tell*.
- We don't mention the person spoken to after the verb *say*.

Direct
'You're in Algeria,' they told him.
*'A search party **will** be sent out **tomorrow**,' he said.*

Reported
*They told him that **he was** in Algeria.*
*He said a search party **would** be sent out **the next day**.*

Reported questions
- The verb moves one tense back from the direct speech tense.
- The subject and verb change position after question words.
- We use *if* or *whether* to introduce *yes/no* questions.

Direct	Reported
*'Where **am I**?' he asked.*	*He asked where ¹_____ .*
*'**Can he** survive?' they wondered.*	*They wondered if **he** ²_____ survive.*

Reported commands and requests
We use *tell/ask* + object (+ *not*) + *to* + infinitive.

Direct	Reported
*'**Don't get** lost,' they told the runners.*	*They told the runners **not to** ³_____ lost.*
*'**Please help me**,' he said to the girl.*	*He asked the girl **to** ⁴_____ **him**.*

> See **Grammar File**, pages 172–173.

2 Write the reported statements in your notebook.

1 'We're feeling nervous about our survival course tomorrow,' they said.
   They said they were feeling nervous about their survival course the next day.
2 'We've never spent a night in the wild before,' they said.
3 'I'm an expert in survival skills,' the instructor told them.
4 'The skills you learn today may save your life,' he said.
5 'You can't sleep in this cave because a bear lives here,' he told them.
6 'I'll teach you to make a shelter,' he said.
7 'We went to a hotel for the night,' they told me.

3 Order the words in these reported questions. Write them in your notebook.

1 any matches / asked / She / had / if / we.
2 We / been / whether / the path / had / destroyed / wondered.
3 was / me / They / what / the matter / asked.
4 gone / had / asked / where / He / a man / everyone.
5 wondered / help / I / who / us / would.
6 if / the weather / was / getting / worse / asked / She.

4 Change the sentences into reported statements, questions, commands or requests. Write each sentence in your notebook. Start with *He* and the verb in brackets.

1 'Would you like to join me on the expedition?' (asked)
   He asked me if I'd like to join him on the expedition.
2 'Last year we had a great time.' (said)
3 'You should definitely come with us.' (said)
4 'Please think about it.' (asked)
5 'Don't worry about the cold temperatures.' (told)
6 'Everyone will wear very warm clothes.' (told)
7 'Can you afford the plane ticket?' (asked)
8 'Please phone Mike and find out more about the trip.' (asked)

They said we wouldn't need a compass.

Other reporting verbs

5 Complete the grammar notes with words from the box.

> refused   go   feeling   congratulated   loved

Verb (+ *that*) + clause e.g. *admit, agree, complain, decide, deny, explain, promise, recommend, suggest, write,* + the verbs of speaking on page 33 *'I love the desert.'* He **explained** that he ¹ _____ the desert.	**Verb + *-ing*** e.g. *suggest, admit, deny* *'I felt scared.'* He **admitted** ² _____ scared.	**Verb + (*not*) *to* + infinitive** e.g. *agree, refuse, offer, promise* *'No, I won't help you.'* She ⁴ _____ to help him.
	Verb + preposition + *-ing* e.g. *apologise for, blame someone for, accuse someone of, congratulate someone on* *'Well done for winning the race, Liz.'* We ³ _____ Liz **on** winning the race.	**Verb + object + (*not*) *to* + infinitive** e.g. *invite, remind, warn, encourage, order, advise* *'Don't go anywhere,' they advised me.* They **advised** me not to ⁵ _____ anywhere.

See **Grammar File**, page 173.

6 Complete the second sentence so that it has a similar meaning to the first sentence.

> Seventeen-year-old Jennifer Graham from New Zealand has nearly finished sailing around the world, all on her own and without stopping. On her satellite phone, she told me about her amazing journey.

1 'I'm sorry I didn't talk to you yesterday,' she said.
She apologised _____ .

2 'There was a big gale,' she told me.
She explained _____ .

3 'Don't sail in the Southern Ocean in April!' she said.
She advised me _____ .

4 'Some adults have been rude about my sailing skills,' she told me.
She complained _____ .

5 'I'm not too young for a journey like this,' she said.
She denied _____ .

6 'I suggest everyone goes on a trip like mine!' she told me.
She recommended _____ .

7 'I will be very happy to get home to New Zealand,' she said.
She admitted that _____ .

8 'Come and celebrate the end of my journey with me,' she said.
She invited _____ .

9 'I'll take you sailing with me soon,' she said.
She offered _____ .

Back up your grammar

7 Read the text and circle the correct words.

Laura Dekker, the schoolgirl who went missing from her home in the Netherlands, has been found.

Last year thirteen-year-old Laura told journalists that she ¹**was planning / to plan** to sail around the world on her own. Her father was encouraging her ²**making / to make** the journey, but the Dutch authorities warned it ³**will / would** not be good for her to spend so much time alone. Many people accused her father ⁴**that he was / of being** an irresponsible parent, and in the end a Dutch court ordered Laura ⁵**she forgot / to forget** about her journey until she was older.

Furious, Laura asked her father if ⁶**she could / she can** ignore the court's order and set off on her adventure. When he refused ⁷**to let / letting** her do that, she decided to run away from home.

Four days ago, she disappeared. In a letter, she told her father that she ⁸**had had / would have** enough of her life in the Netherlands and never ⁹**wanted / had wanted** to come back. She has now been found on the island of St Maarten in the Caribbean.

We are all asking ourselves ¹⁰**if / what** this brave but stubborn young yachtswoman will do next.

More practice on pages 146–147.

Listening

Listening 1

1 You will hear eight short conversations. After each conversation, you will be asked a question. Choose the correct answer, A, B or C.

1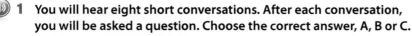

2

3

4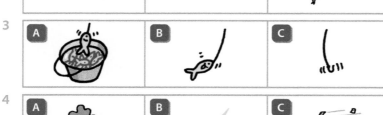

5

6

7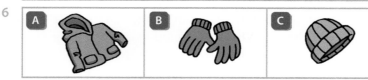

8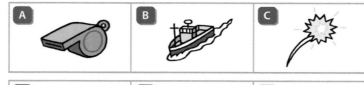

Listening 2

2 You are going to hear an interview with Leo Gardiner, a teenager who went to the South Pole. Listen and complete the answers to the questions.

Listening Tip: completing answers

Before you listen, read the questions and answers carefully and try to guess the missing words.

Questions	Answers
1 What was Leo's ambition as a young boy?	to be an _____
2 What first made Leo want to go to Antarctica?	a visit to _____
3 When did Captain Scott reach the South Pole?	five weeks _____ Amundsen
4 Who encouraged Leo to go on the expedition?	his _____
5 What help did Leo get when he reached the Pole?	A _____ came to collect him.
6 How did Leo transport his clothes and equipment?	on a _____
7 What did Leo miss when he was in Antarctica?	the _____ that he has at home
8 What's Leo's next goal?	to _____ his _____

CHATROOM

Would you like to visit Antarctica? Why/Why not?

Speaking
Solving a problem

1 Work in pairs. Student A: read Situation A below. Student B: read the Information Card for Situation A on page 126. Do both parts of the task.

> ### Situation
>
> I am your friend and I have a problem. Find out what my problem is and offer me some good advice.
>
> ### Task
>
> 1 Look at the pictures below and ask:
> - Who is this person?
> - What is the problem?
> - What are the options?
> - What are the disadvantages of each option?
>
> 2 When you have all the information you need, you should offer some advice to help solve the problem. You can choose one of the solutions in the pictures, or create your own solution to the problem. Remember to use information you have learnt in part 1 to explain your final choice.

A

2 Listen to the recording. What suggestion does the speaker make? Why does she reject the other option? Do you agree with her?

3 Listen again and tick the phrases in the Language Upload box that you hear.

4 Now look at the photos for Situation B and do the task from Exercise 1. Student A: read the Information Card for Situation B on page 127.

B

> ## Speaking Tip: solving a problem
>
> There is no 'right' solution. Any solution is fine, as long as you explain clearly why you have chosen it.

5 Discuss these questions.

1 Have you ever done mountain biking or sailing?
2 Which are the most popular adventure sports for teenagers in your country?
3 What skills do you have that might one day save your life, or the lives of other people?
4 Do you think schools have a responsibility to teach their students to swim and to do first aid? Why/Why not? What other life-saving skills should schools teach?

> ## Language Upload
>
> ### Expressing an opinion
>
> I (don't) think it's a good idea to …
> I'm (not) keen on the idea of … ing.
> I'm (not) sure it would be sensible to …
>
> ### Talking about danger
>
> Anything could happen.
> It would be even more dangerous if …
> You could have a serious accident.
>
> ### Choosing an option
>
> The best option is to …
> All things considered, I think it would be best to …
>
> ### Making an alternative suggestion
>
> Instead of that, I'd suggest … ing.
> Instead, why don't you …?

Writing: Formal email
Before you write

1 Read the writing task and answer the questions below.

> Write an email of application for the expedition advertised below. You can apply as yourself or as an imaginary person.
>
> Write your email in 120–150 words.

VOLUNTEERS FOR EXPEDITION NEEDED!

Destination: the Indian Himalayas
Aim: to collect information about glaciers and plant life in the region
Skills you will learn: ice climbing, mountain survival
Requirements: an excellent level of fitness, an ability to work well in a team

To apply, send an email to <u>youthexpeditions@ himalayas.com</u> outlining:

- your reasons for wanting to take part
- your skills, experience and character traits that will make you a useful member of the team

Selection weekend will be held on May 15th.

1 What sort of text are you going to write?
2 Who is going to read it?
3 Should you use formal or informal language?
4 What information should you include?

2 Read Martha's email. Do you think she is likely to be selected for the expedition? Why/Why not?

New   Reply

Dear Sirs,

1 _____ apply for a place on the expedition to the Indian Himalayas.

2 _____ visit the Himalayas and do something useful. I would really like to participate in your expedition and learn more about the plants and glaciers in the area.

3 _____ an experienced rock climber. I have also been a volunteer in search parties, which has given me a good understanding of mountain safety. I also play hockey for my school. This keeps me fit and has taught me a lot about teamwork. My coach says that my positive attitude has helped my teammates, and that I am mature and hard-working. I'm sure I could be a useful member of your team.

4 _____ invite me to the selection weekend so that I can find out more about the expedition. I look forward to hearing from you.

Yours faithfully,

Martha Jones

3 Now complete the email with these phrases.

a It has always been my dream to
b I am already
c I very much hope you will
d I am writing to

4 Complete Martha's plan for the email.

Writing Plan

Paragraph 1	reason for writing	• apply for a place on the _____
Paragraph 2	reason(s) for my interest in the expedition	• visit the Himalayas to do something _____ • learn more about plants and _____
Paragraph 3	reasons why I'd be a useful member of the team	• _____ rock climber • volunteer in search _____ • team sports at school • positive attitude • _____ and hard-working
Paragraph 4	close in a polite and confident way	• hope to find out more at selection weekend

5 Which of these connecting words are used in Martha's email?

Connecting words

Purpose

so that + clause

I want to join your expedition **so that I can learn** about wildlife conservation.

to/in order to/so as to + infinitive

I've been running every day **in order to improve** my fitness.

6 Complete each sentence with <u>one</u> word.

1 Saskia wanted to go on the expedition in _____ to improve her survival skills.

2 She applied early _____ that she had a good chance of being accepted.

3 The expedition leaders interviewed her _____ as to find out if she'd be a useful team member.

4 They then wrote to her _____ order to tell her she'd been selected.

5 Her parents read all the information carefully so _____ to check it wouldn't be too dangerous.

6 She borrowed her brother's backpack _____ carry all her stuff in.

7 She caught an early train _____ that she would arrive on time for the start of the expedition.

Time to write

7 You are going to write the following email. Read the task.

> Write an email of application for the expedition advertised below. You can apply as yourself or as an imaginary person.
>
> Write your email in 120–150 words.

Young people needed for Amazon adventure!

Destination: the Peruvian Amazon
Aim: to collect information about the wildlife of the region
Skills you will learn: canoeing, jungle survival
Requirements: an interest in animals or ecology, a responsible attitude

To apply, send an email to AndrewSpacey@amazonadventure.com outlining:

- your reasons for wanting to take part
- your skills, experience and character traits that will make you a useful member of the team

Selection weekend will be held on November 9th.

8 Tick the information that you could include in your email.

1 hope to be a vet ☐
2 good at making jewellery ☐
3 father been to Amazon ☐
4 stubborn and pessimistic ☐
5 help at animal rescue centre ☐
6 environmental charity ☐
7 love sci-fi films ☐
8 energetic and sociable ☐

9 Make a plan for your email, similar to the writing plan in Exercise 4. Then write your email. Use the Memory Flash and the Connecting words box to help you.

Memory Flash

Opening a formal letter / email of application	Talking about motivation	Talking about previous experience	Talking about character traits	Closing a formal letter / email of application
Dear Sirs, / Dear Mr Spacey,	It has always been my dream to …	I am already an experienced rock climber.	I am mature and hard-working.	I very much hope that …
I am writing to apply for …	I would really like to …	This experience has given me a good understanding of …	I am sure I could be a useful member of your team.	I look forward to hearing from you.
		This has taught me a lot about …		Yours faithfully, / Yours sincerely,

Vocabulary

1 Circle the correct word.

1   I can't see where I'm going because of the **fog** / **lightning** / **puddle**.
2   The spider vanished behind a rock, but soon **reconsidered** / **reappeared** / **reacted**.
3   If you want to read in the dark, you'll need a **compass** / **flare** / **torch**.
4   Don't climb that cliff unless you use a **rope** / **raft** / **stove**.
5   The **mist** / **flood** / **hail** was hitting my face as it fell.
6   It would have been easier to light the fire if we'd had **whistles** / **matches** / **blankets**.
7   We won't have any more water to drink until we reach the next **dune** / **cliff** / **oasis**.
8   I'd be **hard-hearted** / **heart-broken** / **exhausted** if I had to stop doing the hobbies I love.
9   I'm **terrified** / **baking** / **soaking** that I'll have an accident if I go skiing.
10 If you don't want to be bitten, bring some insect **device** / **repellent** / **rod**.

2 Complete the text with words from the box.

> astonished   attitude   change   delighted
> expeditions   miserable   ordeal
> parachute   recovered   risks

Bear Grylls is ¹_____ with the success of his TV show, *Born Survivor*. Life hasn't always been easy for the TV presenter, however. When he was twenty-one, Grylls jumped out of a plane. His ²_____ didn't open properly, and he broke three bones in his back. Grylls was ³_____ because he thought that such an ⁴_____ meant the adventurous future he'd dreamed of was now impossible. Then he had a ⁵_____ of heart. He decided that, with a positive ⁶_____, anything was possible. He soon ⁷_____ from his injuries. His doctors were ⁸_____ when, only two years later, he became the youngest Briton ever to climb Mount Everest. Since then, he hasn't stopped taking ⁹_____ and he has been on lots of exciting ¹⁰_____ .

Grammar

3 Choose A, B, C or D to complete the sentences.

1   He told her _____ a fire.
    A   to light   C   lighting
    B   that she lit   D   to have lit
2   She asked them where _____ .
    A   was the cave   C   the cave was
    B   is the cave   D   the cave is
3   We all agreed _____ freezing outside.
    A   being   C   to be
    B   that we are   D   that we were
4   He _____ my positive attitude had saved his life.
    A   told that   C   told
    B   said me   D   said
5   They denied that the weather forecast _____ a blizzard.
    A   mentioning   C   had mentioned
    B   mentions   D   to mention
6   I warned him _____ on the expedition.
    A   going   C   not to go
    B   that he doesn't go D   not going
7   We asked them _____ been there before.
    A   had they   C   if they'd
    B   that they'd   D   have they
8   They accused her _____ unnecessary risks.
    A   of taking   C   to take
    B   that she had taken D   that she took
9   I said they _____ rock climbing with us.
    A   should come   C   can't come
    B   not to come   D   will come
10 She complained _____ miserable on the trip.
    A   that she'd been   C   that she's been
    B   to be   D   being

4 Complete the second sentence so that it has a similar meaning to the first sentence, using the word given. Use between two and five words, including the word given.

1   'What do you want to do?' she asked me. **I**
    She asked me _____ to do.
2   They said that they wouldn't walk. **refused**
    They _____ walk.
3   I suggested that he built a shelter. **told**
    I _____ a shelter.
4   He said that I'd started the fire. **blamed**
    He _____ the fire.
5   We decided to have a sip of water. **would**
    We decided _____ have a sip of water.
6   He recommended that we didn't go. **advised**
    He _____ to go.
7   I told you not to forget your GPS device. **reminded**
    I _____ bring your GPS device.

I watch quite a lot of TV, but I prefer live entertainment. I'm lucky living in London. Loads of great bands come here to give concerts, and theatres often have cheap tickets for teenagers.
What about you? What sort of entertainment do you like best?

10 Let Me Entertain You!

Vocabulary Starter
Entertainment (1)

1 Explain the difference between the following.

1. a **TV programme** and a **TV channel**
2. a **movie**, a **play** and a **musical**
3. a **wannabe** and a **star**
4. a **role** and a **costume**
5. to **publish** and to **broadcast**

2 Complete the survey with these words.

> media   radio station   showbiz   autograph
> scenes   special effects   video clips   fan club

Star Surveys

Are you a ¹_____ addict? Let's find out.

ⓐ I can't last twenty-four hours without the radio, TV or other types of ²_____ .   TRUE / FALSE

ⓑ I love it when the DJs on my favourite ³_____ do interviews with pop stars.   TRUE / FALSE

ⓒ I am or have been a member of a band's or star's ⁴_____ .   TRUE / FALSE

ⓓ I've got the ⁵_____ of a famous person written on a piece of paper.   TRUE / FALSE

ⓔ I watch ⁶_____ on the Internet almost every day.   TRUE / FALSE

ⓕ I don't care if a movie is in 3D or has amazing ⁷_____ . It's the stars that make it worth watching.   TRUE / FALSE

ⓖ I've watched my favourite ⁸_____ from my favourite TV shows so often that I know all the words.   TRUE / FALSE

3 Circle True or False in the survey. Then add up your results and read the key on page 126.

CHATROOM

- Who's your favourite pop star or film star? Why do you like him/her? How much would you pay for his/her autograph?
- Describe some of your favourite TV or radio programmes.

Reading

1 Read the article and answer the questions.

1 What did the YouTube video of David Bernal show?
2 Is it easy for David to find work now?
3 In which country is Rebecca popular?
4 Is her dad happy about her success?
5 Why was YouTube started?
6 How many YouTube videos are watched every day?
7 What record does *Charlie Bit My Finger Again!* hold?

2 Read the article again and choose from sentences A–H the one which fits each gap (1–7). There is one extra sentence which you do not need to use.

Reading Tip: missing sentences

Read the missing sentences. Then read carefully the sentences before and after the gaps in the text.

A She has always told him when there have been problems online.
B Calendars with their photos have been published, and people want their autographs.
C Some enter TV talent shows.
D He has also danced in several adverts, including ones for Pepsi® and the iPod®.
E Apart from the pain on the older boy's face, that's really all there is to see.
F And in this weird online world, that's only the start of the problem, it seems.
G YouTube is also a popular site for political comment, and has won an award for its contribution to democracy worldwide.
H David's dance moves were unlike anything they'd ever seen before.

THE POWER OF

1 Millions of people dream of a showbiz career but, in the competitive world of entertainment, being talented isn't enough. The challenge for the determined wannabe is to find a way to stand out from the crowd. [1]_____ Some work hard at making friends in the right places. Others turn to the Internet to show off their talent.

2 Aged twenty-one and studying Art at university, David Bernal enjoyed breakdancing in his spare time. One night, he had one of his dance performances recorded on video then uploaded onto the video-sharing website YouTube. A few people watched it and, despite the low quality of the video, they loved what they saw. [2]_____ They sent the video to friends and before long, it had been watched by millions of people.

3 Since then, David hasn't looked back. An agent took him on, and he was soon appearing on many of the USA's most famous TV chat shows. [3]_____ Often people don't even want to meet him before they hire him. They've seen his dancing on the YouTube video, and that's enough. David's life has been completely transformed by YouTube.

4 So has Rebecca Flint's. Fourteen-year-old Rebecca, whose hobby was to sing and dance dressed up as her favourite manga characters, put some of her performances on YouTube. While living in her home on the Isle of Man, a small island halfway between Britain and Ireland, she became an Internet phenomenon in Japan, and her videos were watched millions of times. A Japanese music company became interested, and Rebecca, who is known online as Beckii Cruel, has just brought out her first album.

5 Her father, police officer Derek Flint, is well aware of the dangers of the Internet, but feels comfortable that Rebecca knows what she is doing. [4]_____ He's very enthusiastic about the opportunities that YouTube has brought his daughter, and so is Rebecca herself. All the global travel and media attention have been a tremendous experience for the whole family.

3 Find words or phrases in the article that match these meanings.

1 give someone a paid job (paragraph 3) _____
2 something very interesting and unusual (paragraph 4) _____
3 collection of songs (paragraph 4) _____
4 very good (paragraph 5) _____
5 around the world (paragraph 5) _____
6 became known to more and more people (paragraph 6) _____
7 place that you get something from (paragraph 6) _____

You Tube® : HOW TO GET FAMOUS IN
ONE MINUTE

6 The idea for YouTube was born in 2005, while three friends were trying to figure out an easy way to upload and share the funny videos they'd taken at a party. Through email and social networking sites, word of YouTube spread quickly, and the site was soon not just a place where people shared homemade videos, but also a source of favourite scenes from popular films and TV shows. YouTube users watch more than a billion clips a day, and that number is increasing every month. It is addictive viewing for anyone who wants to laugh at music videos from the days when their parents were teenagers, see interviews with their favourite stars, or watch endless clips of piano-playing cats and footballing parrots. 5 ☐

7 It can be extremely hard to explain why a particular clip becomes popular while others are ignored. Take *Charlie Bit My Finger Again!*, a fifty-five-second video of two young English brothers. It was only uploaded onto YouTube so that a friend in the USA could see how the boys were growing up. No one ever imagined it could have the massive success that it has. The video shows one-year-old Charlie biting his three-year-old brother Harry's finger. 6 ☐ There's no plot, no clever joke,

and yet it's the most popular video in YouTube's history, with more than 130 million viewings.

8 There are Harry and Charlie fan clubs in several countries around the world, including Lebanon and Belize. 7 ☐ 'It's just crazy,' laughs their father.

YouTube has created some unlikely stars in its time. Who will be next?

Vocabulary

Words from the text
Word formation

1 Read the text below. Use the word in capitals at the end of some of the lines to form a word that fits the gap in the same line.

Oprah!

Oprah Winfrey is one of the USA's biggest stars. Her power in the world of ¹_____ is enormous. When she **ENTERTAIN** makes her ²_____ views known, a **POLITICS** million more people decide to vote for the politician she supports. Her 1993 interview with singer Michael Jackson has had more ³_____ than **VIEW** any other TV interview. She is also a ⁴_____ actress. Her role in the **TALENT** 1985 Steven Spielberg movie *The Color Purple* almost won her an Oscar. Her incredible success seemed ⁵_____ **LIKELY** when she was growing up. As a child, Oprah was very poor. Now, however, she is ⁶_____ rich. She has made **EXTREME** generous gifts to ⁷_____ charities, **END** including a $40 million ⁸_____ to a **CONTRIBUTE** girls' boarding school that she's set up in South Africa.

Dependent prepositions

2 Choose the correct option, A, B, C or D, to complete the sentences.

1 Shawn Corey Carter is known _____ Jay-Z.
   A for   B by   C to   D as
2 I've got to dress up _____ a cat in the show.
   A in   B by   C as   D of
3 We weren't aware _____ his illness until we heard about it on TV.
   A at   B of   C by   D from
4 Actor Heath Ledger, who died at the age of 28, made a huge contribution _____ the film industry.
   A to   B with   C for   D over
5 I'm happy to watch anything apart _____ a horror film.
   A to   B of   C with   D from
6 Upload some of your videos _____ YouTube.
   A onto   B at   C on   D up

Entertainment (2)
Jobs

3 Answer the questions with words from the box.

> agent   stuntman   DJ   make-up artist
> cameraman   director   extra   presenter   critic

Who ...
1 makes sure celebrities look their best for the cameras?
2 introduces clips and guests on TV programmes?
3 does the most dangerous scenes in a film?
4 is part of a large crowd in a film, but doesn't say anything?
5 controls the filming equipment when a film is made?
6 comments on new films, shows, etc. in the media?
7 helps performers and other creative people to find work?
8 gives instructions to the actors and cameramen?
9 plays music on the radio or at dance clubs?

Types of programme

4 Match the speech bubbles with the types of TV programme.

> the news   a chat show   a documentary
> a drama   a talent show   a quiz show

1 What's the capital city of Australia?

2 A man has been arrested for stealing £1 million worth of jewellery from a London department store.

3 That was a fantastic performance – a big improvement on last week. Well done!

4 Please don't leave me, Jen! I can't live without you!

5 When the baby dolphin is born, the mother pushes it up to the air so that it can breathe.

6 So, how did you feel when you were chosen for the role?

CHATROOM

- Which of the jobs in Exercise 3 would be:
  - most interesting?   • most difficult?
  - most likely to make you famous?
- What do you think of the types of programme in Exercise 4? Which do you enjoy, and which do you prefer to switch off?

Phrasal verbs

5 Circle the correct prepositions.

Winning a TV talent show seems like a dream come true. But how easy is it for winners to keep their dream alive and **go** ¹ **on / up** to have a successful career?

When Gareth Gates went on the British TV show *Pop Idol*, he **stood** ² **up / out** from the start. Although he didn't win the competition, he won millions of fans. A big music company **took him** ³ **up / on** and he brought out a few successful songs. Many critics, however, said he **wasn't cut** ⁴ **into / out for** showbiz because he was terrible on chat shows. Soon his fans lost interest, and so did the music company. His career **was** ⁵ **over / out**.

Or was it? A few years later, he was **showing** ⁶ **up / off** his singing voice in a big London musical, and the audience loved him. Careers in pop don't last for ever, but if you have talent, determination and a famous face, the possibilities are endless.

6 Match the infinitive form of the phrasal verbs from Exercise 5 to the definitions below.

1 show something that you are proud of to a lot of people _____
2 be easy to notice because of looking or sounding different from the rest _____
3 start to give someone work _____
4 have the qualities needed for a particular job or activity _____
5 be finished _____
6 do something after you have finished doing something else _____

Comedy

7 Match the expressions with their meanings. Then complete the expressions in the dialogue below.

1 get a joke
2 tell a joke
3 make fun of someone
4 do an impression of someone
5 find someone funny
6 have a sense of humour

a think someone is funny
b copy the speech and behaviour of someone to make other people laugh
c make an unkind joke about someone
d be able to enjoy funny situations and laugh at things
e tell a short, funny story
f understand why a joke is funny

A: Jack's so good at ¹_____ jokes, but Lauren never laughs at them. She has no ²_____ of humour.
B: That isn't true. She just doesn't ³_____ Jack funny.
A: Jack does a really good ⁴_____ of her. Have you seen it?
B: No, but I wish he wouldn't make ⁵_____ of her. Lauren's really clever in a lot of ways. She's just not good at ⁶_____ a joke.

Adjectives with *-ive*

8 Complete the sentences with words from the box.

active   passive   interactive   addictive
massive   competitive   effective

1 For me, watching TV is very _____ . Once the TV's on, I find it very hard to switch it off.
2 My friends and I are really _____ when we do tests. Everyone wants to get the best marks.
3 There's a _____ screen, as big as my house, to watch the concert on.
4 She's very _____ and spends a lot of time doing sport.
5 Social networking sites can be a very _____ way for musicians to attract fans and become famous.
6 When I'm tired, I don't want to make any effort. I want to do something _____ like watching TV.
7 When I'm not tired, I like to do something mentally challenging like an _____ video game.

CHATROOM

• What and who do you find funny? Do you and your friends have the same sense of humour?
• Choose a talented showbiz star that you know about. Tell your partner about his/her life.

Grammar
Relative clauses

1 Read the grammar notes. Then choose the correct options for 1–3 and complete the gaps for 4–7.

Defining relative clauses
- These give more information about the noun they follow. They make it clear who or what we are talking about.

*YouTube started as a site **where people shared homemade videos**.*

*He's very enthusiastic about the opportunities **that YouTube has brought his daughter**.*

*David's dance moves were unlike anything (that) **they'd ever seen before**.*

We ¹ **do / don't** use a comma to separate the relative clause from the rest of the sentence.

We ² **can / can't** use *that* instead of *who* and *which*.

We ³ **can / can't** omit the relative pronoun.

Non-defining relative clauses
- These give extra information that is not essential to identify the person or thing we are talking about.

*Rebecca, **whose hobby was to sing and dance**, uploaded some of her performances onto YouTube.*

*Rebecca, **who is known online as Beckii Cruel**, has just released her first album.*

We use a comma to separate the relative clause from the rest of the sentence.

We can't use *that* instead of *who* and *which*.

We can't omit the relative pronoun.

Relative pronouns
⁴_____ for people, *which* for things, ⁵_____ for people and things, ⁶_____ for possession, *when* for times, ⁷_____ for places, *why* for reasons

See **Grammar File**, page 174.

2 Complete the sentences with the relative clauses (a–f) below. Use commas where necessary.

1 *Titanic* _____ was once the most successful film in history.
2 However, since 1997 _____ another James Cameron film has become even more successful.
3 His 2009 sci-fi film *Avatar* is about a planet _____ .
4 One reason _____ was its incredible use of special effects.
5 The actors _____ did not wear alien costumes or make-up.
6 Instead, their alien appearance was added later by people _____ .

a who are experts in new types of animation
b where humans and aliens are at war
c why the film was so popular
d which was made by Canadian director James Cameron
e that played aliens in the film
f when *Titanic* was brought out

3 Rewrite the sentences using relative pronouns. Add commas when necessary and put the relative pronoun in brackets when it can be left out.

1 Sam Worthington was the Australian actor. He starred in *Avatar*.
The Australian actor <u>who starred in Avatar was</u> Sam Worthington.
2 He had a friend. Her dream was to become an actress.
He had a friend _____ to become an actress.
3 Together, they visited Australia's best drama school. Cate Blanchett and Mel Gibson had studied there.
Together, they visited Australia's best drama school _____ .
4 People were invited to study at the drama school. Sam was one of them.
Sam was one of the people _____ to study at the drama school.
5 Now Sam is the man. All directors want him in their action films.
Now Sam is the man _____ in their action films.

CHATROOM

Test your partner's movie knowledge. Say the name of a film, character, actor, director, or place in a film. Your partner has to make a true sentence about it.
Gotham City   It's the city where Batman lives.

Question tags

4 Read the grammar notes and circle the correct options in the examples.

> If the main verb is positive, the question tag is negative.
> *You've seen that funny film on YouTube,* [1] **have / haven't** *you?*
> If the main verb is negative, the question tag is positive.
> *YouTube didn't exist in 2003,* [2] **did / didn't it?**

See **Grammar File**, page 175.

5 Complete the gaps with question tags.

1 It must be fun working in the film industry, _____?
2 Johnny Depp has never won an Oscar, _____?
3 There'll be a make-up artist, _____?
4 We should go to the cinema more often, _____?
5 She didn't enjoy the film last night, _____?
6 The DVD can't have finished already, _____?
7 Most film stars live in Los Angeles, _____?
8 You weren't in last year's school play, _____?

so, neither and *nor*

6 Read the grammar notes and complete the gaps with *so* or *neither*.

> To agree with a positive or negative statement, we use:
> *so/neither/nor* + **auxiliary verb** + **subject**
> *'I don't like that film.' 'Neither do I.'*
> *David's life has been completely transformed by YouTube, and* **so has Rebecca's.**
> When we are reacting to a positive sentence, we use _____ .
> When we are reacting to a negative sentence, we use _____ or *nor*.
> The subject goes **after** the auxiliary verb.
> The auxiliary verb is always **positive.**

See **Grammar File**, page 175.

7 Complete the gaps with *so, neither* or *nor* and a suitable auxiliary verb.

1 I hate horror movies, and _____ Melissa.
2 'I don't think Brad Pitt is as young as he looks!'
   '_____ I.'
3 'I haven't seen the film.'
   '_____ my parents.'
4 Michael Jackson was famous as a child, and _____ Christian Bale.
5 Kate can't be in the show tonight, and _____ we.
6 The music's great, and _____ the dancing.

Back up your grammar

8 Read the dialogue and complete each gap with **one** suitable word.

A: I'd like to watch a film tonight.
B: Yeah, so [1]_____ I. Have you got anything good on DVD?
A: How about *The Boat That Rocked*?
B: That's about a radio station, isn't [2]_____?
A: That's right. It's about radio in Britain in the 1960s, [3]_____ the only radio station allowed by the government was the BBC. The BBC didn't play the kind of music [4]_____ of our age were interested in.
B: Some of that old music from the sixties is great – the Beach Boys, the Beatles, the Rolling Stones. I love that stuff.
A: [5]_____ do I. But anyone [6]_____ wanted to hear pop music in those days had to listen to pirate radio stations, [7]_____ were broadcast from boats.
B: What happened to the pirate stations eventually?
A: Well, many of the DJs [8]_____ talents had made pirate radio successful started working for a new BBC radio station [9]_____ played pop music. Pirate radio boats weren't around for many years, but they had a dramatic effect on the British music industry.

> **CHATROOM**
>
> Talk about some recent films. Use question tags and *so/nor/neither*.
>
> **A:** *Clash of the Titans* was good, wasn't it?
> **B:** Yes, it was, but I didn't like the scene at the end very much.
> **A:** Neither did I, but I'd like to see …

Listening

Listening 1

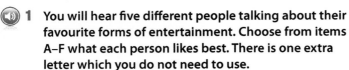

1 You will hear five different people talking about their favourite forms of entertainment. Choose from items A–F what each person likes best. There is one extra letter which you do not need to use.

Listening Tip: multiple matching

An answer is only correct if it matches the speaker's general meaning. Sometimes speakers use words from incorrect answers – don't let that confuse you.

A singing competitions on TV
B watching a music documentary
C a programme that other people in his/her family don't enjoy
D interactive forms of entertainment
E romantic comedy movies
F reading

Speaker 1		Speaker 4	
Speaker 2		Speaker 5	
Speaker 3			

WebSearch

http://myshowbiztalent.com
www.skillset.org/careers

Listening 2

2 You are going to hear people talking in eight different situations. For questions 1–8, choose the best answer, A, B or C.

1 You hear a woman talking about her job. What is it?
   A camerawoman
   B make-up artist
   C actress

2 You hear a couple talking. What does the man want the woman to do?
   A stop being an actress
   B continue being an actress
   C get a job in a café

3 You hear a girl talking about a musical. What did she think of it?
   A It was great.
   B It was OK, but not very exciting.
   C She wishes she'd stayed at home instead.

4 You hear a news report about the film industry. What does the news reporter announce?
   A an accident
   B the winner of a competition
   C the popularity of a new film

5 You hear two people talking about the school holidays. What's the boy planning to do?
   A sell DVDs at the market
   B make costumes for a film
   C be an extra in a film

6 You hear a critic talking about a TV programme. What type of programme is it?
   A a drama
   B a news programme
   C a quiz show

7 You hear someone who works for a music company talking with a singer. Does the company want to bring out any of her songs?
   A yes
   B no
   C maybe

8 You hear a conversation between a young actor and his mother. What is the boy going to be doing soon?
   A getting a new agent
   B acting in a film
   C giving up school

CHATROOM

What are the advantages and disadvantages of being a child actor? Would you like to get acting jobs while you're still at school?

Speaking
Making a decision

1 What are the cinemas near your home like? Do a lot of people go to them? Why/Why not?

2 Two students are doing the task below. Listen to part of their conversation and answer the questions.

> Your local cinema needs more business if it's going to survive. It wants young people to decide what it should do to attract more customers. You must choose one of the ideas in these pictures. First, talk to each other about how effective each idea might be. Then decide which is the best idea.

1 Which picture are they talking about?
2 Who is more enthusiastic about it, the boy or the girl?
3 Do they decide to choose that idea?

3 Listen again and tick the phrases in the Language Upload box that you hear.

4 Work with a partner and do the task in Exercise 2.

Speaking Tip:
Listen carefully to what your partner is saying, so that you can respond appropriately.

5 With a partner, talk about the following questions:

1 How often do you go to the cinema? Would you like to go more often? Why/Why not?
2 How would you describe the type of films you like best? Have you got an all-time favourite film?
3 On the whole, do you find full-length films more or less entertaining than TV shows? Why?
4 How do you feel about film stars earning millions of pounds for each film they're in? Do you think it's fair? Why/Why not?

Language Upload

Managing a discussion

Which one shall we start with?
What about the picture with the …?
Do you think that would make more people go to the cinema?
What other ideas are there?

Expressing and justifying opinions

I (don't) think it's a good idea because …
I (don't) think that would attract a lot of customers.
It seems to me that …
It might make sense.

Agreeing and disagreeing

I don't agree with you there. I think …
Maybe, but we also have to remember that …
You're probably right.
Absolutely!

Making the decision

So you think we should choose that one, do you?
I think the best idea is …
We've decided to choose …

Writing: An essay
Before you write

1 What is your favourite form of entertainment? Why do you like it? What, if anything, do you dislike about it?

2 Read the writing task and answer the questions below.

> People listen to the radio an average of twenty hours per week. Write an essay discussing the advantages and disadvantages of listening to the radio.
>
> Write your essay in 120–180 words.

1 What must you write?
2 What must you give your opinion about?
3 Should you use formal or informal language for the task?

"THERE'S NOTHING WRONG WITH YOUR IPOD, DAD. IT'S JUST TOO EMBARRASSED TO PLAY THE KIND OF MUSIC YOU LIKE!"

3 Read Emily's essay. Do you agree with her arguments and conclusion?

> There are lots of different radio stations for many different types ¹_____ listener, but is the radio good entertainment?
>
> There are many things in its favour. Firstly, you don't need to look at it ²_____ order to enjoy it. Consequently, it can help you through boring jobs like tidying your room. Secondly, there's a lot ³_____ variety on many radio stations. In half an hour you might hear songs, the news and weather, people telling jokes and funny stories, and a competition for listeners. As a result, the radio is good company when you're ⁴_____ your own.
>
> Listening to the radio does have some disadvantages, however. No radio station plays your perfect choice of music all the time, so you will have to listen ⁵_____ music you don't like occasionally. Another disadvantage is that there are often a lot of adverts, which can be very annoying.
>
> However, ⁶_____ my opinion, the advantages outweigh the disadvantages. With the variety of radio stations now available, radio is a great form of entertainment for people of all ages.

4 Now complete the essay with suitable prepositions.

5 Complete Emily's plan for the essay.

Writing Plan

Paragraph 1	introduce the issue	• many different radio _____ • is it good entertainment?
Paragraph 2	explain some advantages	• don't need to _____ at it → can do boring jobs at the same time • a lot of variety (songs, news, _____, jokes, funny stories, _____) → good company
Paragraph 3	explain some disadvantages	• can't choose the music → sometimes have to listen to music you don't like • a lot of _____ → annoying
Paragraph 4	give my opinion	• the advantages outweigh the disadvantages • great form of _____

122

6 Which of these connecting words are used in the essay in Exercise 3? Which are only used in formal language? Which can be used in both formal and informal language?

Connecting words

Result

Jamie works as a DJ. **Consequently**, he gets to meet all the coolest bands.

We don't listen to the radio in the car. **As a result**, we never know where the traffic jams are going to be.

I prefer sci-fi to fantasy. I've **therefore** decided to watch *Star Wars*.

I've got a fantastic new video game, **so** I'll probably be playing it all weekend.

My TV isn't working. **This means that** I can't watch any of my favourite programmes.

7 Complete the sentences about the advantages and disadvantages of TV. Use the connecting words from Exercise 6.

1 There are a lot of adverts on TV. _____ , it can take an hour to watch a forty-minute programme.

2 Becoming a TV presenter is very competitive. _____ those who get work are very good at their job.

3 Most people sit still when they watch TV. _____ , they don't get enough exercise.

4 The people who choose the programmes to show on TV are not teenagers. They _____ struggle to understand what people of our age group like watching.

5 The TV channels for the best sports events cost a lot of money, _____ not everyone can watch them at home.

Time to write

8 You are going to do the following writing task. With a partner, discuss some ideas for the essay.

> Huge amounts of money are spent each year on video games and the consoles to play them on. Write an essay discussing the advantages and disadvantages of playing video games.
>
> Write your essay in 120–180 words.

9 Look at these notes that a student has written for the task in Exercise 8, and decide which points are advantages (A) and which are disadvantages (D).

1 a wide variety of games available ☐

2 interactive – you can take part in a story and create your own virtual world ☐

3 more challenging than passive entertainment ☐

4 addictive – hard to stop once you've started ☐

5 you can take hand-held consoles anywhere ☐

6 new consoles are brought out regularly – expensive if you always want the latest one ☐

7 a great way to pass the time ☐

8 no physical activity needed – not good for health and fitness ☐

10 Make a plan for your essay, using the writing plan opposite to help you. Then write your essay. Use the Memory Flash and the Connecting words box to help you.

Writing Tip: essays

Remember to give a clear personal opinion at the end of your essay.

Memory Flash

Introducing advantages and disadvantages	Sequencing	Giving an opinion
There are many things in its/their favour.	Firstly, …	In my opinion, …
… does/do have some disadvantages, however.	Secondly, …	It's a great form of entertainment for people of all ages.
Another advantage/disadvantage is that …	Finally, …	

Vocabulary

1 Circle the odd one out.

1 news   documentary   critic   talent show
2 agent   stuntman   extra   costume
3 movie   wannabe   play   musical
4 quiz show   drama   chat show   autograph
5 channel   make-up artist   director   DJ

2 Complete the sentences with the correct form of the words in capitals.

1 I'd love to star in a _____ at the theatre, but I'm not _____ enough.   MUSIC / TALENT
2 The _____ makes an important _____ to a TV show.   PRESENT / CONTRIBUTE
3 He's very _____, so he gets _____ unhappy if he doesn't win.   COMPETE / EXTREME
4 There are _____ programmes on TV with boring _____ discussions!   END / POLITICS
5 For me, video games are definitely the most _____ form of _____ .   ADDICT / ENTERTAIN

3 Complete the speech bubbles with words from the box.

> broadcast   find   go on   humour   role
> scenes   show off   stands out   stars

Glee is hugely popular on TV in the USA and around the world. What's the secret of its success?

Its ¹_____, especially Matthew Morrison. He's gorgeous! He plays the ²_____ of a teacher who runs a school singing club.

The dialogue is brilliant. The writers have a great sense of ³_____. The characters ⁴_____ a lot, and I ⁵_____ the things they say so funny!

My friends and I love the music. After the show is ⁶_____ , most of the songs ⁷_____ to be sold on iTunes. We buy them all!

For me it's the dancing that ⁸_____ . I love the ⁹_____ when the characters try out their coolest moves.

Grammar

4 Choose the best option, A, B, C or D, to complete the sentences. Look carefully at the punctuation in the options given.

1 Would you be interested in seeing a film of a _____ like?
  A game
  B game, that you
  C game, which you
  D game you
2 Many video games use a _____ has been taken from a film.
  A story
  B story who
  C story which
  D story where
3 In the past, any _____ was based on a video game was unlikely to be successful.
  A movie, that
  B movie that
  C movie
  D movie, whose
4 The first successful movie based on a video game was _____ came out in 2001 and made Angelina Jolie famous.
  A *Tomb Raider*, which
  B *Tomb Raider* it
  C *Tomb Raider* who
  D *Tomb Raider*
5 Now there are lots of Hollywood _____ want to make video games into films.
  A directors which
  B directors who
  C directors, who
  D directors, that
6 The fantastic quality of the latest games is the main reason _____ this is happening.
  A for   B so   C why   D which
7 The animators and musicians _____ work is used on video games are the best in the world.
  A who   B that   C who's   D whose
8 There are sometimes long queues outside shops on _____ an exciting new video game comes out.
  A the day which
  B the day when
  C the day, when
  D the day, which
9 Video games are a popular form of entertainment, and _____ are movies.
  A so   B neither   C which   D that

5 Complete the dialogues with suitable phrases. Use *so, neither, nor* or a question tag.

1 'That action film wasn't very good, _____ ?'
  'No, it was terrible.'
2 'I can't go to the cinema tonight.' '_____ Jamie.'
3 'I had a great time on the show.' '_____ I.'
4 'He's a cameraman, _____?' 'Yes, I think so.'
5 'They wouldn't want to be TV presenters, _____?'
  'I've no idea.'
6 'She hasn't heard from her agent recently.' '_____ we.'
7 'She does great impressions of film stars, _____?'
  'Yes, she really makes me laugh.'
8 'You should try to get a role in a musical.' '_____ you.'

Activities and Keys

Unit 3, Vocabulary Starter, page 29, Exercise 3

1 FACT. This happened to the future King Hussein of Jordan in 1951. His grandfather, who had told him to wear the medal, was killed in the attack.
2 FICTION. Many New Yorkers believe it is fact, however.
3 FICTION. This is one of the most famous stories from Ancient Greece. Most historians believe that there really was a long war between the Greeks and the Trojans, but no details are known.
4 FACT. The first flies went into space in 1947, followed by the first monkey in 1948.
5 FICTION. The famous sixteenth century play by William Shakespeare was based on this story, which first appeared in fifteenth century Italian writings.

Unit 3, Speaking, page 37, Exercise 1

Picture 1

Type of story: sci-fi adventure
Setting: the planet Zadoc, thirty-ninth century, home to some clever but peace-loving aliens
Characters: **Col (the hero)** an alien from Zadoc, and captain of a spaceship
               Gad (the heroine) Col's assistant, also from Zadoc
               The Jords (the villains) a group of scary aliens from a distant planet
Plot: The Jords want to kill everyone on Zadoc and live there themselves, but Col and Gad have a clever plan to send them back home.

Picture 2

Type of story: detective thriller
Setting: Los Angeles, 2012
Characters: **Slash (the villain)** a dangerous and ambitious criminal
               Rick (the hero) a police detective who has been secretly working for his criminal brother Slash; he's in love with Susie
               Susie (the heroine) a police detective
Plot: Slash thinks Susie knows too much, and decides to have her killed. Only Rick can save her.

Picture 3

Type of story: historical adventure
Setting: the city of Rome, second century AD
Characters: **Scorpus (the hero)** a young actor; actors in Rome are poor and unimportant
               Flavia (the heroine) a girl from an important Roman family, and secretly Scorpus's girlfriend
               Macrinus (the villain) a powerful Roman politician; he wants to marry Flavia because her father is rich
Plot: Scorpus uses his acting skills and is mistaken for a rich man ... until Macrinus finds out the truth.

Picture 4

Type of story: teenage romance
Setting: North High School, USA, 2010
Characters: **Stefanos (the hero)** a Greek teenager who moves to the USA; he loves football, but football is mostly played by girls at his new school.
               Maddy (the heroine) the best footballer at North High
               Luke and Lisa (the villains) twins who think they rule the school; they're very nice-looking but not very kind
Plot: Lisa wants Stefanos to be her boyfriend. When Stefanos becomes friendly with Maddy, Lisa uses her brother Luke to get revenge.

Unit 5, Speaking, page 61, Exercise 5

English teacher's rolecard

Suggested prompts:

The problem is, you can't miss half the class each week.
Is there any way you could catch an earlier bus?
Are you sure there isn't another way to get to class?
I might be able to put you into my later class.

Finally agree to a new class time.

B

Solar-powered Tent

A tent for the twenty-first century camper, powered by the sun

Features:
- wireless internet connection
- charger for electronic gadgets
- heating system in the floor of the tent
- lights up by remote control if you're trying to find it in the dark

Recommended price: £599

Unit 9, page 109, Speaking, Exercise 1

Situation A Information Card

Who the person is	My friend, Katie	
What the problem is	Katie and I have gone mountain biking in the woods. We have got lost and it is now getting dark. We have no bike lights. We have to decide what to do next.	
Solutions	Keep on cycling.	Spend the night in the forest, and try to find our way home tomorrow.
Disadvantages	We might have an accident. We might get even more lost.	Our families will be worried all night. We haven't got food, drink or sleeping bags, and it's quite cold at night.

Unit 10, page 113, Exercise 3

KEY
6–7 true: You're a showbiz addict. You know a lot about your favourite stars, but make sure you find time for some other hobbies.
3–5 true: You're interested in showbiz, but it doesn't control your life. That's a good thing – as long as you're not hoping for a media career.
0–2 true: What planet are you living on?! It's great to have your own interests, but conversation may be difficult if you ever come to Earth for a visit.

D

Origami DVD player

A big-screen DVD player that folds up to the size of a normal CD

Features:
- screen 24 cm x 18 cm
- weighs only 40g

Recommended price: £119

Unit 9, page 109, Speaking, Exercise 4

Situation B Information Card

Who the person is	My friend, Alfie	
What the problem is	Alfie and I are half-way through a non-stop round-the-world sailing race. We're currently in the lead, and about 200km from the nearest coast. However, there's been a storm and our flares and some of our food have fallen into the sea.	
Solutions	Keep going with the race.	Sail to the nearest coast and buy more food and flares.
Disadvantages	We won't have enough to eat if the race takes longer than expected. We can't set off flares if we get into trouble.	We won't be able to compete in the race any more. We won't achieve our goal of sailing round the world without stopping.

1 Read the text below and decide which answer, A, B, C or D, best fits each gap.

New   Reply

Hi Emma,

I've just got back from my first day at my new school. It was ¹_____! There are loads of people in my class that we knew when we were little!

Megan Taylor was there – remember her? She looks completely different now. She isn't ²_____ any more. She's really slim and she wears ³_____ to hide her freckles. She's got shoulder-⁴_____ hair now too. I hardly recognised her! Her ⁵_____ hasn't changed though. She's still really naughty. I don't think she's very ⁶_____ with the teachers!

The Kennet ⁷_____ were there too. They told me to say 'hi' to you. They still look ⁸_____, and they're really good-looking. They've got ⁹_____ blond hair and tanned skin. Very cute!

They introduced me to a friend of theirs called Jody. She was really ¹⁰_____ and friendly, and we had a lot in ¹¹_____. She suggested we should meet ¹²_____ after school some time, but I don't know if she was just being ¹³_____. I gave her my phone number, and I really hope she gets in ¹⁴_____. It would be great to be friends with her.

Anyway, talk soon!

Love

Daisy

1	A challenging	B straight	C fair	D brilliant
2	A overweight	B elderly	C wavy	D motivating
3	A clothes	B a beard	C make-up	D eyebrows
4	A long	B height	C length	D short
5	A appearance	B look	C tradition	D personality
6	A popular	B embarrassing	C extraordinary	D spectacular
7	A ancestors	B strangers	C twins	D pets
8	A cautious	B identical	C brave	D informative
9	A generous	B spiky	C skinny	D relaxing
10	A outgoing	B painful	C handsome	D curly
11	A like	B culture	C tribe	D common
12	A up	B with	C out	D off
13	A polite	B dull	C unbearable	D pretty
14	A mobile	B talk	C touch	D hold

2 Use the phrases below (A–H) to complete the conversations. Use each option only once. There are two options you do not need.

A change my mind	B on time	C part-time	D on my own
E time flies	F chill out	G work out	H from time to time

1 A Are you sure you don't want to come?
   B I think so, but I'll tell you if I _____ .
2 A Oh no! What are we going to do now?!
   B Hey, _____ , Lucy! There's nothing to worry about.
3 A Sorry I'm late.
   B It's OK. I'm used to it. You're never _____ .
4 A Where do you like going at the weekend?
   B I go to the bowling alley _____ .
5 A I hate doing my homework _____ .
   B Me too. Do you want to come and do it at my house?
6 A I never have any money!
   B Why don't you get a _____ job that you can do at the weekends?

3 **Choose the correct option, A, B, C or D to complete each gap.**

1 She _____ up in New Zealand, but she lives in France now.
   A went   C brought
   B grew   D born

2 She's got six _____ – two brothers and four sisters!
   A siblings   C nephews
   B parents   D nieces

3 I bought a lovely _____ of gloves yesterday.
   A two   C pair
   B partner   D couple

4 I've lost _____ with all my friends from primary school.
   A childhood   C seeing
   B touch   D close

5 We've got the same mum but different dads, so we're _____ .
   A brothers-in-law   C twins
   B stepbrothers   D half-brothers

6 There's some fascinating new art at the _____ in town.
   A hall   C stadium
   B temple   D gallery

7 I've been studying all weekend. I'd love some time _____ .
   A up   C off
   B out   D on

8 'How long is a _____ ?'
   'A thousand years.'
   A decade   C millennium
   B century   D age

9 'When did Matt Damon first become famous?'
   'In 1997 or 1998, I think. Sometime in the _____ 1990s, anyway.'
   A high   C late
   B after   D top

10 We usually spend a week at a seaside _____ every summer.
   A resort   C rink
   B spot   D alley

4 **Use the word given in capitals at the end of some of the lines to form a word that fits in the gap in the same line.**

WANTED:
Swimming Pool Attendant

Is it your [1]_____ to work in sport and leisure?   AMBITIOUS

Then this might be the perfect job for you. Because of the

[2]_____ in the popularity of   GROW
Pancroft Pool, we are looking for

someone with [3]_____ and   MATURE
[4]_____ to join our team of   SELF-CONFIDENT

attendants. Dangerous diving

[5]_____ a lot of accidents   CAUSE
at swimming pools, and the

[6]_____ that result can be very   INJURE
serious. It is the attendant's

[7]_____ to keep swimmers safe   RESPONSIBLE
in the pool area and [8]_____   ADVICE
people about the dangers of breaking
the rules. If you are a good swimmer

and can [9]_____ that you are a   PROOF
[10]_____ , hard-working and   SENSE
[11]_____ person, we'd like to   ENERGY
hear from you.

Please apply in writing by 12th May to:
The Manager, Pancroft Pool, Park
Street, Pancroft, DH1 4HL

We will reply to everyone, but please be
[12]_____ . *Choosing the right*   PATIENCE
person for the job will take some time.

5 Choose the correct option, A, B, C or D to complete each gap.

1 My dad's always _____ people embarrassing things about me.
  A tells   C telling
  B tell   D be telling

2 Have you got _____ ?
  A a stepfather   C the stepfather
  B stepfather   D some stepfather

3 You'll have to get _____ it.
  A used to   C used
  B use to   D be used to

4 I _____ he's a bit mean.
  A am thinking   C was thinking
  B think   D am thought

5 It turned out _____ was my second cousin.
  A that Lily   C a Lily
  B the Lily   D when Lily

6 I _____ by my grandparents at the moment.
  A am being brought up   C brought up
  B was brought up   D am bringing up

7 _____ to enjoy going to safari parks when you were younger?
  A Used you   C Would you
  B Did you   D Did you use

8 It was _____ exam of the year.
  A a last   C last one
  B last   D the last

9 What _____ at seven o'clock?
  A you were doing   C were you doing
  B you do   D did you

10 They never _____ after sunset.
  A are playing tennis   C play tennis
  B play the tennis   D are playing the tennis

6 Read the text below and think of the word which best fits each gap. Use only one word in each gap.

Four years ago, 19-year-old Jeffrey Lawal-Balogun ¹_____ having a bad day. 'I was coming home from college ²_____ I saw a number 28 bus,' he remembers. 'I started running for ³_____ bus but I just missed it.'

A teenage girl saw him and realised that he was fast … very fast. She introduced herself ⁴_____ him and said he should get in touch with her running club.

Jeffrey followed her advice and now, four years later, he ⁵_____ one of the fastest 200-metre runners ⁶_____ Europe.

The change in Jeffrey's life is amazing. Before that encounter in the street, he ⁷_____ often play a bit of football in the park. He ⁸_____ to run ahead and hold the bus for his friends too, but he only ever ran for fun. Now he ⁹_____ several kilometres every day and goes to races all around the world. It's hard work, but he has ¹⁰_____ used to it. He feels very lucky to be a sportsman.

At the moment, he ¹¹_____ living with other British runners in South Africa. And the teenage girl? She's not ¹²_____ stranger any more. She's Jeffrey's girlfriend.

7 Complete the second sentence so that it has a similar meaning to the first, using the word given. Use between two and five words, including the word given.

1 She's very generous. **person**
She's _____ .

2 Before the Internet, people used to find things out at the library. **would**
Before the Internet, people _____ at the library.

3 He lost his keys during his walk home from school. **while**
He lost his keys _____ home from school.

4 We're finding our Maths very hard at the moment. **understand**
We _____ our Maths at the moment.

5 Seeing you with a fringe is strange for me. **used**
I _____ seeing you with a fringe.

6 It isn't always easy being a teenager. **life**
_____ not always easy for teenagers.

7 We had a picnic the day before yesterday. **ago**
We had a picnic _____ .

8 She felt very scared at the time of the accident. **happened**
She felt very scared _____ .

8 Complete the sentences with the correct form of the verb in brackets.

What really annoys you?

Homework! I ¹_____ (try) to do my French homework at the moment, but I ²_____ (not understand) any of it. It's impossible! And even when the homework's easy, I still ³_____ (get) into trouble about it. Last week, I got to school and ⁴_____ (realise) that my geography homework ⁵_____ (sit) on the kitchen table at home. My Geography teacher ⁶_____ (give) me loads of extra work because of that.

People who aren't polite. I ⁷_____ (walk) to the bus stop this morning when someone pushed past me. He ⁸_____ (eat) a banana while he was walking, and some of the banana ⁹_____ (got) on my clothes. Yuk! And the man ¹⁰_____ (not stop) to say sorry. How rude!

Football. Conversation with my friends ¹¹_____ (be) so dull at the moment because they ¹²_____ (always talk) about football, football, football. They ¹³_____ (have) no idea how boring that is! I ¹⁴_____ (hate) football!

1 Read the text below and decide which answer, A, B, C or D, best fits each gap.

Come to Mumbai, India's most exciting city!

Sightseeing

The spectacular Gateway of India building is Mumbai's most famous ¹_____ , but you'll also want to see the business district with its ²_____ skyscrapers. The beautiful underground temples on Elephanta Island are another popular ³_____ , a short ferry ride from Mumbai ⁴_____ .

Bollywood

Mumbai is the centre of India's 'Bollywood' film industry, so you shouldn't miss a trip to the cinema while you're in town. Every film is a ⁵_____ , so you can be sure that true love will win and the horrible ⁶_____ will be punished ⁷_____ his bad behaviour! An ⁸_____ to Film City is also a great ⁹_____ , giving you the chance to have lunch where the films are made and drive past the homes of Bollywood's most popular actors. Many film fans will also want to go on a guided ¹⁰_____ of Dharavi, the poorest district of Mumbai, which became famous as the ¹¹_____ for the film *Slumdog Millionaire*.

Food

Mumbai is famous for its restaurants, so make sure you ¹²_____ some spicy pav bhaji and other local specialities.

1	A arrival	B deck	C fantasy	D landmark
2	A optional	B modern	C essential	D shared
3	A destination	B roundabout	C souvenir	D speciality
4	A airport	B cabin	C platform	D harbour
5	A romance	B thriller	C biography	D horror story
6	A hero	B victim	C passenger	D villain
7	A on	B at	C for	D to
8	A elevator	B exception	C enquiry	D excursion
9	A experience	B departure	C return	D novel
10	A tale	B tour	C test	D fiction
11	A alien	B fact	C setting	D plot
12	A blame	B taste	C stroll	D glance

2 Read the texts and complete each gap with the correct word, A, B or C.

1

Thank you for your booking enquiry. We can offer you a _____ on 26th April for £45 per person per night.

A twin room
B departure gate
C cupboard

2

Please take your _____ , passport and tickets to the check-in desk at least two hours before your flight leaves.

A petrol
B luggage
C cruise

3

Everyone interested in the life of actress Mia Meadows will be pleased to hear that she has written her _____ .

A historical novel
B adventure story
C autobiography

4

Drivers are asked to leave their vehicles in the _____ at the back of the building and not in front of the gate.

A subway
B flat
C car park

3 Choose the correct option, A, B, C or D to complete each gap.

1 Hey, look! It's snowing. Let's get out the _____ .
   A jet ski   B sledge   C yacht   D van
2 Sorry I'm late. I was _____ up by an accident on the motorway.
   A held   B queued   C picked   D got
3 I haven't got a lot of money, so I'll be staying in a _____ hotel.
   A luxury   B single   C budget   D ensuite
4 We'll get in before noon if we take the _____ train.
   A cable   B hot air   C high-speed   D self-catering
5 I'd love to go scuba _____ one day.
   A rafting   B diving   C snorkelling   D hitchhiking
6 You can't rely on your dad's car – it's always breaking _____ .
   A up   B on   C over   D down
7 We aren't in the same class, so we've _____ seen each other this year.
   A hardly   B hard   C lately   D late
8 'I love you,' she _____ quietly in his ear.
   A screamed   B yelled   C stammered   D whispered
9 If you _____ the test, you'll have to take it again in September.
   A catch   B make   C fail   D mistake
10 She stood and _____ at him, too angry to speak.
   A studied   B limped   C glared   D crept

4 Use the word given in capitals at the end of some of the lines to form a word that fits in the gap in the same line.

Amelia Earhart

Amelia Earhart took her first [1] _____ in a plane in 1920, **FLY**
and it was an [2] _____ experience for her. Her **FORGET**
[3] _____ to try flying as a child was now a distant memory, **REFUSE**
and by the time she had been brought [4] _____ back to **SAFE**
land, her only ambition was to take flying lessons. Helped
by a [5] _____ of money from her mother, she soon **GIVE**
made a [6] _____ with a flying teacher. **BOOK**
This was the start of a great career. In 1932 she became
the first woman to fly on her own from America to Britain,
and was soon a [7] _____ for millions of fans. After **HERO**
her first [8] _____ journey, she planned to fly around **HISTORY**
the world. At the [9] _____ of the first 35,000 km of the **COMPLETE**
trip, everything seemed to be going [10] _____ , but her **GOOD**
[11] _____ from Papua New Guinea in 1937 was the last **DEPART**
[12] _____ that anyone had of her. Her plane disappeared **SEE**
somewhere in the Pacific, and has never been found.

5 Read the text below and think of the word which best fits each gap. Use only one word in each gap.

'By the time you read this, I will ¹_____ been dead for exactly a hundred years. I will ²_____ waiting for you tonight at midnight.'

Keiran stared at the strange, curly writing ³_____ amazement. It was on a piece of paper that he had found in a hole in the wall of his new bedroom. For months he had ⁴_____ looking forward to moving into this strange old house, which ⁵_____ been a train station in the early twentieth century. Now he wasn't sure that he wanted to be here.

He went to bed early that night, but at midnight he suddenly ⁶_____ up. He heard the hissing sound of an old train, but when he rushed to the window there was nothing there. He went back to sleep.

The next morning there was a note on his bed, in the same curly writing. 'The next train ⁷_____ at midnight tonight. Be on it or you ⁸_____ be sorry!'

That night he slept badly. 'What's going on?' he wondered in the morning. 'Why ⁹_____ I been dreaming about trains all night?'

There was another note. 'You have ¹⁰_____ warned! Now I'm ¹¹_____ to come for you.'

He heard the distant sound of a train. It got louder and louder until, in horror, Keiran saw a train appear through his bedroom wall. It ¹²_____ come for him.

6 Choose the sentence, A, B, C or D which is closest in meaning to the first sentence.

1 We've been having problems with our car lately.
   A The problems with our car started a short time ago and are still going on.
   B Our car wasn't working very well recently, but now it's OK.
   C One day our car didn't work very well.
   D Our car often breaks down late at night.

2 We won't decide about the cinema until Jack phones.
   A We've already decided about the cinema.
   B Jack will phone when we've decided about the cinema.
   C Jack won't phone until we decide about the cinema.
   D We'll wait for Jack to phone before we decide about the cinema.

3 When he joined our team, he had already played a lot of football.
   A He joined our team and then played a lot of football.
   B He played a lot of football and then joined our team.
   C He was playing in a match at the time that he joined our team.
   D When he joined our team, he planned to play a lot of football.

4 By June 30th, you'll have finished all your exams.
   A All your exams will finish on June 30th.
   B Your last exam will finish on or before June 30th.
   C You're going to take all your exams on June 30th.
   D You won't start your exams before June 30th.

7 Choose the correct option, A, B, C or D to complete each gap.

1 At this time tomorrow, we _____ on the beach.
  A will sunbathe
  C sunbathe
  B will be sunbathing
  D are sunbathing

2 Are you going to finish your homework before you _____ out?
  A are going
  C will go
  B are going to go
  D go

3 I _____ him twice before, but I don't know him very well.
  A have been meeting
  C had met
  B have met
  D had been meeting

4 The tram _____ every fifteen minutes from the coach station.
  A is setting off
  C sets off
  B will be setting off
  D will have set off

5 I had never believed in ghosts before I _____ that girl in the mirror.
  A had seen
  C had been seeing
  B saw
  D have seen

6 _____ been taken for a ride on a snowmobile?
  A Is she going to
  C Will she
  B Has she ever
  D Does she ever

7 Sarah arrived at six o'clock, but James _____ .
  A had already been going
  C has already gone
  B already went
  D had already gone

8 I can't help you tomorrow because I _____ my grandparents.
  A will visit
  C am visiting
  B visit
  D have visited

9 We were all wet because we _____ football in the rain.
  A had been playing
  C have been playing
  B have played
  D will have played

10 Please _____ and see me off at the station?
  A are you going to come
  C will you be coming
  B will you come
  D will you have come

8 Complete the second sentence so that it has a similar meaning to the first, using the word given. Use between two and five words, including the word given.

1 They've arranged to meet up with Ella tonight. **are**
They _____ with Ella tonight.

2 I ran onto the platform, but I was too late to catch the train. **already**
I ran onto the platform, but the train _____ .

3 She doesn't want to stay at school until the age of eighteen. **she**
She doesn't want to stay at school until _____ eighteen.

4 We were tired after working all day. **had**
We were tired because _____ working all day.

5 I'll tell you the moment I hear from him. **soon**
I'll tell you _____ I hear from him.

6 This is my first visit to Sweden. **never**
I _____ Sweden before.

7 When Cara gets here, we'll have finished. **time**
By _____ here, we'll have finished.

8 When did you start learning the guitar? **been**
How long _____ the guitar?

1 Use the word given in capitals at the end of some of the lines to form a word that fits in the gap in the same line.

Actors and their hidden talents

All through his ¹_____, Tom Cruise was a determined   CHILD
sportsman. It was a big ²_____ when, in his late   DISAPPOINT
teens, a knee injury made ³_____ in sports   PARTICIPATE
⁴_____ impossible. He tried out some other hobbies,   COMPETE
and soon he was ⁵_____ to act in the school play. He   INVITE
made a great ⁶_____ on the audience, and now, of   IMPRESS
course, he's a famous actor … but in most of his films we
see him running really fast. Perhaps, in his head, he's
still a school sportsman.

Film star Johnny Depp also has hidden talents. In fact, he
left school early to be the ⁷_____ in a band. Two   GUITAR
weeks later he almost changed his mind, but his
headteacher ⁸_____ him from returning to school.   COURAGE
Instead, he advised him to express himself ⁹_____   CREATE
and follow his dreams. It was through his ¹⁰_____ with   FRIEND
actor Nicholas Cage that he eventually became ¹¹_____   INTEREST
in acting, but watch his film *Chocolat* and you'll see that
his ¹²_____ skills haven't been forgotten.   MUSIC

2 Choose the correct option, A, B, C or D to complete each gap.

1 He needs to _____ the Kenyan runner if he wants to win.
   A defend   B overtake   C sprint   D score
2 He really hurt my _____ .
   A feel   B feeling   C feelings   D feels
3 The coach has a great _____ with the players.
   A relationship B relation   C relative   D relate
4 If everyone is in the club except Tom, he'll feel _____ .
   A tripped up   B left out   C handed in   D denied
5 Sylvia loves creating new clothes, so she's hoping to do a course in _____ design.
   A pottery   B web   C carpentry   D fashion
6 'How's the match going?'
   'Our team is in the _____ !'
   A win   B victory   C lead   D pass
7 They're building some new tennis _____ in town.
   A courts   B pitches   C tracks   D courses
8 I think you should tell him _____ .
   A truth   B true   C the truth   D the true
9 Jewellery making doesn't really _____ to me, I'm afraid.
   A attract   B ignore   C take   D appeal
10 I'm going to do more exercise from now _____ .
   A off   B up   C on   D out

3 Read the text below and decide which answer, A, B, C or D, best fits each gap.

When Kerry Jamieson went to a new school, she quickly had a
¹_____ of great friends. Kerry was an ²_____ at chess.
Before she could tell her friends about her hobby, however, she
found out about a ³_____ called Toby. Her friends were
mean ⁴_____ Toby because he was in the school chess club.
Perhaps Kerry should have stuck ⁵_____ this boy, but she
didn't. When her friends laughed at Toby, she ⁶_____ .

A year later, she had to play against Toby in a chess competition.
She ⁷_____ him easily, and won the whole competition.
She asked Toby not to tell anyone, but Toby wasn't very good
at ⁸_____ secrets. ⁹_____ of her hobby soon spread
around the class. She finally ¹⁰_____ to her friends that
she played chess. She expected her friends to ¹¹_____ her
and was amazed when, instead, they organised a night out to
celebrate her ¹²_____ in the competition. 'If you enjoy chess,
it must be a cool game,' they said.

	A		B		C		D
1	colleague		membership		gang		crush
2	ex		expert		audience		adult
3	classmate		partner		partnership		friendship
4	to		for		at		in
5	up to		into		up for		out of
6	joined in		caught on		signed up		went on
7	won		lost		beat		drew
8	giving		making		keeping		holding
9	Rings		Sculptures		Pitches		Rumours
10	denied		admitted		praised		criticised
11	reject		lose		serve		defeat
12	tie		creation		victory		neighbourhood

4 In the following sentences, one of the underlined words or phrases (A, B, C, or D) is wrong. Circle the one that is incorrect and write the correct form underneath.

1 He should have(A) pass(B) the ball earlier, but it's too late now because he's been(C) tackled(D).

_____

2 She's always had(A) a passion of(B) music and could(C) be a famous composer(D) one day.

_____

3 If you don't want to take(A) the show seriously, you'd(B) better not make(C) part in(D) it.

_____

4 He encouraged(A) her going(B) outside and get some(C) fresh air(D).

_____

5 I don't(A) mind running(B) but I can't(C) stand to play(D) volleyball.

_____

5 Read the text below and think of the word which best fits each gap. Use only one word in each gap.

the Blizzards

The *Blizzards* gave their first UK concert last night and I regret [1]_____ say that it was the worst concert I've ever been to. I'm usually a big fan of this band, so I was expecting [2]_____ have a great night. Unfortunately, however, the lead singer, Baz, was ill and [3]_____ not sing. In my opinion the concert [4]_____ have been cancelled, but instead the band [5]_____ the drummer, Danny, take Baz's place. It must [6]_____ been difficult for him, but it was even more difficult for the audience. Danny [7]_____ forgetting the words, and [8]_____ to start one song three times before he got it right. If you're planning to go to a *Blizzards* concerts, you had [9]_____ check that Baz [10]_____ able to sing. If he isn't, there's [11]_____ point buying a ticket. Trust me – you [12]_____ rather eat spiders than listen to Danny's singing.

6 Complete the second sentence so that it has a similar meaning to the first, using the word given. Use between two and five words, including the word given.

1 Playing a musical instrument isn't easy. **play**
   It isn't easy _____ a musical instrument.

2 I'm sure he isn't a bully. **can't**
   He _____ a bully.

3 Someone cut her hair in town last week. **had**
   She _____ in town last week.

4 We regret not working harder for our exams. **should**
   We _____ harder for our exams.

5 I don't think I've met him before. **remember**
   I _____ him before.

6 He didn't bring his phone because it wasn't necessary for him to phone anyone. **need**
   He didn't bring his phone because he _____ anyone.

7 They never allow me to wear my favourite clothes. **let**
   They _____ my favourite clothes.

8 I'd like a glass of water, please. **may**
   Please _____ a glass of water?

7 Choose the correct option, A, B, C or D to complete each gap.

1 Last year, I _____ to have extra Maths lessons.
  A was having   C had
  B must   D needn't

2 She often makes excuses to avoid _____ her homework.
  A have done   C doing
  B do   D to do

3 We mustn't _____ him the letter.
  A to forget sending   C to forget to send
  B forget sending   D forget to send

4 They _____ to come with us, but they're not sure yet.
  A might   C could
  B may be able   D have suggested

5 He doesn't deserve _____ in the team.
  A being   C have been
  B to be   D be

6 I tried _____ the match but I couldn't.
  A winning   C win
  B to win   D to have won

7 I think I might _____ here before.
  A have been   C to be
  B was   D being

8 They can't _____ a bit anxious about it.
  A to feel   C have to feel
  B help to feel   D help feeling

9 She's really proud of _____ such good marks in the test.
  A getting   C have got
  B get   D to get

10 You _____ to take up a new hobby.
  A should   C could
  B might   D ought

8 Use the expressions below (a–f) to complete the gaps in Column A.
The descriptions given in Column B will help you.

a I don't really think you should
b You must not
c Could you
d I think I'd rather
e You needn't have
f Please let me

COLUMN A	COLUMN B
1 _____ have it done by someone else.	Expressing a preference
2 _____ ask him on my behalf?	Request from a student to a teacher
3 _____ phone her again today.	Gently discouraging a friend from doing something
4 _____ try it out.	Asking for permission to do something
5 _____ do that again. Do you understand?	Order from a headteacher to a student
6 _____ worried about me. I'm fine.	Explaining that something wasn't necessary

1 Use the word given in capitals at the end of some of the lines to form a word that fits in the gap in the same line.

Clothes of the future

You've probably never tried wearing a computer, but if you
did, you'd soon be making ¹_____ that it wasn't very   COMPLAIN
²_____ . The future may be very different, however.   COMFORT
³_____ are working on material with tiny wires inside,   INVENT
which can be used to make computers and other high-tech
gadgets. It feels like ⁴_____ material, and it can be   TRADITION
made into ⁵_____ clothes that would cause no   STYLE
⁶_____ to the wearer, but the wearer could also use   EMBARRASS
these ⁷_____ clothes to search the Internet, play   EXPERIMENT
music or provide information about the body's health.
The experiments have been very ⁸_____ and computer-   SUCCEED
clothes are available to buy – if you're ⁹_____ enough.   WEALTH
But scientists are ¹⁰_____ to make the clothes cheaper   DETERMINE
and ¹¹_____ . Their aim? To create clothes that can make   GOOD
their own electricity every time the wearer bends an arm or
leg. Now that would be ¹²_____ !   USE

2 Choose the correct option, A, B, C or D to complete each gap.

1 I need a belt for these trousers. May I _____ yours?
  A lend   B borrow   C look after   D dress up

2 Will you be paying _____ credit card?
  A for   B by   C at   D on

3 Why has he got that horrible _____ on his head?
  A glove   B sandal   C bracelet   D baseball cap

4 He's got a _____ games console.
  A new Japanese fantastic   C fantastic Japanese new
  B Japanese fantastic new   D fantastic new Japanese

5 A lot of _____ are made of silk.
  A necklaces   B earrings   C scarves   D rings

6 That big, heavy camera will never sell. A camera has to be _____ .
  A transparent   B portable   C bendy   D woollen

7 I love stripy clothes. Something colourful is nicer than _____ white.
  A plain   B glamorous   C tight   D cotton

8 Please can you buy me some chicken at the _____ ?
  A baker's   B greengrocer's   C butcher's   D jeweller's

9 Maybe the handle would stay on the cup if you used stronger _____ .
  A panels   B robots   C glue   D varnish

10 My new top's got short _____ so it'll be great for the summer.
  A buttons   B hoods   C sleeves   D collars

3 Read the text below and decide which answer, A, B, C or D, best fits each gap.

¹_____ such as the train, plane and car have changed the world, but many experts think that the bicycle has brought us just as many changes.

This ²_____ form of transport first appeared in the 1860s. Early bicycles had ³_____ front wheels, and it was difficult to turn the ⁴_____ and ⁵_____ at the same time. Designers soon ⁶_____ better bikes, however, and in the 1890s they were everywhere. Cities were ⁷_____ , as people were now able to travel further to their place of work. Women cyclists couldn't wear their usual long skirts, so ⁸_____ trousers called 'bloomers' became ⁹_____ , to the horror of many husbands and fathers! In the early twentieth century, cars became available, but they cost a ¹⁰_____ and buying petrol to power the ¹¹_____ was expensive too. In contrast, most ordinary people could ¹²_____ a bike.

1	A	Inventing	B	Invents	C	Inventions	D	Inventors
2	A	wind-powered	B	high-tech	C	remote-controlled	D	environmentally-friendly
3	A	stretchy	B	filthy	C	ancient	D	enormous
4	A	hooks	B	wires	C	pedals	D	pump
5	A	steer	B	charge	C	mend	D	vanish
6	A	wound up	B	came up with	C	tried on	D	did up
7	A	dressed up	B	transformed	C	looked after	D	wasted
8	A	sticky	B	spotless	C	baggy	D	ancient
9	A	trendy	B	gorgeous	C	hideous	D	shiny
10	A	sample	B	bargain	C	fashion	D	fortune
11	A	engine	B	handle	C	controls	D	switch
12	A	pay	B	afford	C	waste	D	spin

4 Complete the sentences using the correct form of the words in brackets.

1 His _____ in his science exams was a big disappointment. (fail)
2 There are a lot of _____ people at my new school. (friend)
3 There's a _____ that I'll be in London next week. (possible)
4 Her _____ leather boots look fabulous. (shine)
5 I'm _____ at French so I always make lots of mistakes. (use)
6 Would you like to make an _____ to see a doctor? (appoint)
7 It's a very _____ picture, with lots of red, green and yellow paint. (colour)
8 It's _____ to say you're eighteen when you're only fifteen. (honest)
9 The _____ at the market shout really loudly to attract customers. (trade)
10 You can only take that games console back to the shop if you've still got the _____. (receive)
11 I'm sure you'll pass the test with _____ colours. (fly)
12 I need some bread, but the _____ closed an hour ago. (bake)

5 **Read the text below and think of the word which best fits each gap. Use only one word in each gap.**

Harrods, Britain's ¹_____ famous department store, has been selling to London's richest customers for more ²_____ a century. It is still as popular ³_____ it ever was, with about 15 million customers a year.

The first Harrods food shop was opened in 1849. By the late 1880s, the store had become ⁴_____ in size and included a bank as well as departments for food, make-up and pens. There ⁵_____ now said to be 330 different departments. Over the years, an enormous range of products have ⁶_____ sold there. A young lion was ⁷_____ from the store in 1969 and lived in a flat nearby for six months before it had to ⁸_____ taken to a ⁹_____ suitable home in Kenya. Now trading in wild animals ¹⁰_____ been banned in the UK, but perhaps you'd be interested in Harrods' most recent new product, gold bars. Sadly, you won't be able to afford ¹¹_____ heaviest bar ¹²_____ you have £300,000 in your pocket! You could, however, buy a ¹³_____ expensive chocolate bar for £9.95.

6 **Choose the correct option, A, B, C or D to complete each gap.**

1 He always wears that ugly colourful shirt. I wish he _____ !
   A doesn't   B wouldn't   C hadn't   D wasn't

2 Fleece clothes are a good choice if _____ cold.
   A it'll be   B only   C it's   D it's going to be

3 We've decided not to go scuba diving after all, but we'll bring a waterproof camera with us
   _____ we change our minds.
   A unless   B as long as   C providing   D in case

4 _____ the gadget, the easier it is to lose.
   A The smallest   B Tiny   C The smaller   D Tinier

5 If the plane had been invented earlier, Christopher Columbus _____ flown to America.
   A could have   B will have   C had been   D was

6 Metal money is believed _____ used for the first time 3000 years ago, in China.
   A to have   B to have been   C that it was   D that it had

7 Imogen is _____ ambitious person I know.
   A the less   B the least   C less   D most

8 If the nail varnish _____ brighter, maybe more people would want to buy it.
   A would be   B is   C will be   D was

9 It will be _____ from the highest quality leather.
   A made   B make   C making   D been made

10 Supposing you had £1000, what _____ it on?
   A did you spend   B was spent   C would you spend   D had been spent

7 Complete the second sentence so that it has a similar meaning to the first, using the word given. Use between two and five words, including the word given.

1 I regret lending him all my money. **only**
If _____ him all my money.

2 He's not as friendly as he used to be. **less**
He's _____ he used to be.

3 The shoes are said to have been designed by Coco Chanel. **that**
It is said _____ by Coco Chanel.

4 They must put a zip on that jacket. **be**
A zip _____ on that jacket.

5 We won't be able to afford it if I don't get a job. **unless**
We won't be able to afford it _____ a job.

6 He only knew about it because he went to the chemist's. **if**
_____ to the chemist's, he'd never have known about it.

7 It's bouncier than any other ball in the world. **the**
It's _____ ball in the world.

8 We'll bring some food provided we get to the supermarket in time. **long**
We'll bring some food _____ to the supermarket in time.

8 Read the text and complete the gaps with the correct word, A, B, C or D.

If you're interested in robots, ¹_____ the new Robot Room at the Museum of Science. I went there for a couple of hours yesterday and I wish ²_____ able to stay longer.

The ³_____ of the robots is Topio, a human–like machine from Vietnam. Visitors ⁴_____ the chance to play table tennis against him. ⁵_____ lost my match, I'd have been very, very embarrassed, but luckily he wasn't ⁶_____ to beat as I'd feared. The moving ball was ⁷_____ the cameras in his 'eyes', but his arm movements needed to be ⁸_____ .

Another interesting robot was a dog called Barclay. ⁹_____ you are to Barclay, the friendlier he is. If you ¹⁰_____ at him or sound angry, he walks away and hides. He has fur, looks very cute, and makes ¹¹_____ mess than a real dog. If I had a spare £1000, I ¹²_____ one.

	A	B	C	D
1	you love	you are loving	you'll love	you loved
2	I'd been	I would be	I'm	I've been
3	more interesting	less interesting	as interesting	most interesting
4	give	have given	are given	had been given
5	If I	Unless I	If I'd	Unless I'd
6	as hard	harder	hardest	harder than
7	saw	seen by	seen for	see by
8	as fast as	faster than	as fast	faster
9	The kind	The kinder	The kindest	Kind
10	shout	will shout	would	shouted
11	the less	the least	less	least
12	would definitely buy	had definitely bought	definitely bought	will definitely buy

1 Use the word given in capitals at the end of some of the lines to form a word that fits in the gap in the same line.

There's a great singing competition on TV at the moment, with girls who want to be the star of a ¹_____ in a | MUSIC
London theatre. The ²_____ , Dan Spence, has a | PRESENT
great sense of humour, and the girls are so ³_____ . | TALENT
They're really ⁴_____ , too, because winning the show | COMPETE
is ⁵_____ important to them. They all know they're | EXTREME
⁶_____ to get another chance to become famous. | LIKELY
When the experts' comments about their songs aren't
positive, it's hard for them to ⁷_____ their confidence. | GAIN
It's amazing how often they ⁸_____ , though, and | COVER
sing much better the following week. The two girls who perform
worst have to ⁹_____ at the end of the show and sing | APPEAR
again, and then one of them has to leave the show. It's
really sad seeing how they ¹⁰_____ when they lose, but | ACT
in general the programme is great ¹¹_____ . It's really | ENTERTAIN
¹²_____ to watch! | ADDICT

2 Choose the correct option, A, B, C or D to complete each gap.

1 The sand _____ in the desert look like big yellow hills.

  A glaciers   B cliffs   C oases   D dunes

2 My big sister's been taken _____ as a TV make-up artist.

  A up   B out   C over   D on

3 We should bring a first aid _____ in case there's an accident.

  A stove   B device   C kit   D net

4 The _____ was so strong that it blew down a tree outside our house.

  A hail   B gale   C downpour   D mist

5 If only we had _____ to help us light a fire!

  A a raft   B a blanket   C a whistle   D matches

6 Maybe you're just not _____ out for a career in showbiz.

  A got   B found   C cut   D known

7 'It's too dark to see anything!'
'Here, use my _____ !'

  A sunscreen   B torch   C parachute   D rod

8 He can do really good _____ of famous people.

  A impressions   B fun   C jokes   D contributions

9 Do you think we should build _____ somewhere?

  A a shelter   B a flare   C an SOS   D a sip

10 I got all the answers right on the _____ show!

  A chat   B quiz   C talent   D critic

3 Read the text below and decide which answer, A, B, C or D, best fits each gap.

The film *2012* starts in the ¹_____ heat of an underground science station in India, where it has been discovered that life as we know it will soon be ²_____ . The US President and his ³_____ advisors are made aware ⁴_____ the problem. They have ⁵_____ ships built secretly in ⁶_____ under the Himalayas, to prepare for the terrible ⁷_____ that will soon cover the Earth with water.

A radio ⁸_____ called Charlie finds out about the coming disaster and ⁹_____ the information to anyone who'll listen. Jackson is one of the people who listens to Charlie's radio station and, when the worst happens, Jackson and his family manage to ¹⁰_____ the ordeal.

This ¹¹_____ has been very popular around the world. With its exciting plot, ¹²_____ action scenes and fabulous ¹³_____ effects, it has helped to make its German ¹⁴_____ , Roland Emmerich, Europe's most successful filmmaker ever.

1	A freezing	B	soaking	C	baking	D	starving
2	A off	B	over	C	above	D	down
3	A political	B	furious	C	passive	D	interactive
4	A at	B	with	C	by	D	of
5	A massive	B	astonished	C	delighted	D	exhausted
6	A icebergs	B	puddles	C	streams	D	caves
7	A blizzards	B	floods	C	thunder	D	fog
8	A cameraman	B	extra	C	agent	D	DJ
9	A publishes	B	uploads	C	broadcasts	D	contributes
10	A survive	B	navigate	C	stand out	D	show off
11	A media	B	channel	C	documentary	D	movie
12	A miserable	B	heartbroken	C	non-stop	D	terrified
13	A special	B	active	C	play	D	showbiz
14	A fan	B	wannabe	C	director	D	drama

4 Decide on the best answer, A, B or C to complete the sentences.

1 He told us to stay _____ , not to explore.
  A putting   B put   C puts
2 Why didn't you bring a _____ bag to keep you warm at night?
  A sleeping   B sleep   C sleeper
3 My grandmother keeps herself _____ – she walks at least five kilometres every day.
  A actual   B acting   C active
4 The tree looks black and burned because it's been hit by _____ .
  A lightning   B lighting   C light
5 I'm so bored of his _____ stories about fishing!
  A ending   B ended   C endless
6 The clip has had a lot of _____ , but there may only be a few people watching it again and again.
  A views   B viewings   C viewers

5 Read the text below and think of the word which best fits each gap. Use only one word in each gap.

In 1971, a plane ¹_____ had been flying over the Amazon Rainforest crashed to the ground. Everyone on the plane was killed apart ²_____ seventeen-year-old Juliane Koepcke. One of Juliane's eyes was injured and ³_____ were her shoulder and arm, but amazingly she could still walk. She wondered if a search party ⁴_____ ever find her, but decided ⁵_____ this was unlikely. Instead Juliane, ⁶_____ parents were both biologists and had taught her jungle survival skills, decided ⁷_____ follow streams and rivers until she found help. She walked for eleven days. The crocodiles in the rivers didn't scare her and ⁸_____ did the enormous jungle insects, but she later admitted that she ⁹_____ been very close to death. She was eventually found by some woodcutters, ¹⁰_____ took her by boat to a town ¹¹_____ she could be given medical attention.

6 Choose the correct option, A, B, C or D to complete each gap.

1   He'd never done that before, _____ ?

    A   would he   B   wouldn't he   C   had he   D   hadn't he

2   'They were extras in the film.'
    '_____ Rosie.'

    A   So were   B   So was   C   Neither were   D   Neither was

3   She accused me _____ no sense of humour.

    A   of having   B   to have   C   that I had   D   having

4   He asked _____ his autograph.

    A   to want   B   for wanting   C   did we want   D   whether we wanted

5   I _____ wait for me.

    A   told to   B   told them   C   told them they   D   told them to

6   Freddie said _____ be there.

    A   that he would   B   that he   C   he's going   D   me that he's going to

7   They promised _____ on the quiz show, but later they had a change of heart.

    A   going   B   to go   C   they go   D   for going

8   The movie _____ last night was terrible.

    A   that saw   B   which saw   C   I saw   D   who I saw

9   That's the boy _____ dad's a stuntman.

    A   who's   B   that's   C   whose   D   that

10   The play *Romeo and Juliet*, _____ can see at the theatre next week, was written by William Shakespeare.

    A   you   B   that you   C   who you   D   which you

7 Read the dialogue and complete the gaps with the correct word, A, B, C or D.

It's freezing tonight, ¹_____ ?

Yes. The weather forecast said it ²_____ cold. Shall we light a fire?

That's a good idea ... but where can we put it? I did a survival course once, and the instructor advised ³ _____ very careful with fires. We don't want it to spread.

That area ⁴_____ Jemima's sitting might be a good place. There are no trees nearby.

OK. I'll go and get some wood ⁵_____ put on it.

⁶_____ I. And Jemima can help us too, ⁷_____ ?

I don't know. She was a bit moody earlier. She refused ⁸_____ with putting up the tent. Maybe we should just do it ourselves.

1	A is it	C isn't it
	B yes, it is	D it isn't
2	A will be	C to be
	B was going to be	D is going to be
3	A to be	C us being
	B we were	D us to be
4	A where	C whose
	B which	D that
5	A we can	C who we
	B for	D which
6	A So do	C Nor can
	B Neither will	D So will
7	A can she	C can't she
	B neither can she	D so can she
8	A to help	C that she helped
	B helping	D not helping

8 Complete the second sentence so that it has a similar meaning to the first, using the word given. Use between two and five words, including the word given.

1 'Did you see her last week?' he asked us. **we**
  He asked us _____ her last week.
2 I think the cliff is too dangerous. Do you agree? **it**
  The cliff is too dangerous, _____ ?
3 He said he hadn't taken unnecessary risks. **denied**
  He _____ unnecessary risks.
4 It's easier for people to be successful in showbiz if their parents are famous. **whose**
  It's easier for people _____ to be successful in showbiz.
5 She advised me to keep a positive attitude. **said**
  She _____ keep a positive attitude.
6 Jane couldn't go on the expedition. We couldn't go on the expedition either. **nor**
  Jane couldn't go on the expedition, and _____ .
7 I heard it on the news at six this morning. You were still asleep then. **when**
  I heard it on the news at six this morning, _____ still asleep.
8 'Don't lose your compass!' he said to me. **told**
  He _____ my compass.

147

Word List

UNIT 1

People

adopt
ancestor
birth
childhood
first cousin
grandparent
great-aunt
great-grandparent
great-uncle
half-brother
have (something) in common
identical
inherit
lonely
lose touch
mother-in-law
nephew
niece
only child
relative
second cousin
sibling
similar
stepbrother
stepmother
twin

Reading text

definitely	several
encounter	stranger
long for	

Prepositions

by email
compared to
for the first time
get in touch with
introduce (someone) to
the same as
the worst thing about (someone/something)

Phrasal verbs

bring up	meet up
chill out	turn out
find out	work out
grow up	

Personality
Adjectives

ambitious	honest	naughty
brave	loyal	outgoing
cautious	mean	polite
energetic	modest	romantic
generous	moody	sensible

Word formation: nouns from adjectives

ambitious ▶▶ ambition
cautious ▶▶ caution
creative ▶▶ creativity
generous ▶▶ generosity
honest ▶▶ honesty
impatient ▶▶ impatience
loyal ▶▶ loyalty
mature ▶▶ maturity
modest ▶▶ modesty
responsible ▶▶ responsibility
self-confident ▶▶ self-confidence

Appearance

beard	nose
blond	overweight
cheek	pale
chin	ponytail
curly	pretty
cute	scar
dark	shoulder-length
elderly	skinny
eyebrow	slim
fair	spiky
forehead	straight
freckles	tanned
fringe	tattoo
good-looking	teenage
handsome	ugly
lip	wavy
make-up	well-built
middle-aged	wrinkles
moustache	

UNIT 2

Life experiences

adolescent	motivating
brilliant	painful
ceremony	popular
challenging	relaxing
culture	spectacular
dull	tradition
embarrassing	tribe
extraordinary	unbearable
fascinating	wedding
informative	weird

Reading text

bruise	crop	panic
bullet	inspire	wasp
coward		

Word formation: nouns and verbs

advice ▸▸ advise	injury ▸▸ injure
cause ▸▸ cause	proof ▸▸ prove
dive ▸▸ dive	result ▸▸ result
growth ▸▸ grow	shot ▸▸ shoot

Collocations

a pair of gloves	head-first
a wasp sting	in total
any more	on my own
change my mind	

Time
Times of day

dawn	midnight	sunrise
dusk	noon	sunset

Expressions with *time*

from time to time	part time
full time	time flies
in time	time off
on time	time's up

Dates

AD	the day before yesterday
BC	in the early twentieth century
century	in the late 1950s
decade	in the Middle Ages
millennium	the year before last
in prehistoric times	

Days out

aquarium	ice rink
art gallery	museum
beauty spot	picnic
bowling alley	safari park
concert hall	seaside resort
fire	stadium
fireworks	temple
have a meal out	zoo

UNIT 3

Stories (1)

adventure story	historical novel
alien	horror story
autobiography	plot
biography	revenge
comic book	romance
detective story	science fiction (sci-fi)
fact	setting
fairy tale	superhero
fantasy	thriller
fiction	vampire
hero	victim
heroine	villain

Reading text

chase	interfere	rescuer
deliver	passenger	response

Verb–noun collocations

catch my eye	make an exception
fail a test	move out of the way
have an accident	take a step

Compound words

lifestyle	open-mouthed
mid-air	popcorn
mid-sentence	

Stories (2)
Adverbs

badly	gently	lazily
early	hard	reluctantly
enthusiastically	hardly	safely
far	late	well
fast	lately	

Verbs
Ways of looking

glance	stare
glare	study
peer	

Ways of speaking

hiss (quietly but angrily)	whisper (softly)
scream (in terror)	yell (loudly)
stammer (nervously)	

Ways of walking

creep	rush
limp	stroll
march	

Verbs + prepositions

believe in	mistake (someone/
blame (someone) for	something) for
disagree with	punish (someone) for
laugh at	rely on

UNIT 4

Transport (1)

arrival	guidebook	sledge
backpack	guided tour	snowmobile
cable car	high-speed train	spacecraft
coach (vehicle)	hot air balloon	speedboat
departure	jet ski	tram
destination	landmark	van
excursion	luggage	yacht
ferry	return	

Reading text

district	immigrant	notify
duration	itinerary	skyscraper
guarantee		

Word formation: verbs and nouns

book ▸▸ booking	experience ▸▸ experience
complete ▸▸ completion	give ▸▸ gift
correct ▸▸ correction	refuse ▸▸ refusal
enquire ▸▸ enquiry	see ▸▸ sight

Adjectives

common	historic	optional
essential	modern	unforgettable

Transport (2)
Places

cabin	departure gate	platform
check-in desk	harbour	ticket office
deck	passport control	

Phrasal verbs

break down	put (someone) up
get in	queue up
hold (someone) up	see (someone) off
pick (someone) up	set off

British and American English

apartment (US)	lift (UK)
car park (UK)	motorway (UK)
closet (US)	parking lot (US)
cupboard (UK)	petrol (UK)
elevator (US)	roundabout (UK)
flat (UK)	subway (US)
freeway (US)	traffic circle (US)
gas (US)	underground (UK)

Accommodation

bed and breakfast	luxury hotel
budget hotel	self-catering
campsite	shared bathroom
double room	single room
ensuite bathroom	twin room
hostel	

Activities

go on a cruise	hitchhike
go scuba diving	shop for souvenirs
go sightseeing	sunbathe
go snorkelling	taste the local specialities
go white-water rafting	

UNIT 5

Relationships (1)

bully	headteacher
call (someone) names	hurt (someone's) feelings
classmate	keep a secret
coach (person)	make a good impression on
colleague	make excuses
ex	neighbour
flatmate	spread rumours about
gang	teammate
get (someone) into trouble	tell lies
have a crush on	tell the truth

Reading text

be on (someone's) side / stick up for	freedom
cheat / copy	pick
commitment	regret
	relax

Useful phrases

a word of warning	in the long run
feel left out	in your spare time
from now on	on your behalf

Phrasal verbs

give up	pick on	stick up for
hand in	run out of	trip up

Word formation
Suffixes *ship* and *hood*

adult ▶▶ adulthood	member ▶▶ membership
child ▶▶ childhood	neighbour ▶▶ neighbourhood
father ▶▶ fatherhood	partner ▶▶ partnership
friend ▶▶ friendship	relation ▶▶ relationship

Relationships (2)
Adjective + preposition

anxious about	interested in	pleased with
bored of	jealous of	popular with
guilty about	mean to	proud of

Verb antonyms

accept	discourage	pay attention to
admit	encourage	praise
criticise	ignore	reject
deny		

Verb and prepositions

accuse (someone) of	find out about
apologise (to someone) for something	interfere in
	result in
care about	tease (someone) about
confide in (someone)	treat (someone) like
depend on	

Free time

(do something) casually
(do something) physically demanding
(do something) to a high standard
appeal to
attract
enthusiastic about
expert
express yourself creatively
get some fresh air
have a passion for
hooked on
instructor
productive
take (something) seriously
technique

Reading text

forthcoming	junior
guest	social event
jam	talent

Word formation: verbs and nouns

create ▶▶ creation	compete ▶▶ competition
imagine ▶▶ imagination	celebrate ▶▶ celebration
participate ▶▶ participation	invite ▶▶ invitation
disappoint ▶▶ disappointment	equip ▶▶ equipment

Phrasal verbs

catch on	join in	try out
go on	sign up	take part in

Hobbies
Music

audience	lead singer
composer	microphone
drummer	musical instrument
guitarist	rehearsal
keyboard player	

Visual arts and crafts

animation	jewellery making
carpentry	pottery
digital photography	sculpture
fashion design	sketching
filmmaking	web design

Sport

attack	football	score
baseball	golf	serve
basketball	half-time	shoot
be in the lead	hockey	sprint
beat	horseracing	tackle
boxing	lose	tennis
course	motor racing	tie
court	overtake	track
cricket	pass	victory
defeat	pitch	volleyball
defend	ring	win
draw	running	

UNIT 7

Gadgets

Bubble Wrap	robot
environmentally-friendly	roundabout
games console	solar panel
glue	solar-powered
high-tech	touch-sensitive
lightweight	transparent
nail varnish	Velcro
portable	waterproof
remote-controlled	wind-powered

Reading text

ban	remove
fur	trigger
horrify	vanishing
packaging	vital

Word formation

determine ▶▶ determination ▶▶ determined
experiment ▶▶ experiment ▶▶ experimental
fail ▶▶ failure ▶▶ failed
invent ▶▶ invention/inventor ▶▶ inventive
succeed ▶▶ success ▶▶ successful
use ▶▶ use ▶▶ useful/useless

Useful phrases

a bright idea
come to nothing
get (something) for free
keep an open mind
pass (something) with flying colours

Machines, gadgets and inventions
Verbs

bend	spin	transform
charge	steer	vanish
mend	store	

Machine parts

button	handle	pump
controls	hook	switch
engine	pedal	wire

Phrasal verbs

bring out	figure out	plug in
come up with	fold up	wind up

Adjectives
Adjectives ending in -y

bendy	fizzy	sticky
bouncy	shiny	stretchy

Extreme adjectives

ancient	filthy	spotless
enormous	gorgeous	tiny
fabulous	hideous	

UNIT 8

Shopping

auction house	jeweller's
baker's	market stall
bargain	newsagent's
butcher's	offer
chemist's	online seller
complaint	post office
customer	receipt
department store	sample
dishonest	shop assistant
fashion boutique	shopping mall
greengrocer's	supermarket
hypermarket	trader

Reading text

float	spot
interrupt	tunnel
rare	window-shop
solution	

Word formation: nouns and adjectives

colour ▶▶ colourful	possibility ▶▶ possible
comfort ▶▶ comfortable	style ▶▶ stylish
embarrassment ▶▶ embarrassed	tradition ▶▶ traditional
friend ▶▶ friendly	wealth ▶▶ wealthy

Collocations

a bite to eat	make an appointment
casual clothes	the most (adjective) in the world
cost a fortune	

Money
Verbs

afford	earn	save
borrow	lend	waste
buy	pay	

Prepositions

borrow (something) from	pay for (an item)
lend (something) to	spend (something) on
pay by (cheque/credit card)	waste (something) on

Clothes
Accessories

baseball cap	earrings	ring
belt	gloves	sandals
bracelet	hood	scarf
button	necklace	sleeve
collar	pocket	zip

Adjectives

baggy	glamorous	stripy
checked	leather	tight
cotton	plain	trendy
denim	silk	woollen
fleece	spotty	

Phrasal verbs

do up	get out of	look after
dress up	grow out of	try on

UNIT 9

The great outdoors

build a shelter	oasis
cave	puddle
check the weather forecast	purify the water
cliff	sand dune
glacier	send an SOS
go on an expedition	send out a search party
iceberg	set off a flare
keep a positive attitude	stream
light a fire	survive an ordeal
navigate with a compass	take risks
need medical attention	

Reading text

beetle	official
eagerly	pierce
get your bearings	puzzled
herd	skull

Verbs with the prefix re-

react	recover
reappear	regain
reconsider	

Useful phrases

blow up (of a storm)	non-stop
head for	sip of water
lose sight of	stay put

Survival

Equipment

blanket	insect repellent	rope
camping stove	matches	sleeping bag
first aid kit	mosquito net	sunscreen
fishing rod	parachute	torch
GPS device	raft	whistle

Weather

blizzard	fog	lightning
downpour	gale	mist
flood	hail	thunder

Extreme adjectives (2)

astonished	freezing	soaking
baking	furious	starving
delighted	miserable	terrified
exhausted		

Expressions with *heart*

(someone's) heart sank

(someone's) heart's in the right place

hard-hearted

have a change of heart

heartbroken

UNIT 10

Entertainment (1)

autograph	role
broadcast	scene
costume	showbiz
fan club	special effects
media	star
movie	TV channel
musical	TV programme
play (n)	video clip
publish	wannabe
radio station	

Reading text

album	source
global	spread
hire	tremendous
phenomenon	

Word formation

contribute ▶▶ contribution	likely ▶▶ unlikely
end ▶▶ endless	politics ▶▶ political
entertain ▶▶ entertainment	talent ▶▶ talented
extreme ▶▶ extremely	view ▶▶ viewer

Dependent prepositions

apart from	known as
aware of	make a contribution to
dress up as	upload (something) onto

Entertainment (2)
Jobs

agent	director	make-up artist
cameraman	DJ	presenter
critic	extra	stuntman

Types of programme

chat show	news
documentary	quiz show
drama	talent show

Phrasal verbs

be cut out for	show off
be over	stand out
go on to	take (someone) on

Comedy

do an impression of someone	have a sense of humour
find someone funny	make fun of someone
get a joke	tell a joke

Adjectives with -ive

active	interactive
addictive	massive
competitive	passive
effective	

Grammar File

Unit 1

Present simple, Present continuous

Form	Use	Example
Present simple I give He/she gives Do you give? Does he/she give? He/she doesn't give They don't give **Passive:** They are given	• permanent situations • general truths • regular actions or habits • timetables (future) • with stative verbs (see below)	They **come** from London. It **rains** a lot in winter. I never **play** tennis on Fridays. The plane **leaves** at nine o'clock. I **don't know** the answer to the question.
Present continuous I'm eating We're eating Is he/she eating? Are you eating? I'm not eating They aren't eating **Passive:** It is being eaten	• actions that are happening at the moment • temporary situations • future arrangements • habits with *always* (often annoying)	The boys **are playing** football at the moment. Dad **is travelling** abroad a lot this year. **Are you having** a party on Saturday? They**'re always arguing** about his homework!

Notes

1 Adverbs of frequency and adverbial phrases

• Time phrases commonly used with the present simple:
always, normally, usually, often, sometimes, rarely, never, once/twice a week, most of the time, all the time, every day, on Saturdays, etc.

• Time phrases commonly used with the present continuous:
at the moment, right now, these days, today, this evening, tomorrow, next summer, on Saturday, always (for an annoying habit), etc.

Stative verbs

Stative verbs are verbs that are not normally used in the continuous form. Here are some of the most common stative verbs:

Feelings	*dislike, hate, like, love, trust*
Thinking / believing	*agree, believe, find (= think, feel), guess, imagine, know, realise, remember, suppose, think, understand*
Wanting	*hope, need, prefer, want, wish*
Senses (often used with 'can')	*feel, hear, see, smell, taste*
Being	*appear, be, look (= seem), seem*
Having	*belong to, have, own*
Other	*mean, promise*

Stative verbs with change in meaning

Some stative verbs are also used in the present continuous to describe actions.
There is a change of meaning:

I **think** she's really nice. (= believe)
I**'m thinking** about the test tomorrow. (= considering)
Do you **see** that boat over there? (= ability to see something)
We**'re seeing** our friends next weekend. (= visiting)
I **have** some good DVDs. (= own)
I**'m having** pizza with my friends tonight. (= eating)

Articles

Form	Use	Example
a / an + singular countable noun	• something or someone which is not specific • one of many • something or someone mentioned for the first time • jobs • certain numbers	*There's **a** girl outside.* *I'd like **a** piece of cake.* ***A** man rang last night.* *She's **a** doctor.* ***a** hundred, **a** thousand, **a** million*
the + singular or plural, countable or uncountable noun	• something or someone specific • something or someone unique • something or someone mentioned before • the names of rivers and certain countries • superlatives • musical instruments • certain phrases • parts of the day • place names	***The** girl who lives next door is outside.* *You're **the** winner of our competition.* *A man rang. **The** man wanted to speak to you.* ***the** Amazon, **the** UK, **the** USA, **the** Netherlands* *It was **the** best day of my life.* *I can play **the** piano.* *see **the** sights, they look **the** same, etc.* *in **the** morning / afternoon / evening* ***the** beach*
no article	• things or people in general • the names of people, towns and most countries • sports and activities • school subjects • certain time expressions • certain phrases • meals • possessive adjectives	*Life is short.* *Nerea lives in Spain.* *He's been playing tennis.* *I love Geography.* *last year, next week, at night* *at home, by car, on holiday, etc.* *breakfast, lunch, dinner* *My best friend lives here.*

Unit 2
Past simple, Past continuous

Form	Use	Example
Past simple I liked Did you like? He didn't like **Passive:** It was liked	• completed actions at a specific time in the past • a sequence of completed actions in the past • past habits or regular past events • situations or states in the past	*After the meeting, he **got** in the car and **drove** off.* *Yesterday I **played** tennis, **ran** ten kilometres and **swam** for an hour.* *We **went** swimming every day in the summer.* ***Did** you **live** in France when you **were** younger?*
Past continuous I/He/She was eating You/We/They were eating **Passive:** They were being eaten	• actions in progress at a particular time in the past • two actions in progress at the same time in the past	*At ten o'clock in the morning, they **were swimming** in the lake.* *He **was playing** his music quietly but it **was** still **annoying** her.*
Past continuous vs Past simple	• an event that was in progress when another event happened • an unfinished action (past continuous) interrupted by a short action (past simple) • the background information (past continuous) and events (past simple) in a story	*I **was sitting** in the caravan when suddenly it **started** to rain hard.* *I **was watching** TV when the lights **went off**.* *The sun **was shining** and everyone on the beach **was enjoying** the nice weather.*

Notes

1 **Time phrases commonly used with the past simple:**
   at that moment, suddenly, then, when

2 **Time phrases commonly used with the past continuous:**
   while, as, when, at that time, meanwhile

3 **Stative verbs (see Unit 1) cannot be used in the past continuous.**

Used to, would

Form	Use	Example
used to + infinitive	• past habits and regular past events that don't happen any more • past states that are no longer true	*Grandma **used to** walk to school every day when she was a child.* *There **didn't use to** be so many cars on the roads.* ***Did you use to** like bananas?*
would + infinitive	• past habits and regular past events that don't happen any more	*Every summer we **would** stay in a caravan by a lake.*

Notes

1 *Used to* acts like a normal, regular, past simple verb. It forms questions and negatives with the auxiliary *did* and drops the final –d in both forms.

2 *Would* is not used for past states.

3 *Would* with a past meaning is not commonly used in the question or negative form.

Form	Use	Example
be used to	• to say that something is no longer strange because we have experienced it so often	*I **wasn't used to** walking to school so I got very tired.* *They **are used to** doing lots of homework so they don't complain.*
get used to	• to say that something is becoming less strange because we have been experiencing it	***Have you got used to** your new school yet?* *You'll soon **get used to** sleeping in your new bed.*

Notes

1 Tenses of *be* and *get* are formed in the normal way and are followed by *used to* + noun, pronoun or *-ing* form.

Unit 3
Present perfect simple and continuous, Past simple

Form	Use	Example
Present perfect simple I've seen He/She's seen Have you seen? Has he/she seen? We haven't seen They haven't seen **Passive:** We have been seen	• states and completed actions at an unstated time in the past • states and actions that began in the past and continue up to now • actions completed recently • repeated actions in the recent past • with expressions like *the first, the best, the worst*	*I've **travelled** by boat but I've never travelled by plane.* *I've **been** friends with her since last year.* *I've **just had** a dance lesson and I'm exhausted.* *She's **seen** that film five times.* *It's the best book I've **ever read**.*
Present perfect continuous I've been walking He/She's been walking Have you been walking? Have they been walking? He/she hasn't been walking We haven't been walking	• actions that began in the past and continue up to now • longer actions in the recent past, where the results can still be seen	*It's **been snowing** heavily since last night.* *We've **been working** together on a school project so now we know each other really well.*
Present perfect simple / continuous vs Past simple	• Present perfect simple or continuous: states and actions at an unstated time in the past • Past simple: states and actions at a known time in the past	*My dad **has visited** lots of different countries. In October, he **went** to Japan.*

Notes

1 The present perfect continuous is not used in the passive form.

2 Time phrases

  • Commonly used with the present perfect simple:
    already, yet, just, ever, never, for, since, before, how long, today, recently, lately, this week/month/year
  • Commonly used with the present perfect continuous:
    how long, for, since, today, recently, lately, all morning/afternoon/day/week, etc.

3 *been / gone*

  Remember the difference in the present perfect simple between *been* and *gone*.
  *I've **been** to London. (= I've visited London in the past but I'm not there now.)*
  *She's **gone** to London. (= She is visiting London and is there now.)*

Past perfect simple and continuous, Past simple

Form	Use	Example
Past perfect simple I had eaten He/she had eaten Had you eaten? Had he/she eaten? We hadn't eaten They hadn't eaten **Passive:** It had been eaten	• a past action that was completed before another past action • an action that was completed before a specific time in the past	*By the time we arrived, most of the guests had already left.* *It was nine o'clock. My parents had finished their meal and they were watching TV.*
Past perfect continuous I'd been playing He/she'd been playing Had you been playing? Had they been playing? We hadn't been playing They hadn't been playing	• to say how long something continued, up to a time or event in the past • for a longer action that was completed before a specific time in the past, where the results could still be seen	*We had been going out for three months when she told me she loved someone else.* *We had been walking for half an hour and we were very tired.*
Past perfect simple / continuous vs Past simple	• to show the sequence of events, when one event happens before another	*I had already gone to bed when the phone rang.* *She had been looking for her keys for ages before she found them on the bookcase.*

Notes

1 **The past perfect continuous is not used in the passive form.**

2 **Time phrases**

- Commonly used with the past perfect:
  by the time, as soon as, when, after, already, ever, never, (not) … before
- Commonly used with the past perfect continuous:
  before, until, for a long time / for ages, all day/evening, etc.

3 **When the order of events is clear from the context of the sentence, the past perfect is not necessary.**
We left the café and, a few minutes later, we met our friends in the street. NOT ~~We had left the café…~~

4 **If two events happened before another past action, the auxiliary** *had* **is normally only used once.**
By the time my mum got home I had done the washing up and cooked dinner. NOT ~~had cooked.~~

5 **In dependent clauses, the past simple can be used after a past perfect verb.**
*I arrived home and realised that someone had stolen the TV **while I was out / while I had been out**.*

Unit 4
The future

Form	Use	Example
Future simple I'll visit Will she visit? They won't visit **Passive:** He will be visited	• facts about the future • decisions made at the moment of speaking • offers, promises, requests, refusals • predictions	*Tomorrow **will be** March 3ʳᵈ.* *I **won't have** the fish, I'**ll have** the spaghetti.* ***Will** your dad **bring** us home after the cinema?* *No, I **won't lend** you my iPod!* *You'**ll enjoy** the party because all your friends **will be** there.*
Future perfect simple I'll have finished Will you have finished? She won't have finished **Passive:** It will have been finished	• actions that will be completed before a certain time in the future	*I'**ll have finished** my homework by nine o'clock.*
Future continuous He'll be travelling Will they be travelling? We won't be travelling	• actions that will be in progress at a certain time in the future	*This time next month, we'**ll be skiing** in Switzerland!*
going to I'm going to see Is she going to see? They aren't going to see **Passive:** It's going to be seen	• future plans and intentions • predictions based on present evidence	*What **are you going to** get your sister for Christmas?* *Oh no! That was our bus! Now we'**re going to** be late.*
Present continuous	• fixed or personal arrangements	*We'**re having** a meal out in town this evening.*
Present simple	• timetabled events	*What time **does** the concert **start**?*

Notes

1 **The future continuous is not generally used in the passive form.**

2 **Phrases commonly used with the future simple:**
probably, I'm sure, I think, I expect, I hope

3 **Time phrases commonly used with the future perfect:**
by the time, by 2020, by next year, by the end of the week

4 **Time phrases commonly used with the future continuous:**
in five years' time, this time next week

5 *Shall* **is used for offers and suggestions, instead of** *will.*
***Shall** I take the dog for a walk?*
*Where **shall** we meet tomorrow?*

Future time clauses

We use **present tenses** to talk about a future time in clauses after these words:
when, while, before, after, as soon as, by the time, until, the moment

*She's going to get a job **when she leaves** school.*
*We're going to have a lot of fun **while they're staying** with us.*
***Before I go** to Rome, I'm going to visit Venice.*
*They'll be really tired **after they climb** the Eiffel Tower.*
***As soon as I hear** from him, I'll tell you.*
*It'll be dark **by the time we land** at the airport.*

*She won't do it **until she feels** more confident.*
***The moment it arrives**, we'll bring it to show you.*

Notes

1 **The present perfect is also possible in future time clauses.**
*When I'**ve finished** my homework, I'm going to watch TV.*

Unit 5
Modals

Modal verb	Use	Example
should / ought to	• advice	You **should** try to do more exercise. We **ought to** go for a long walk.
can	• ability • permission	Jocelyn **can** cook really well. **Can** Joe and Dan stay here tonight?
be able to	• ability	Dan **is able to** teach us yoga.
can't	• present impossibility	That **can't** be your mum! She looks so young!
could	• present and future possibility • permission (polite)	Yes, that **could** be the new gym teacher. **Could** I go to the cinema tomorrow?
may	• present and future possibility • permission (polite)	We **may** be late home this evening. **May** I go to Jane's party at the weekend?
might	• present and future possibility	It **might** rain later.
must	• present certainty • obligation or necessity	He **must** be tired after all that hard work. You **must** eat well in order to stay healthy.
have to / need to	• obligation or necessity	We **have to** drink lots of water every day because it's good for our bodies. I **need to** be on time for the plane.
mustn't	• prohibition (not allowed)	You **mustn't** eat chocolate after every meal!
don't have to / don't need to / needn't	• lack of necessity (not necessary)	You **don't have to** go to the gym every day; three times a week is enough. You **don't need to** do your homework tonight – you can do it tomorrow. You **needn't** pay me back – it's a present!

Notes

1 **Most modal verbs have one form and don't change.**
   *He **must** take more care about what he eats.*
   The semi-modals (*have to, need to* and *be able to*) change according to person and tense.
   *He **doesn't have to** go to work today.*

2 **There is little difference between *must* and *have to*. We use *must* more often to talk about a decision we have made ourselves about what is necessary and *have to* for a decision someone else has told us is necessary.**
   *I **must** eat less fast food.*
   *The doctor says I **have to** improve my diet.*

3 ***Mustn't* and *don't have/need to* do not mean the same.**
   You **mustn't** go into that room. (It isn't allowed.)
   You **don't have to / don't need to** go into that room. (It isn't necessary.)

4 **There are two negative forms of *need to*: *don't need to* and *needn't*. They have the same meaning.**

Past modals

Modal verb	Use	Example
should have / ought to have + past participle	• regret or criticism about the past	*You agreed to look after the cat so you **should have** fed her every day while I was away.* *We **ought to have** offered to help Mum when she wasn't well.*
could / was able to + infinitive	• ability in the past	*Ten years ago, Dad **could** touch his toes, but he can't now!* *She **was able to** speak three languages before the age of five.*
can't have + past participle	• impossibility about a past situation	*That round-the-world cruise **can't have** been cheap!* *You **can't have** studied – you only got 12%!*
could have + past participle	• possibility about a past situation	*Peter **could have** broken the window – he was playing football in the garden.* *You **could have** come camping with us, you know.*
may/might have + past participle	• possibility about a past situation	*Andrew didn't come to school today; he **might have** been ill.* *Lisa **may have** been at the party. I didn't see her, so I'm not sure.*
must have + past participle	• certainty about a past situation	*You **must have** had an amazing holiday in Australia.* *Sam **must have** left already because all the lights in the house are off.*
had to + infinitive	• obligation or necessity in the past	*They **had to** climb for five hours to get to the top of the mountain.*
didn't have to / didn't need to + infinitive	• lack of necessity or obligation in the past	*The trekking group **didn't have to** carry their own bags.* *They **didn't need to** take the bus because it was only a five-minute walk.*

Notes

1 We use *was/were able to* to say that somebody managed to do something on one occasion (usually something that was not easy).
*He **was able to** pass his exams the second time.* (We cannot use *could* in this case.)

2 We use *didn't have to / didn't need to* + infinitive whether or not the action happened.
*I **didn't need to** study last night so I watched TV instead.*
*I **didn't need to** study last night, but I read through my school work anyway.*

We only use *needn't have* + past participle if the action happened but was probably not necessary.
*Thanks for buying the food, but you **needn't have bought** it. We've already got plenty.*

3 We use *wasn't/weren't allowed to* to talk about prohibition in the past (see *Allow*, unit 6).
*When I was ten I **wasn't allowed to** stay up after ten o'clock.*

Unit 6

-ing form vs *to* + infinitive

Form	Use	Example
verb + *-ing* (gerund)	• as the subject of a sentence	***Watching*** *too much TV is not good for your health.*
	• after prepositions	*Are you good <u>at</u> **making** things?*
	• after certain verbs	*Jamie <u>enjoys</u> **playing** computer games.*
	• after certain expressions	*It <u>isn't worth</u> **learning** Swedish, because Swedish people speak such good English.*
to + infinitive	• after certain verbs (with or without an object)	*Did you <u>manage</u> **to join** the tennis class?* *We <u>expected</u> him **to arrive** earlier.*
	• after certain adjectives	*I was the <u>first</u> **to hear** the news.*

+ *-ing*	+ *to* + infinitive
admit avoid be worth can't help can't stand delay deny discuss dislike enjoy feel like finish give up imagine involve keep (on) look forward to (don't) mind miss practise risk suggest there's no point in	afford agree allow appear arrange ask choose continue decide deserve encourage expect fail forget help hope learn manage offer plan pretend promise refuse seem tend want would like would prefer
+ *-ing* OR *to* + infinitive with no change of meaning	+ *-ing* OR *to* + infinitive with a change of meaning
begin hate love prefer start	regret remember stop try

Notes

1   **Some common adjectives followed by an infinitive with *to* are:**
difficult, easy, excited, first, happy, last, likely, sad, surprised

2   **Some verbs can be followed by either the *–ing* form or the infinitive with no change of meaning. For others, the meaning changes depending on the structure used.**

regret
I regret going skiing yesterday because I didn't enjoy it. (I am sorry about something I've done.)
I regret to tell you that you haven't been chosen for the national team. (I am giving bad news and I am sorry about it.)

remember
He **remembered locking** the doors. (He locked the doors and then he remembered that action.)
He **remembered to lock** the doors. (He remembered first and then he locked the doors.)

stop
He **stopped buying** chocolate every day. (He was buying chocolate every day and then he stopped.)
He **stopped to buy** chocolate every day. (He stopped (at a shop) first and then he bought the chocolate.)

try
They **tried talking** to Joe but he wouldn't listen. (They were experimenting to see if it worked.)
They **tried to talk** to Joe but he wouldn't listen. (It was a difficult thing to do.)

Infinitive without *to*

Form	Use	Example
let + object + infinitive (without *to*)	• give permission	*Jack's parents **won't let him try** horseriding.*
make + object + infinitive (without *to*) Passive: *be made* + *to* + infinitive	• create an obligation	*The teacher **made the students do** the exercise again.* *The students **were made to do** the exercise again.*
would rather + infinitive (without *to*)	• give a preference	*Jack **would rather go** horseriding than play football.*
had better + infinitive (without *to*)	• give advice	*You **had better** walk home before it gets dark.*

Notes

1 *let* and *allow*.

- *let* has a similar meaning to *allow*, but *let* can only be used with an object. Compare these pairs of sentences:

   *Do they **allow skateboarding** in that park?*
   *Do they **let people skateboard** in that park?*

- Remember that we don't use *to* after *let*, but we need *to* after *allow*.

   *My mum **doesn't allow me to go** out during the week.*
   *My mum **doesn't let me go** out during the week.*

- *Let* is not used in the passive, but the passive form of *allow* is very common.

   *I'**m not allowed to go** out during the week.*

2 Remember that we use *to* + infinitive with the passive form of *make*, but we don't use *to* with the active form.

   *They **made me tell** the truth.*
   *I **was made to tell** the truth.*

The causative

Have / Get + object + past participle	*Get* + agent + *to* + infinitive + object
*They **get** the house **painted** every three years.*	*They **get** my uncle **to paint** the house every three years.*
*She **got** extensions **put** in her hair last week.*	*She **got** her hairdresser **to put** extensions in her hair last week.*
***Have** you **had** your hair **cut**? It looks nice!*	***Have** you **got** your hairdresser **to cut** your hair? It looks nice!*
*She **had** already **had** the car **fixed** by the time I arrived.*	*She **had** already **got** the mechanic **to fix** the car by the time I arrived.*
*Do you think they'**ll get** a swimming pool **built** in the garden?*	*Do you think they'**ll get** the builders **to build** a swimming pool in the garden?*
*You **should get** your satellite **moved**.*	*You **should get** someone **to move** your satellite.*
*I hate **getting** my teeth **cleaned**.*	*I hate **getting** the dentist **to clean** my teeth.*
*I'd like **to have** my photo **taken**.*	*I'd like **to get** a professional photographer **to take** my photo.*

Note

1 We use the causative when we arrange for somebody else to do something for us.

Unit 7

Conditionals: zero, first, second, third

Form	Use	Example
Zero conditional *if* + present simple // present simple	• general truths	*If I **get up** very early, I**'m** always tired by lunchtime.* *Food **goes** bad if you **don't keep** it in the fridge.*
First conditional *if* + present simple // will/ can/may/might/ could//should/imperative	• events that we expect to happen in the future	*If she **doesn't like** the present, I**'ll buy** her something else.* *If you **are** free tomorrow evening, we **could go** to the cinema.* *If you **like** the CD, **buy** it!*

Second conditional
if + past simple // would/
could/might
	• imaginary, hypothetical
	  or unlikely situations in
	  the present or future
	• giving advice
		*If my dad **knew** how to fly a plane, he**'d have** his own
		helicopter!*
		*If I **went** to your party on Saturday, I **might wear** my new dress.*
		*If I **were** you, I**'d buy** those trainers.*

Third conditional *if* + past perfect // would/ could/might have	• unreal situations in the past	*If I **hadn't been** ill yesterday, I **wouldn't have missed** the maths test!* *If he **had played** in the match, we **could have won**.*

Notes

1 **The *if*-clause can come before or after the main clause in the sentence. If it comes after the main clause, we don't use a comma.**

   *If we **had** a dog, I**'d be** really happy.*
   *I**'d be** really happy if we **had** a dog.*
   *If Paul **hadn't had** a great voice, he **wouldn't have** become a singer.*
   *Paul **wouldn't have** become a singer if he **hadn't had** a great voice.*

2 **We sometimes use continuous instead of simple tenses.**

   *If you **were living** in another city, I'd really miss you.*
   *We'll stay at home if it**'s raining** in the afternoon.*
   *If he**'d been concentrating**, he wouldn't have lost the match.*

3 **To give advice, we often use *If I were you* (instead of *If I was you*).**

Alternatives to *if*	Example	*Meaning*
unless (= if not)	I won't go **unless** you go. He won't pass his exams **unless** he works hard.	I won't go if you don't go. He'll only pass his exams if he works hard.
as long as providing provided (= only if)	She'll have a great time **as long as** James is there. It'll be safe to eat **providing** it's cooked properly. I'll go **provided** you give me a lift home.	She'll only have a great time if James is there. It'll only be safe to eat if it's cooked properly. I'll go but only if you give me a lift home.
supposing (= imagine the situation that)	Supposing no one turns **up**, what will you do?	Imagine the situation if no one turns up. What will you do?
in case (= because it's possible that)	Take an umbrella **in case** it rains.	Take an umbrella because it's possible that it will rain.

Notes

1 *Unless, as long as, providing, provided* and *in case* are generally used with the first conditional. *Supposing* can be used with the first, second and third conditional.

   *Supposing you **won** the lottery, what **would** you do?*
   *Supposing you **had been caught** cheating in your exams, what **would** your parents **have said**?*

2 *On condition that* is a more formal way of saying *providing*.

   *You will be allowed to have a party here **on condition that** there are no more than twenty guests.*

3 We can use *Suppose* instead of *Supposing*, but with two separate sentences.

   ***Supposing** your bike was stolen, **h**ow would you get home?*
   ***Suppose** your bike was stolen. **H**ow would you get home?*

Wish / if only

Form	Use	Example
I wish / If only + past simple	• a wish or regret about the present	**I wish** I **had** an electric guitar! **If only** the holidays **were** longer! **I wish** I **could** run really fast.
I wish / If only + would	• a complaint about the present or a desire for something to change in the future	**I wish** they **would** stop shouting! **If only** the weather **would** get warmer!
I wish / If only + past perfect	• a regret about the past	**I wish** I **hadn't spoken** to him like that. **If only** I **hadn't dropped** tomato sauce on my best jeans!

Notes

1 Don't confuse *wish* and *hope*!

   *I **wish** (hope) you happiness!*
   *I **hope** (wish) you will be happy!*

2 We don't use *wish + would* about our own habits.

   *I **wish** I **could** stop biting my nails. NOT would stop*
   *I **wish** I **wasn't** always late. NOT wouldn't always be late*

Unit 8
The passive

	Active	Passive
Present simple	They **lock** the door every night.	The door **is locked** every night.
Present continuous	They **are watching** the shop.	The shop **is being watched**.
Past simple	The burglars **broke** the window.	The window **was broken** by the burglars.
Past continuous	They **were making** a film.	A film **was being made**.
Present perfect	The police **have found** a white van.	A white van **has been found** (by the police).
Past perfect	No one **had** ever **seen** the monster	The monster **had** never **been seen**.
Future simple	Thousands of people **will visit** Stonehenge this summer.	Stonehenge **will be visited** by thousands of people this summer.
Future perfect	By the end of the week, the new restaurant **will have served** seven thousand customers!	Seven thousand customers **will have been served** at the new restaurant by the end of the week!
Modals	You **mustn't use** the TV after ten o'clock.	The TV **mustn't be used** after ten o' clock.
-ing forms	Celebrities **like** people **recognising** them in the street.	Celebrities **like being recognised** in the street.
Infinitives	We **have to give** these library books back.	These library books **have to be given** back.

Notes

1 We use the passive to describe what happens to people or things, when we want to focus on the action rather than the person who does it, and when we don't know who does it. It is often used in news reports and historical accounts.

2 To form passives, we use the verb *to be* in the correct tense and the past participle of the main verb.

3 If it is important to say who completed the action, then we use *by* added to the end of the sentence.
*The pyramids were built **by the Egyptians**.*

4 Questions in the passive are formed by using the question form of the verb *to be*:
*Who **was** chosen for the school team?   Where **have you been** employed before?*

5 Some verbs can have two direct objects; they can have two passive forms.
Dan sent me two text messages.
*I **was sent** two text messages by Dan.   Two text messages **were sent** to me by Dan.*

Impersonal structures

It + passive + *that* + clause	**It is believed** that the dinosaurs were killed by a meteorite. **It is said** that carrots are good for your eyesight. **It was thought** that the Earth was flat.
Subject + passive + *to* + infinitive	Dinosaurs **are believed to have been killed** by a meteorite. Carrots **are said to be** good for your eyesight. The Earth **was thought to be (have been)** flat.

Notes

1 Several different verbs can be used with this structure:
say, think, believe, expect, understand, claim, know, etc.

2 This structure is used when it isn't important to state who the people saying or thinking are.

Adjective	Comparative	Superlative
quick big nice	quicker than bigger than nicer than	the quickest the biggest the nicest
happy	happier than	the happiest
impressive	more impressive	the most impressive

Notes

1 **Remember the irregular adjectives!**

good – better – the best
bad – worse – the worst
far – further/farther – furthest/farthest
little – less – the least
much/many – more – the most

2 **We use the comparative form to compare one thing or group of things with another.**

*My brother's **taller than** me.*
*These books are **more difficult than** last year's books.*

3 **We use the superlative form to compare one thing or group of things with a number of others. Superlatives are often used with *ever* and present perfect and past perfect tenses.**

*My friend Maria is **the best** in the class.*
***The most important** thing is to be confident about what you can do.*
*The USA is **the most interesting** country I've ever visited.*
*It was **the nicest dress** she'd ever seen.*

4 **We use *(not) as ... as* to compare one thing and another.**

*Their new flat **isn't as big as** their old one.*
*He's **as intelligent as** his sisters.*

5 **We can also use *less ... than, the least* (+ adjective) to compare one or more things with other things.**

*These boots are **less** heavy **than** those boots.*
*= These boots are **lighter than** those boots.*
*The **least** difficult part of the test is the Speaking, I think.*
*= The **easiest** part of the test is the Speaking, I think.*

6 **We can use *the* + comparative, *the* + comparative to say that two changes happen together.**

***The hotter** the weather, **the more** water you should drink.*
***The older** she gets, the **more beautiful** she becomes.*

Unit 9
Reported statements

Direct speech	Reported speech
Present simple She said, 'I **feel** tired.'	Past simple She said (that) she **felt** tired.
Present continuous She said, 'I'**m watching** TV.'	Past continuous She said (that) she **was watching** TV.
Past simple She said, 'I **played** tennis.'	Past perfect She said (that) she **had played** tennis.
Past continuous She said, 'We **were studying** hard.'	Past perfect continuous She said (that) they'**d been studying** hard.
Present perfect She said, 'I'**ve seen** that film before.'	Past perfect She said (that) she'**d seen** that film before.
will She said, 'I'**ll go** for a walk.'	would She said (that) she **would go** for a walk.
is going to She said, 'I'**m going to** phone Sam.'	was going to She said (that) she **was going to** phone Sam.
must She said, 'I **mus**t go home.'	had to She said (that) she **had to** go home.
can She said, 'I **can** run fast.'	could She said (that) she **could** run fast.
may She said, 'I **may** watch a film.'	might She said (that) she **might** watch a film.

Notes

1 After present, future and present perfect reporting verbs, e.g. *says, has asked* etc., the verb form is generally the same as in direct speech.

Ben: 'I'**ve found** the keys.'
Ben says he'**s found** the keys.

2 In reported speech, we often need to change the pronoun e.g. *I, he, us,* etc.

'**I** saw them in the shopping centre,' she said.
She said that **she** had seen them in the shopping centre.

3 Place/time words may change in reported speech:

yesterday → the day before / the previous day
tomorrow → the following day / the next day
now → then / at that time
today → that day
this → that
these → those
here → there
next → the following
ago → before / previously
last → the previous

4 Infinitives do not change in reported speech.

'I want **to have** an ice cream,' said Saskia.
Saskia said (that) she wanted **to have** an ice cream.

5 We can use *say* and *tell* (and other verbs) to report statements. When we use *say* we don't use an object. When we use *tell* we use an object.

Ben **said (that) he would** bring a picnic.
Ben **told me (that) he would** bring a picnic.

Reported questions

Wh- questions	
Direct speech	Reported speech
Question word + auxiliary verb + subject + verb '**Where are you going**?' I asked. '**What did you do**?' he asked.	Question word + subject + verb I asked him **where he was going**. He asked me **what I had done**.
Yes/No questions	
Direct speech	Reported speech
Auxiliary verb + subject + verb '**Can you help** me?' I asked. '**Does he like** chocolate?' she asked.	If/Whether + subject + verb I asked him **if he could help** me. She asked **whether he liked** chocolate.

Notes

1 We use *if* or *whether* to introduce *yes/no* questions.

2 We often use *ask* to report a question. *Wonder* can also be used.

   'Have you seen her anywhere?'
   He **wondered** if I'd seen her anywhere.

3 The tense changes as for reported statements.

4 For reported questions/offers with *shall*, *shall* changes to *should*.

   *'**Shall** I open the window?'*
   She asked if/whether she **should** open the window.

Reported commands and requests

Direct speech	Reported speech
Imperative **'Open** it!' he said. **'Don't say** anything!' I said. 'Please **lend** me some money,' she said.	*(not) to* + infinitive He told her **to open** it. I told them **not to say** anything. She asked me **to lend** her some money.

Notes

1 We usually introduce a reported command with *tell* and a reported request with *ask*.

2 We always use an object after *tell* and *ask*: *I told them, They asked their parents*, etc.

Other reporting verbs

Form	Verbs	Examples
Verb (+ *that*) + clause	admit, agree, complain, decide, deny, explain, hiss, promise, recommend, scream, stammer, suggest, whisper, write, yell	'It's not fair,' he complained. → He complained that it wasn't fair. 'We'll help,' they promised. → They promised that they'd help.
Verb + *-ing*	admit, deny, suggest	'I didn't break it,' she said. → She denied breaking it. 'Let's go to the beach,' he said. → He suggested going to the beach.
Verb + preposition + *-ing*	apologise for, accuse someone of, blame someone for, congratulate someone on	'I'm sorry I shouted,' she said. → She apologised for shouting. 'Sam stole my mobile,' he said. → He accused Sam of stealing his mobile.
Verb + *(not) to* + infinitive	agree, offer, promise, refuse	'OK. I won't take any photos,' he said. → He agreed not to take any photos. 'We can take her to the station,' they said. → They offered to take her to the station.
Verb + object + *(not) to* + infinitive	advise, encourage, invite, order, remind, warn	'You shouldn't buy it!' they said. → They advised me not to buy it. 'Don't forget to bring a map,' he said. → He reminded them to bring a map.

Notes

1 To use the structures *admit / deny* + *ing* and *agree / promise* + *to* + infinitive, the subject of both verbs must be the same. If the subject is different, use *that* + clause.

   'I made the phone call,' I admitted.
   → I **admitted making** the phone call. OR
      I **admitted that I**'d made the phone call.

   'He made the phone call,' I admitted.
   → I **admitted that he**'d made the phone call.

Unit 10
Relative clauses

Relative clauses give more information about the noun.

Relative pronoun	Use	Example
who	to refer to people	*I know some people **who** spend all their free time watching TV!* *Terry Jones, **who** lives in Brighton, is an excellent guitar player.*
that	replaces *who* or *which* in defining relative clauses only	*Have you got the book **that** I lent you last week?*
which	to refer to things	*Where's the CD **which** I was listening to?* *These football cards, **which** I collected when I was young, are worth something now.*
whose	the possessive of *who* or *which*	*I met someone **whose** brother is a famous photographer.* *Henry, **whose** new book I am reading, won a prize in a writing competition.*
where	to refer to places	*That's the house **where** we used to live.* *London, **where** my cousin lives, is a great city to visit.*
when	to refer to time	*Do you remember the day **when** there was a fire at the school?* *Last July, **when** they were in Paris, John asked Polly to marry him!*
why	to refer to reasons	*Do you know the reason **why** he left so early?*

Notes

1 **Defining relative clauses** make it clear who or what we are talking about

- We don't use commas.
- *that* can replace the relative pronouns *who* or *which*.
- We can omit the relative pronouns *who, which* and *that* when they are the object of the relative clause not the subject.
*Where's the **book (that)** I was reading?*   *That's the **girl (who)** I met last week.*
- We can omit *when* and *why* in defining relative clauses, but we cannot omit *whose* or *where*.
*That was the **day (when)** I took my exam.*
*I know a **shop where** you can buy cheap clothes.*

2 **Non-defining relative clauses** give extra information about something. The information is not necessary to understand who or what we are talking about.

- We use commas.
- We don't usually use *that*.
- The relative pronoun cannot be omitted.

Question tags

Present simple	You love skiing, **don't you**? She doesn't play tennis, **does she**?
	He isn't happy about it, **is he**? I'm late, **aren't I**?
Past simple	We didn't say that, **did we**? They went to France, **didn't they**?
	You were there, **weren't you**?
Past continuous	He was living in Athens at the time, **wasn't he**?
	They weren't sleeping, **were they**?
Present perfect	You haven't met him, **have you**? It's been difficult, **hasn't it**?
Past perfect	She hadn't seen it, **had she**? They'd already finished, **hadn't they**?
Futures	You'll come, **won't you**? She's going to find out, **isn't she**?
	We won't be sitting at home, **will we**?
Modals	She can't do it, **can she**? You should get a job, **shouldn't you**?
Passives	It was made in China, **wasn't it**? They've been sent the letter, **haven't they**?
Imperatives	Tidy your room, **won't you**? Don't forget your bag, **will you**?
Let's	Let's go out tonight, **shall we**?

Note

After a positive statement, the question tag is usually negative.
After a negative statement, the question tag is usually positive.

so, neither and *nor*

Initial statement	Response
I love skiing.	**So** do Brandon and Lara.
I don't often eat out.	**Neither/Nor** do I.
I went to France last year.	**So** did we.
My mum didn't like the concert.	**Neither/Nor** did mine.
My sister's going to study Spanish.	**So** is my brother.
I'm not going to worry about the exams.	**Neither/Nor** am I.
I've been to Egypt.	**So** have I.
She hasn't been to Egypt.	**Neither/Nor** has anyone else in the class.
Jimmy can play the guitar.	**So** can Katia.
You can't play the guitar.	**Neither/Nor** can you.
They'll be late this evening.	**So** will I.
I won't be late this evening.	**Neither/Nor** will we.

Notes

We use *so* to agree with a positive statement.
We use *neither* or *nor* to agree with a negative statement.

Pearson Education Limited
Edinburgh Gate
Harlow
Essex CM20 2JE
England
and Associated Companies throughout the world.

www.pearsonelt.com

© Pearson Education Limited 2011

The right of Fiona Beddall to be identified as author of this Work has been asserted by her in accordance with the Copyright, Designs and Patents Act 1988.

First published 2011
Eleventh impresssion 2020

ISBN: 978-1-4082-7281-7

Printed by CPI Group (UK) Ltd, Croydon CR0 4YY

Set in: Myriad Pro 10/14pt

We are grateful to the following for permission to reproduce copyright material:

Extract on page 79 adapted from Hamster inspires teenage inventor, http://news.bbc.co.uk/cbbcnews/hi/newsid_4180000/newsid_4185400/4185420.stm, BBC News Online

In some instances we have been unable to trace the owners of copyright material, and we would appreciate any information that would enable us to do so.

Illustration Acknowledgements

Illustrated by Beehive Illustration Limited (Chris Simpson pages 10, 13, 22, 32, 33, 35, 58, 74, 75, 83, 107); **Bill Ledger pages** 16, 20, 30, 41, 60, 71, 76, 77, 93, 100, 113; **Andy Peters pages** 11, 21, 33, 36, 45, 59, 62, 77, 81, 88, 104, 108, 121.

Picture Credits

The publisher would like to thank the following for their kind permission to reproduce their photographs:

(Key: b-bottom; c-centre; l-left; r-right; t-top)

Alamy Images: 115l, ACE STOCK LIMITED 15cr, 53cr (Above), Alibi Productions 5cl, Rex Argent 89cr (Above), Blend Images 54tr, Howard Davies 109cr, 127br, Tomas del Amo 109cl, 126cr (Below), Danita Delimont 18tr, Dinodia Images 5r, Bruce Farnsworth 111cr, Mark Hamilton 89cl (Above), Blaine Harrington III 110cl, Iconsinternational. Com 48tr, ICP 41cl (Above), ICP 91bl, image100 17cl (Below), INSADCO Photography 109tr, 127cr, INTERFOTO 80bl, Gregory James 73tr, Janine Wiedel Photolibrary 54cr, Justin Kase zsixz 97cr, Geraint Lewis 113cr (Below), Karel Lorier 55tr, MBI 98r, MIXA 34r, nobleIMAGES 24tr, 41l (Above), Papilio 18c, Paul Thompson Images 49tr, David Pearson 89c (Above), Pepbaix 44bl, PhotoSpin, Inc 41c, Chuck Place 17tl, Dave Porter 79cl (Below), Robert Harding Picture Library Ltd 97cl, RubberBall 6-7c, Stocktrek Images, Inc. 46bc, David Taylor 17cl, Adina Tovy 49cl, travelstock44 91cl (Above), Visions of America, LLC 90tr, Jim West 25cl, 65c, Pete M. Wilson 36tr; **Corbis:** Hervé Collart / Sygma 18r, Toby Melville / Reuters 97bl, Gideon Mendel 84cr, Ocean 27cl, Pressefoto ULMER / Kurt Schorrer / dpa 97cr (Below), Sampics 66cr; **Getty Images:** 26tr, 115r, BMP / Stock Image 14tr, Bongarts 69tr, Will Conran 117l, Michael Dunning 24bl, Joey Foley 113cr (Above), Holly Harris 53cl (Above), Andrew Hobbs 25bl, Huntstock 9bl, Joel Kiesel 65t, Kos Picture Source 109cr (Above), 127bl, Hans Neleman 109bl, 126br, PictureNet Corporation 17l, Ryuichi Sato 30br, Astrid Stawiarz 116tl, Noel Vasquez 56cr, White Packert 25cl (Above), Brad Wilson 50tr; **Randy Glasbergen:** 47tr, 122tr; **Innespace Productions LLC:** 85cl; **iStockphoto:** 5l, 29cr, 41cl, 42-43c, 49l, 49cl (Above), 53tr, 54tl, 60tl, 61tl, 67br, 70bl, 77c (Above), 77cl (Above), 79tl, 94bl, 95bl, 96bl, 101l, 103b; **Kobal Collection Ltd:** 20th Century Fox / Paramount / Wallace, Merie W. 118l, Hammer 36tl, HBO 37bl, Paramount Television 37tc, United Artists 29tr, Walt Disney Pictures / Walden Media 29cl; **Orange:** 126; **Orange/ M&C Saatchi:** 126tl; **Pearson Free Image:** 41c (Below), 48tl, 89tr, 90tl, 96tl, 101tr, 102tl, 108tl; **Photolibrary.com:** Comstock 68tr, Corbis 13tr, Alex Hibbert 108cr (Above), Image Source 5tr, 6tl, 12cl, Image100 25cl (Below), moodboard RF 37cr (Above), Eri Morita 49tc, David Oliver 37bc, Nigel Pavitt 48tc, Photodisc 49tl, 89cl, Purestock 61tr, Stockbyte 17cl (Above), 57cr, Mike Tittel 109cl (Below), 126cr; **Press Association Images:** Barry Batchelor / PA Archive 79tr, Bruno Press 107cr, Anja Niedringhaus / AP 130br; **Rex Features:** 20thC.Fox / Everett 29cl (Above), 118br, 124bl, 9r, 9bc, 112bl, Bauer Mar / Everett 9c, Everett Collection 30tl, Eye Ubiquitous 91tr, Neale Haynes 65cl, ITV 119tr, Jen Lowery 9br, Miramax / Everett 29c (Above), Charles Pertwee 77cl, Picture Perfect 23tr, John Powell 54cr (Below), SNAP 21bl, 36tc, Neil White 65cr; **Science Photo Library Ltd:** DR JEREMY BURGESS 78cr (Above); **SuperStock:** moodboard 53l; **Thinkstock:** 17tr, 18tl, 24tl, Hemera Technologies 65tr, 66tl, 72tl; **thumbsupuk.com:** 85; **Trevor Baylis Brands PLC:** 86c

Cover images: *Front:* **Alamy Images:** Chris Rout; **Getty Images:** Joel Kiesel; **Rex Features:** Charles Pertwee; *Back:* **Alamy Images:** Alibi Productions; **Photolibrary.com:** Age Fotostock / Marcos Welsh

All other images © Pearson Education

Every effort has been made to trace the copyright holders and we apologise in advance for any unintentional omissions. We would be pleased to insert the appropriate acknowledgement in any subsequent edition of this publication.